500 BEACONS

THE U3A STORY

Third Age Press

ISBN 1 898576 81 5
First edition

Third Age Press Ltd, 2004
Third Age Press, 6 Parkside Gardens
London SW19 5EY
Managing Editor Dianne Norton

Layout design by Dianne Norton
Printed and bound in Spain
by Bookchase, London

For more information about the U3A in the UK contact:
University of the Third Age
19 East Street, Bromley BR1 1QH
Tel: 020 8466 6139 Fax: 020 8466 5749 www.u3a.org.uk

500 BEACONS

~

THE U3A STORY

Eric Midwinter

Third Age Press

Dedication

For my co-founders, teachers and friends,
Peter Laslett and Michael Young,
in admiring and affectionate memory

Contents

One: INTRODUCTION

A year or so ago Jeremy Paxman asked the contestants on *University Challenge* a leading question, the gist of which was 'what educational institution was introduced from France into the United Kingdom in 1982 by Michael Young, Peter Laslett and Eric Midwinter?' Glory beckoned – but glory is a fickle jade, for none of the boneheaded students knew the answer. Still, it was a kind of cultural recognition, rather like the celebrity accolade of being the guest on *Desert Island Discs*. U3A had become a topic of everyday converse. No longer were people referring to it confusedly as the University of the Third World. U3A had landed.

This is the story of that extraordinary adventure in social co-operation. This is the tale of the beginning and growth of this self-mobilising exercise in the provision of education for older people, those in the Third Age. This is both the chronological and the thematic account of how the U3A movement grew to its present dimensions of over 500 groups and some 140,000 members in the twenty-one years since its inception. It may sound overly sentimental to suggest that it is the compound of 140,000 individual stories, but such is the truth, for, without that recognition by all these thousands of older people that here was an agency serving their needs and aspirations, there would be no tale to recount.

It is certainly a highly localised endeavour. It is certainly the story of 500 ventures in district determination, with resolute individuals in all those many neighbourhoods toiling to make a success of each new U3A group. It is, in the slightly ambiguous terms of political journalese, a 'bottom-up' movement, with very many of the initiatives deriving from the localities and with the central element seeking to lend a hand as and when required. Although it would scarcely be practicable or sufficiently diverting to wade through the discrete histories of 500 U3A groups, there must be no doubt that this localised aspect is of major import. A conscious attempt has been made, from the annals of many of them, to provide the essence of some of these undertakings. That is not to downplay the efforts of the central body, formally the Third Age Trust, in the rapid growth of the movement. The relationship of the core and its hundreds of out-riding adherents has been a symbiotic one, each element drawing sustenance from the other.

The response to the author's request for information about local U3As was overwhelming, even a little nerve-wracking, as the accumulated material eventually rose two feet from the floor of his study. These details have, of course, been indispensable for the statistical analysis in the third part of the book, especially in regard of the numbers and range of interest-groups arranged by U3As and the very new knowledge about the through-put of members since the origins of U3A in 1982. Moreover, this huge scale of examples amply demonstrates the astounding array of ways in which U3As have come into being. This store of information has also furnished useful evidence of how U3As communicate with their members. In terms of statistical validity, the more the merrier . . . these findings are based on details provided by upwards of 190 U3As representing just short of half of the total national membership. All this makes it an extremely solid sample and we are indebted to all the officers of the relevant U3As for giving so kindly of their time and knowledge in these respects.

Conscious of the promise that this history would concentrate on the localities, the true bedrock of the movement, a mental vow was sworn to mention, if only in a passing phrase, as many as possible of the U3As that were kind enough to provide this information. The unexpectedly high response rate has made this pledge a difficult one to fulfil. One had hoped to sustain a reasonably lucid narrative thread and it soon became obvious that this might be imperilled by the insertion of dozens of parochial illustrations, which, while special in themselves, particularly to the contributing U3A, must, by some yardsticks, appear similar. That said, the effort has been made to deploy these localised cameos to strengthen and colour this account of the nationwide U3A movement and offer some flavour of its essentially decentralised nature. In an attempt to avoid any added confusion, much of the countervailing and vexed tale of 'regional' and 'area' politics and actions has been subsumed within one chapter, late on in the text.

There is a difficulty in writing history on the hoof. When the events are all neatly completed, when one comes, for instance, to write the story of the Seven Years War of 1756-63 or the life of Henry II, all is done and dusted and one is able to judge something of the necessary perspective. When one studies an ongoing phenomenon, such as the U3A in the UK, that luxury is denied the historian. One is unable to ascertain whether the U3A movement is still in its infancy or has already reached adulthood; no one can estimate what proportion of the final tally will be these first 22 years. One ruefully might recall that there is said to be in Chinese history a period known as 'the 600 Years Confusion'.

More immediately, and with such a bustling organisation, one is caught out by new and daily events: much has happened since research for the book began. History suddenly becomes something nearer to current affairs and one finds oneself more in the role of the war correspondent than the analyst of battles fought long ago. It is, then, perhaps in the nature of such an exercise that a little more prominence has been given to the origins and earlier years of the U3A in the UK, for the later events are still, so to speak, ongoing and maybe many readers will be more familiar with the 'current affairs' than the 'history' of U3A. That said, a fairly long scrutiny of the present position, together with some attempt to crystal ball the future, form the closing two chapters.

Another cause of authorial anxiety has been the overall construct of this study and to what extent a conventional academic structure, with all the paraphernalia of footnotes and referencing, should be adopted. Apart from several secondary sources, probably 250 people have contributed information and it was feared that a heavy-handed approach to formal referencing would have proved extremely disruptive of straightforward readability. This book is aimed primarily at the general U3A audience, not, for instance, at a more narrowly professional clientele of students of educational history, much as one hopes these might find something of value herein. One recalls Noel Coward's opinion that a footnote at the bottom of the page, when engrossed in reading, is the equivalent of someone ringing the front door bell when one is upstairs making love in the bedroom.

Thus it was determined to opt for a freely running text, unencumbered with overmuch scholarly apparatus. On very many occasions, the citation of references has been made explicit in the ongoing text, while, by way of proper compromise, an extensive list of sources, both personal and documentary, has been appended. One trusts this balance of accessible text and referential back-up will be accepted as a suitable and consensual approach.

Notice must also be taken of the international component, for the British U3A movement is part of a worldwide phenomenon. Notable among these global relationships is the link with Australia. Having examined the possibilities, the Australian protagonists opted for the Anglo-Saxon model, rather than the French template, and now the Australian U3As have a strong membership. It is understood that, some years back, a character, Harold, in the popular Australian soap, *Neighbours*, was, in the script, described as being chairman of his local U3A.

When it comes down to the awesome judicature of street-cred, *Neighbours* assuredly has the edge on *University Challenge*. Only with a Weatherfield or a Walford U3A, their committees either enjoying a hot-pot in 'the Rover's Return' or a punch-up in 'the Queen Vic', could we compete with that degree of populist penetration. Nevertheless, few will doubt that the British U3As are here to stay.

William Makepeace Thackeray subtitled his worldly-wise masterpiece, *Vanity Fair,* 'a novel without a hero'. This work of non-fiction is a text without a villain. Well, there may be one or two. In general, however, it is difficult to find anyone concerned in the 21 years of U3A history whose motives could be suspected of anything other than trying to sustain the movement according to their own dictates. This does not mean that there have not been quarrels and disagreements, some of them extremely fiery and acutely personal, for this has been a very human process and some of the controversies have been and remain real and significant ones. The arguments and the failures have not been glossed over. Nonetheless, the basic narrative stance has been to describe, in what the author firmly believes to be deservedly praiseworthy tones, the positive contributions of the hundreds of Third Agers, some of whom, sadly, have died, who have contributed to this remarkable story. It is a book with many heroes . . . and many heroines.

In 1980 it was estimated that, at any one time, only 200,000 older people in the United Kingdom were involved in any form of regular adult education, broadly defined. In the year 2004 a number equating to almost three-quarters of that figure alone were participating in U3A activities. It is tale well worth the telling.

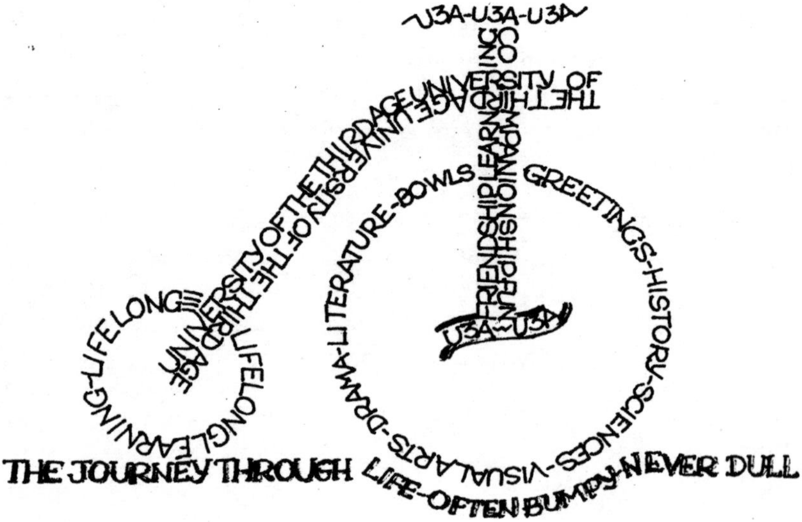
U3A-U3A-U3A
UNIVERSITY OF THE THIRD AGE UNIVERSITY OF
LIFELONG
LIFELONG LEARNING
FRIENDSHIP LEARNING
U3A-U3A
DRAMA-LITERATURE-BOWLS
GREETINGS-HISTORY-SCIENCES-VISUAL ARTS-
THE JOURNEY THROUGH LIFE-OFTEN BUMPY-NEVER DULL

Part One

THE BRACING 1980S

Two: Before the Beginning

Perhaps only Third Agers will now recall the simplistic formula employed in the Mickey Rooney/Judy Garland movies of mid 20th century. After but a few minutes consideration, the triumphal *cliché* was exclaimed: 'let's do the show right here in the barn!' Moments later a beautifully choreographed musical extravaganza appeared before our eyes in the raven-black of a thousand Gaumonts and Odeons.

Would that the origins of the British version of the University of the Third Age were as clear-cut and expedient. The notion – older people organise their own educational activities – appears straightforward enough, but a complex web of political, social and other strands went into its making. Just as the layperson in the Roman Catholic confessional seems to be a simple idea, yet one that is predicated on two thousand years of theological and cultural inquiry, so does U3A in the UK similarly have a rather more complicated set of intellectual and practical antecedents than what first sight might indicate.

U3A is the confluence of several streams of thought and analysis and, in its very existence, it is the exemplar of several concepts about the way society should be organised. However pretentious this might sound, for a small knot of older people enjoying a humble French conversation class or a musical appreciation session in one of their number's home, that is exactly the case. For a full understanding of the *nuances* of the precedents and starting-points of the organisation, it really is necessary to invite the patient reader to defer the gratification of watching U3As spring up in vast and speedy numbers. Without some grasp of the defining precepts something of the whole style and colour of the movement may easily be lost.

By way of agenda for such a discussion, the following items might be listed. First, there was the recognition that, for most individuals in developed societies and, thereby, as a proportion of any national population, what might loosely be termed older age plays a larger part than hitherto. Along with this quantitative growth in what came to be called the Third Age, there arose a belief that, as opposed to the negative vibrations relating to the desuetude and decline of human beings in the face of the ageing process, one should discover, in this later phase of life, positive virtues of self-fulfilment. However, what was significant in this revelation of the Third Age was its social and cultural novelty, with the corollary that such a brand-new phenomenon should or would evoke its own pristine responses, not least in the formulation of newborn institutions.

Second, there was the concept of social mutuality or co-operation. This was no new idea. Even only to describe it in its industrial setting – and there were several precedents, some reaching back to medieval times – the outstanding success of the retail and wholesale co-operative movement, in the hundred years after its foundation in Rochdale in 1844, is sufficient testimony to its longevity. Nonetheless, the mainstream argument about the organisation of modern society had tended to be a conflict of the dictates of private choice and commercial enterprise with the dogmas of public need and governmental edict. Only occasionally had 'the third way' (if one may re-coin a phrase) of decentralised action, with local communities seizing the levers of their own civic provision, been attempted or allowed.

Third, there was the idea of recurrent education. Despite the efforts of adult educators, this was a notion of relative freshness, for the public provision of education had been persistently related to the preparation of children and young people, ostensibly for their place in work and society. It was, then, largely a matter of social investment and, although some 'topping up' might be sometimes required for vocational or even leisure purposes, few entertained the view that education should be life-long because life was long. There was little acceptance that the national educational service, like its capitalised health counterpart, should be offering intellectual succour across the age-ranges.

The U3A precept clearly incorporated these three notions and did so deliberately and not by happenstance. There might have been a Third Age agency that was mutually based but dealt with, say, volunteering; or one that was educationally focused but without the co-operative element. Equally, there might have been – there have been - other ventures that similarly included two of the three principles. It is important to recall that U3A is critically defined by reference to the triple doctrines of the Third Age, of mutualism and of recurrent education.

Perhaps a useful way of tracing these ideas in fuller vein would be to introduce the three founding fathers of the U3A in the UK, for, in more or less degree, these three hypotheses were consciously implicit in their working and professional lives. It might be more accurate to envisage two founding grandfathers and one founding father, for Eric Midwinter would insist on regarding himself as the disciple of the two older men whom he looked upon as his Gurus.

Born in the Manchester area, the son of a fireman, in 1932, he became very much aware of Peter Laslett's scholarly prestige during his own Cambridge historical studies and later research in social history, while, as an educationalist, he was equally soon alert to the promptings of Michael Young, in particular his award-winning satire, *The Rise of the Meritocracy*. In 1968 Eric Midwinter was recruited to run the Liverpool component of a national project that grew out of the Plowden report on primary education, a project that aimed to develop educational schemes of community and parental involvement in socially deprived areas. Michael Young was chairman of the national project committee and Eric Midwinter was soon drawn into the intriguing circle of Michael Young's social inventiveness, to wit, the world of the Advisory Centre of Education (he later became its chairman), the National Extension College, the International Extension College and like agencies. Here he also met Peter Laslett. ACE and NEC were Cambridge-based and Peter Laslett was an assiduous advisor to them. It was at this time that Peter Laslett was increasingly turning his keen-eyed attention to the demographic studies that were to have such worldwide significance.

In 1975 Michael Young, as befitted the originator of *Which*, became the founder-chairman of the National Consumer Council, which, at its onset, was given a special remit to campaign for the rights of vulnerable consumers, especially in the public sector. Eric Midwinter was appointed head of the NCC Public Affairs Unit, with a broad brief to experiment, *inter alia*, in the field of self-help. He very clearly remembers a visit from Peter Laslett during this time. Peter Laslett told him in characteristically forthright tones to forget all his prior obsessions with children and youth. Old people, pronounced Peter Laslett, are the new wonders. The issue of older age would soon be the fashionable one and any right-thinking social analyst should get in on the ground floor. Thus tipped off by one of his twin Mentors, Eric Midwinter kept open a weather eye and, in 1980, found himself Director of the Centre for Policy on Ageing, a recently devised think-tank devoted to the social challenge of older age. He was fully wedded into the Young/Laslett axis.

At first and superficial sight, it might be tempting to align the three great U3A principles with each of the founding figures; the demographer; the social entrepreneur; the educationalist. The truth is, however, much more intricate than that, for, if in slightly varying degrees of intensity and from slightly differing angles of attack, the threesome subscribed wholeheartedly to the three defining guidelines. For example, Peter Laslett's vigorously held opinion that those in the Third Age should not be subservient to authority but be ready and willing to organise their own affairs chimed in neatly with Michael Young's steadfast and consistent view about the essential value of ordinary people running their own lives and agencies.

Possibly the most effective manner of screening through this interplay, particularly of the life and work of the two older Founders, would be to revisit the descriptions of their influence that Eric Midwinter composed at the sad time of their deaths, only weeks apart, over the winter of 2001/2002.

Michael Young 1915 – 2002

It has been a rough season for co-founders of the British U3A movement. I last saw Michael Young at the impressive and ceremonial funeral of Peter Laslett in the imposing chapel of Trinity College, Cambridge.

The order of service leaflet ended: Tea will be served in the Master's Lodge. Michael, his woolly bobble hat looking out of sorts against the stately gowns of the fellows and the dignified uniforms of the porters, muttered: 'let's find a little cafe and have a scone and a cup of tea'. We walked across the road and parked ourselves in a comfortable teashop. This was characteristic of Michael. He was ever anxious to escape from ritual and protocol and rediscover normalcy.

He had not altogether found Peter's service satisfactory, feeling that, for all its sonorous tones, it had not quite caught the essence of that vividly enthusiastic man. We chatted about Peter. Michael, already failing badly in health, was naturally distressed at the loss of his energetic sparring partner.

For the hundredth time – yet it was always fresh and vital – he expounded on the need to match concept and action, to dream up the vision but to sustain the impetus for detailed implementation. That was the long-held faith of possibly the most effective social innovator of the last 60 or so years.

He asked, with his usual genuine concern, about my own activities and said, very simply, that his own chief pleasure was playing with his small daughter. He had some purchases to make – I suspect for that same small daughter –so he crossed the street to the shops and I took the bus to the station. We had said good-bye.

All his thought, all his incisive writing, all his brilliantly conceived schemes, all his astutely handled initiatives were guided by a salient method. He was a utopian socialist. His thinking stemmed from the views of 19th century radicals like Robert Owen, Saint-Simon or Charles Fourier, with their hatred of massive institutionalism, be it in the hands of the public authority or of the large commercial company.

Another of that number, Etienne Cabet, wrote: If we are asked: What is your science? – We reply, Fraternity. What is your principle? – Fraternity. What is your theory? Fraternity. – What is your system? – Fraternity. Yes, we maintain that Fraternity is everything. Michael Young never deviated from this philosophy over the six decades of his active life.

A devout egalitarian, he retained to his dying day (during which, in the shadow of imminent death, he contrived to do six hours work) an unbudgeable belief in the capacity of the man, woman and child on the Clapham omnibus to organise their own affairs in localised concert with one another, if only they were allowed the resources, the tools and, perhaps most important of all, the encouragement. In every one of his manifold enterprises one may trace this sterling, humane and deeply moving faith in his fellow men and women.

Diffident in many ways, he was defiant and robust in his defence of this principle and enormously resourceful and agile in putting it into practice. The track record of previous utopian socialists was not too dazzling, and perhaps his extra ingredient was constantly to find a spot in the existing social fabric where he could insert his innovative communitarian notion and enable it to adhere in reasonable comfort. That degree of superb judgement, allied to a colossal intellect and that unfailing energy in the cause, made Michael Young the supreme craftsman of social invention.

Eric Midwinter & Michael Young

Above all, his own natural instinct favoured mortal ordinariness. Unspoilt, mild of temperament, mellow humoured and courteously moderate in his personal dealings, he was, perhaps without ever realising it, the equable model for the friendly, co-operative sort of communities he believed we should all find a substantial improvement on our current lot.

He was one of the founders of the U3A, of course, but of much else as well, including the Consumers Association and the Open University. He drafted Labour's 1945 manifesto, the blueprint for the revolution of the Attlee administration, and his book The Rise of the Meritocracy *was one of the main influences in the demise of the 11-plus examinations.*

On that last occasion we met, we talked about U3A, and his sense of pride in its achievements was manifest. He spoke of the marvellous moment at Norwich in 1999 when we three co-founders had conferred upon us the title of Founder Member Emeritus. Of the scores of organisations and institutions that Michael Young begat, not one more fundamentally represents him than U3A - in structure, style, method and mood - the determining motif of his life work. All of us should rejoice in how harmoniously it embodies his civilised and compassionate designs.

Peter Laslett 1915 – 2002

'I AM the most privileged person you know', Peter Laslett used to say, truthfully enough, when I met him in his Trinity College rooms, seated on the chair presented to him by Prince Charles, glancing at the priceless portrait of John Locke's mistress, and munching the tasty cake, the recipe for which has been passed from chef to college chef for centuries.

He was also one of the busiest and most enthusiastic persons I knew. He once explained to me that he had three lives. The morning was spent on political philosophy, Peter's original field, where he became the acknowledged world expert on the 17th century masters, like Thomas Hobbes, Robert Filmer and, in particular, John Locke. The afternoon was given over to the Cambridge Group for the History of Population and Social Structure, which he helped found in 1964 and henceforth directed, another arena in which he found global fame and the locus of his most influential book, the evocative The World We Have Lost *(1965).*

The evening was for his Third Age campaigning, a third theme that gave him international prominence, for he introduced the thesis of the sequence of ages into British thinking. In all this he was quietly helped by his wife, Janet Crockett Clark, whom he married in 1947; she, and their two sons, survive him.

A restless reformer, he was, in chief, responsible for creating the BBC Third Programme, before, with Michael Young, crusading for the establishment of the Open University – and then co-founding the U3A.

Thomas Peter Ruffell Laslett was the child of a Baptist manse in Watford, and perhaps some of that old-style nonconformist vigour typified his approach, at once intellectually stringent and yet immensely generous in his desire to bring cultural and educational well-being to wider audiences. He advised me to forget all that nonsense about children and youth; old age is the coming subject - and, within months I found myself director of the Centre for Policy on Ageing, which, among other things, acted as charitable vehicle for U3A until its own status was legally determined.

Peter Laslett

We obtained a grant of some £10,000 from the Nuffield Foundation. Having subsidised an Easter School in Cambridge that led to the creation of some baker's dozen of U3As, we split the rest of the money between a national headquarters (Dianne Norton's 'spare' room) and, as our local window, the Cambridge U3A. Nearly 20 years later the triumph has been astonishing, although Peter was always embarrassed by the self-excommunication of the Cambridge U3A.

Peter Laslett remained a trenchant, if affectionate, critic of all the institutions with which he was concerned, fulminating about Cambridge University, about the Open University and, indeed, the U3A. Having benefited in his demographic studies from massive volunteer assistance on ancient parish registers, he had hoped the U3A would give rise to large-scale and profound research explorations.

At the end, however, you can tell what was closest to his heart from a short line in the notice of his death. 'All donations to the Third Age Trust.'

Before analysing the three distinct streams of U3A thought in a little more detail, it is worth pausing a moment to emphasise that, despite deriving enormous intellectual and emotional inspiration from the French example of the university-sponsored U3A, the question of a direct British equivalent was never really contemplated by the founding trio. In later years a rumour contrived to emerge suggesting it was only after the failure to persuade the University of Cambridge to organise something like a French-style U3A that a more humdrum model was hurriedly devised. The truth is that assistance was sought from the University and it was not much forthcoming – but the help sought was for the homemade version, not for a continental design. It is also true that the Founders believed fervently that the universities and other educational providers should be more liberal in their recruitment of older people as students, but that was more a complement to, not a substitute for, the self-help U3A. There was one robust moment, during early meetings, when Peter Laslett said that tutors and colleges that refused to offer free tuition to retired people, who, as he asserted had already paid their dues in a lifetime of taxes, should be 'pilloried in the press'.

It would have been, in any event, naïve to think that the British Universities, in the early 1980s, would have been, if only for financial reasons, able to associate themselves with an experiment of the French kind. Beyond that, the interested parties in the few universities and polytechnics that recognised the concept of older age provision were themselves mainly wedded to the self-help ideal. Moreover, the English founding trio were deeply conscious of what, with all respect to the mighty achievement of the French U3As, they regarded as something of a weakness. In effect, one could only have a U3A were a regular university conveniently situated, in contrast to the belief that a local U3A might be formed anywhere there were sufficient persons of good will and like mind, while, with the French U3A, the power still lay too much on the side of the professional authority.

What Eric Midwinter chiefly remembers of that springtime of conjectural seed sowing is the harmony of thought. That is not to say there were no arguments. Whenever such stubborn controversialists as Michael Young and Peter Laslett met, the one mildly tenacious, the other trenchantly obdurate, it was no place for those of a nervous disposition. Nevertheless, the squabbles were about tactics. There was never a hint of division on the overall strategy. Indeed, there was hardly a debate about the overarching pattern. The three men came to the planning table with remarkably similar concepts of how one might proceed: older people deserved educational facilities and older people should manage their own educational facilities.

To ensure that the historical and philosophic frame of reference is properly rehearsed, it is time now to scrutinise more closely both the data and application of the three flows of U3A thought and practice, beginning with a glance at the pragmatic meaning of the Third Age as it affected, and as it continues to affect, British society.

It was the essential genius of Peter Laslett that drew together the strict disciplines of history and sociology to describe and explain a global demographic trend of unprecedented impact – and, in the case of Britain, to do so over a thousand year period; and then, from his glittering resource of political acumen, to develop an ideological rationale to meet its importunate challenge. He succeeded in investing the rather nebulous view that 'people were living longer' with something akin to academic rigour.

There is still idle talk of a 'demographic time-bomb', but, as Peter Laslett acidly insisted, it had been detonated in the 1950s, presumably with a silencer attached. It was in that post-war era that the United Kingdom officially became an 'ageing society', as assessed by the proportion of its population who were over 60. In effect, the ratio of older people trebled over the 20th century from the 6% of the Edwardian era. Now the figure is close to 20%, with a European Community of something over 18% and a global figure of 10%. Peter Laslett was at pains to elucidate the reasons for this change, in particular scotching the vague feeling that some sort of radical switch had occurred, affecting the race or even the species.

He demonstrated that people, as a whole, were not living longer, but that many more people were surviving to lead normal lives. Paradoxically, it might be argued that it was not so much people living longer as people dying later. From his vast researches, much of it helped by the kind of voluntary assistance he would later see as an inspiration for U3A activity, he was able to demonstrate that 'living longer' was not a fresh phenomenon. From the Battle of Hastings in 1066 to the Battle of the Somme in 1916, the British count of over 60s had risen as high as 10% and never dropped lower than 6%. Britain had always had a modicum of old people, some of them even challenging the natural human maximum of about 115 or 120, a maximum that was not being seriously challenged, species wide, at the onset of the 21st century.

The illusion had partly arisen because of a confused interpretation of the actuarial figures for life expectancy at birth. In earlier centuries this average had been seriously lowered by the huge number of deaths in infancy. To take a sadly exaggerated illustration, in parts of Liverpool in the 1840s life expectancy had been as poor as 17, because over 80% of deaths occurred in childhood and adolescence. Few people, of course, actually died at 17 and some of those who survived those often fatal years lived to riper ages. Thus, asserted Peter Laslett, it was the survival to enjoy a natural life-span that explained the vast change in Britain's demography, and not some biological bonus to life itself. In 1900, out of a UK population of 41m, 156,000 people died before the age of one. In 1990, out of a UK population of 57m, 128,000 died before the age of . . . 65.

In 1900 one was the dangerous age; now only one in seven deaths occur in the pre-65 age-bracket. As Peter Laslett was wont belligerently to declaim: 'the old have monopolised death.' Many people are surprised to learn that expectancy of life at 60 is not much better now (about four or six years according to gender) than in 1900. The trick is survival to 60 and it is one that the later generations have wonderfully mastered. If one glances at the national median age, that is, the point above and below which half the population find themselves, then one finds it has risen from 24 in 1850 to 38 in 2000.

Peter Laslett also pointed out that another prime reason for the growing proportion of older people was the declining proportion of younger people, defined as those under 16. This dwindled over the 20th century from 32% to 20%. Indeed, one curio is that the ageing of the population has been associated with a declining birth-rate, from 35:1000 in 1850 and 30:1000 in 1900 to 12:1000 today. Through vastly improved life-styles and other social apparatus, we have discovered the knack of reproducing ourselves more efficiently. Of course, the huge numbers assembled in the post-60 age-range presses on the natural maximum. There were about 250 centenarians in 1950. There are about 8000 now. The estimate for 2030 veers wildly between 34,000 and 45,000.

Nonetheless, and looking ahead to mid-21st century, a strange symmetry presents itself over a two hundred years period. In 1840 46% of the population were under 20 and 6% were over 60; in 2040 it is calculated 23% of the population will be under 20 and 29% over 60. In each case the percentage between 20 and 60 is 48%, solid testimony to Peter Laslett's insistence that one must look at the demographic figures in perspective.

This is a crucial vision if one is, as Peter Laslett was, ready to analyse the social ramification of the bare demographics. The adroit shift from a construct based on birthdays to one founded in civic engagement was the sublime consequence. Concisely summarised as a breakdown by 'stage', not 'age', the subsequent scrutiny of the whole life-cycle in relation to social and economic involvement was the key to this social critique. Thus there emerged the structural design of the First Age of socialisation, the Second Age of work and family-rearing and the Third Age when the burden of vocational and familial cares had been completed. Peter Laslett also differentiated, not without controversy, between a Third Age of independent older age and a Fourth Age of dependence, the better to emphasise the positive aspects of much of later life. In everyday practice, the U3A has not felt it necessary to use that distinction and, for purposes of this analysis, the two have been subsumed.

For the relatively sudden trebling of the proportion of older people in the UK coincided with, in historical time, as speedy a reduction in their working and parenting duties. It is this coincidence that makes the Third Age designation such a special one. This socio-economic transformation is sometimes summed up by the joint metaphors of 'the gold clock' and 'the empty nest'. As part of the vast diminution in working hours, days, weeks and years, ongoing since the middle of the 19th century, there came the comparatively modern device of retirement, something unknown to the main bulk of the population before the turn of the 20th century. Driven by the rapid technological changes of the last century and a half and, on occasion, by the pressures of economic depression, late redundancy and early retirement, allied with official retirement statutes and agreements meant that, by the 1980s, the decade of the launch of the British U3As, 31% of those aged 55/59 and 58% of those aged 60/64 were no longer in paid work.

It should be stressed that this also meant that 3.5m men and women still remained in employment after their 55th birthdays, a sizeable minority of them over 70; indeed, surveys indicate more people over 70 enjoying permanent work than suffering permanent incapacity. This serves to justify the value of the 'stage' construct, for the tyranny of the 'age' diktat often gives a false impression of how older people disport themselves. It is worthy of note, for example, that three-quarters of people over 60 report themselves as in fairly good or very good health in a society that still tends too willingly to align oldness with illness.

As for 'the empty nest', the 1900 average of a little more than three children per family has dropped to a current average of just under two. In 1900 the average age of the mother when the last child was 15, that is, on the verge of, at least, notional adulthood, was 50. Now it is 45. Even allowing for the greater involvement of children in college courses and so forth, the majority of children have now reached what parents may feelingly view as a theoretical rather than a practical independence while those parents are still in their late 40s or early 50s.

Taking into account these varied yardsticks, one might hazard the guess that, of Britain's 15m over-55s, 12m may be said to be in the Third Age, again, it is stressed, by no means all of them. In turn, they represent a largish fraction of the 80m Third Agers resident in the unenlarged European Community. Eric Midwinter was able to furnish Peter Laslett, just before his death, with an approximate calculation about the changing character of 'stages' in the British population. Using a number of different sources, including school registrations and pauper totals, he arrived at the following estimates:

Year	% in First Age	Second Age	Third Age
1850s	14	84	2
1900s	21	76	3
1950s	21	67	11
2000s	24	55	21

Perhaps the most astonishing element in that table is not just the growth of the Third Age but also the shrinking nature of the Second Age, as the machinations of longer pre-work and post-work phases invades the primacy of the working life. Peter Laslett was right to hail this dual demographic and social revolution as unprecedented. For all human history and across all human geography, the salience of adult life had revolved around work and child-rearing. For the first time ever, a substantial proportion of adults were not only freed from those chores but were thus liberated for a considerable period. We had already reached the juncture where people were retired for as long as they had worked; now we were approaching the point where people were retired for as long as they had previously lived. Some commentators, anxious to emphasise the dramatic quality of the happening, were even beginning to talk of the Third Age as 'post-adult', in that adult life previously had been defined precisely in terms of what Third Agers had foregone, namely, employment and parenting.

Given 12m persons, over a fifth of the nation, literally spread over fifty years of age, one is not dealing with a homogenous group. Some of the traditional indicators, such as health, as we have noted, or income (some 3m edge towards poverty; some 1.5m are among the richest echelon in the country) are unhelpful. The main definer is their Third Agery. They are, technically, at leisure, in the sense that they are liberated from the chafing shackles of the work-place and the nursery. Curiously, this inner actuality of 'retirement' had been largely ignored by social gerontologists, well-versed, as they were, in many of its peripheral aspects, such as finance, housing and health. The sheer question of how they utilised their time, energy and talents had rarely been examined. One recalls the comment of the anthropologist, Margaret Mead, that, were anthropologists fish, the last thing to be discovered would be water.

Thus, next, to a further twist in the argument, for, despite this newfound leisure, surveys constantly suggested that older people were not effectively attuned to it. This was worrying, for it coincided with germane research that leisure usage, especially of a self-enhancing and participative kind, was as important a factor in quality of life measures as the conventional standards of physical well-being, income and accommodation. It was calculated, in the late 1990s, that average adult Europeans had, with all the hours and minutes totted together, the equivalent of 3000 'leisure' days before retirement and 8000 days afterwards. British time-studies suggested something similar, with, on average, the retired person predictably having twice as much leisure availability each week as the working person, counting in the essentials of sleep, shopping, domestic chores and the like.

Repeated investigations demonstrated a low level of active involvement in leisure activity among older people, whether it were going for a walk or going to the opera. Ominously, as the years drew by, older people overtook children as the nation's chief television watchers, by the 1990s clocking up a weekly ration of almost 40 hours a week, bizarrely close to the sort of working week many of them had recently forsworn. In fact, watching television was, in most studies, the only leisure activity where older people were ahead of the younger generations. The post-war 'automation' that caused social policy analysts to pause for thought about the amount of free time that was available, had led to a widespread scrutiny of leisure provision – but most of it had been directed at the working population. Commentators, such as the astute and perceptive gerontologist, Miriam Bernard, with her concept of 'hurdles to participation', further explained the several reasons for this seeming inertia in older age. Interestingly, a leading cause noted in many such comments was the cultural obstacle. Older people, believing the propaganda about senescence, felt obliged to play out the role of old age and withdrew to the sidelines, into the ante-chambers of society. In Eric Midwinter's phrase, 'they were not only the victims, they were part of the conspiracy.'

Nothing was more guaranteed to make Peter Laslett's intellectual blood boil than what he regarded as the wastage of millions of people with millions of skills and talents. His was a moral crusade. He regarded the sidelining of older people as unethical and his combine of intellectual grasp and moral fervour was well nigh unstoppable. Nonetheless, no one has more fundamentally espoused the anti-ageist cause than Michael Young. Because the subject of ageism has been raised mainly by those in the 'old age' industry, it has been a predominantly 'old age' issue, but Michael Young spotted that the basic problem was the arbitrary usage of age to mark off what we might or might not do throughout the life-span. He made the point forcefully at the British Association in 1990, insisting that 'age stratification' and the use of birthdays as 'public events' were no less wrong than assessments based on gender or race or sexual orientation. He declared that age should be 'something very personal, a private matter' and brought under the scope of data protection legislation.

It is worth pressing that point as one turns to the second of the elements in the build-up towards the launch of the U3A in the UK, that is, the notion of mutual aid, properly associated with Michael Young. For it is right to note that he was extremely alert to the distinctive 'age' issues, just as Peter Laslett was alive to the virtues of self-help agencies and the benefits of recurrent education. In short, and to repeat a point already introduced, although the three founders had, on the face of it, a particular stance, they were each wedded inexorably to the other two strands, in thought and practice.

Michael Young was assuredly the key thinker in terms of new social organisation. In fact, he stands fair to be counted in line with the famous communitarians of the 19th century when it comes to the pragmatic as well as the theoretical exposition of popular democracy. He saw mutual aid as both the supplement to and the humaniser of the collective provision of the state. He was suspicious of what he called 'giantism', that is, the tendency for institutions to become uncomfortably and monstrously large, and, thereby, anonymous, over-bureaucratic and inanimate. It is worth mentioning that he castigated not only the large-scale public bodies but also the vast private corporations and – for they had something of this character in the 1970s when this thinking was being developed – the massive trades unions. In this he followed the line of one of his mentors, R H Tawney, who famously asserted that the opposite of centralised public ownership (what in the 1940s and afterwards was tagged 'nationalisation') was not only private enterprise, but also what he termed 'decentralised public ownership'. This came close to Michael Young's view that, where services were local, it was easier for them to retain a human countenance and for the users to maintain some degree of control.

It was a definitive 'middle way'. So much of political contest and social conflict was either government or business *versus* employees. The important third group – the consumers – had few rights and little representation. Michael Young would take as an example a row in the National Health Service, with management and professional staff locked in mortal combat. The patients would lie supine in their hospital cots unable to influence the debate one way or the other. One of Michael Young's creations, the College of Health, was a direct response to this particular problem, but he ranged very widely, with bulk buy groups (a development in which Eric Midwinter was very much concerned), with a motorists' co-operative, and with the 'brain train', small study clubs for commuters, which had a particular resonance for U3As, as well as with engagement with the public services. With his clear-cut view that consumers should be in the van of authority and control, he was predictably enthusiastic about older people taking control of their own activities.

But why education? That might now seem a surprising question, but it is a necessary one. As Director of the Centre for Policy on Ageing, Eric Midwinter and his staff were developing a series of initiatives, among which education was but one, aimed at a more life-enhancing Third Age, crucially seeing the older person as active citizen rather than passive social casualty. With Peter Laslett exercised about the rights and merits of those in the Third Age across a similarly wide field and Michael Young likely to pop up with an experiment in the most unexpected arena, it was not inevitable that education would be the chosen realm for action. Conceivably, a case might have been made out for a venture into the political sphere, into the volunteering nexus, into – another of Michael Young's passions – the visual and performing arts *per se*, or into domestic tasks from shopping to DIY.

There were perhaps two reasons why education served to be the salient feature. In the first place, it was the common denominator of the three men's interests: it was the issue that had joined them together – Michael Young and Peter Laslett in their concern for distance teaching, not least their prominent, their indispensable, part in the creation of the Open University; Michael Young and Eric Midwinter in the struggle to develop educational progress in socially desolated areas; all three in connection with the Advisory Centre for Education and other like Youngian bodies. Education was a natural trysting-post for the trio.

In the second place, there was a groundswell of activity in the world of continuing and adult education itself. Central to this was Peter Laslett's research, which he undertook in 1979, courtesy of a grant from the Elmgrant Trust and the National Extension College, both agencies with a Michael Young imprint. This led to the highly significant publication of *The Education of the Elderly in Britain*, which included a swingeing assault on the paucity of provision for that age-echelon that had, in childhood and youth, earlier suffered so disastrously in the schooling stakes: 'they are the least educated community of native English speakers', claimed Peter Laslett. His study embraced *An Educational Charter for the Elderly*, which was actually first published in *New Society*, 13 March 1980.

The Charter made five demands: a fair share of the educational budget; a general recognition that education should not be so obsessively youth oriented; access for older people to all educational institutions; the establishment of a distance education system for older people ; and the wide acknowledgement of 'the cultural and intellectual importance' of older people. Peter Laslett also included a far-sighted proposal that a specific TV channel for older learners should be established. He was enraged by the generational injustice that had dismissed the elders in our society with a miserly schooling and then, after using their hard-earned taxes to pay for the hugest bonanza ever in educational expenditure, had dismissed them again with meagre rations in old age.

At much the same time other educators were getting the Third Age bit between their teeth. Under Michael Young's aegis at the National Consumer Council, Eric Midwinter had drafted a paper on 'Senior Colleges', what he later apostrophised as 'Ruskins for the Retired', in 1978 – and there are signs in 2003 that something like this might be happening – while adult tutors in general were seizing the opportunity. Prominent among them in the London area was the ebullient and highly respected Brian Groombridge, an associate of Peter Laslett's and a close friend of Eric Midwinter and Michael Young. Following some research into the co-operative movement and education, he had, earlier in his career, become, under Michael Young's *Which* banner, the first Director of the Research Institute for Consumer Affairs (RICA). He was now to become involved very closely with the ongoing discussions and was to prove a major influence on U3A developments, especially in the important metropolitan region. Indeed, as early as 1960, Brian Groombridge, now Professor of Adult Education in the University of London, had raised many of these issues in his far-sighted *Education and Retirement; an Enquiry into the Relevance of Education to the Enjoyment of Leisure in Later Life*. This was funded by the Nuffield Foundation – a charity that was destined to play a major role in U3A's early story – and published by the National Institute of Adult Education.

Another meaningful London-based player was Sidney Jones of the then North London Polytechnic. His pioneer work with older learners, in particular his successful experience with the visual arts as a means of stimulating elderly hospital patients, rightfully attracted attention. The gist of his findings were recorded in *Education for the Elderly* (two articles in *The Technical Journal* in 1975) and, in 1976, under the auspices of the Beth Johnson Foundation, Stoke-on-Trent and the Department of Education of the University of Keele, his publication, *Liberation of the Elders.* His contribution to later U3A debate and development was ever measured, perceptive and good-humoured.

Another significant step was taken in 1981 when representatives of the 'old age' charities and adult education academics came together to form FREE, the Forum on the Rights of Elderly People to Education, an information service and pressure group promoting the thesis that older people should have improved educational chances. This was convened on the suggestion of Sally, now Lady, Greengross, the imaginatively bright Director of Age Concern England, at the North London Polytechnic on 18 January 1981.

This was, in part, the formalisation of a looser network of experts in these fields that had been exploring the question in an *ad hoc* fashion since 1976. One of its interests had been the success of the American Elderhostel programmes, with their *motif* the linkage of holidays and learning for older people. In 1980 some of this group made overtures to SAGA about the possibility of a British equivalent, but this came to nothing, and thus there came the suggestion to start an information network. Their names made up something of a roll-call of the radically aware scholars and 'old age' experts of their day, many of whom were to offer significant assistance to the general and unfolding theme of the education and British older people. It is proper to note at this point that, currently, Brian Groombridge is co-editing with Jim Soulsby, of the National Institute of Adult Continuing Education (and himself with a plot-line in the U3A story) preparing a history of the wider canvas of educational opportunity for older people in the United Kingdom, in which, of course, the U3A has a decent but by no means exclusive portion. This promises to serve as an instructive backdrop to the more specific tale of U3A.

Brian Groombridge, Frank Glendenning, of the University of Keele, later the founder of the Association of Educational Gerontology and a wise and prime influence with the Beth Johnson Foundation, Eric Midwinter and Peter Laslett were members of FREE, while its Coordinator was the Canadian-born social scientist, Dianne Norton. The Forum, otherwise completely lacking funds, was generously taken under the wing of Age Concern England, and the Coordinator role was incorporated into her post of Education and Leisure Officer at Age Concern England. Impressed by her networking and her energetic professional skills, Peter Laslett and Eric Midwinter would soon invite Dianne Norton to adopt the administrative role in the putative U3A project that was now emerging, and she accepted. This completed the quartet that was to be responsible for the mounting of a national U3A movement in the United Kingdom. This was in April 1981. It was Peter Laslett, consummate drafter of the intellectual-cum-political case, who penned the FREE Manifesto, highlighting the duties of the public sector in this respect, whilst also underlining the primacy of the Third Ager as citizen and likely contributor to the solutions. Dianne Norton and Eric Midwinter were among its signatories, all of them notables in the field of adult education.

Of course, the French University of the Third Age set-up was vital in stimulating the thinking. L'Université du Troisième Age (UTA), was instigated at Toulouse in 1972 under the gifted leadership of Pierre Vellas. A successful summer school for retired people in that year prefaced the very first Third Age University at Toulouse in 1973, quickly followed by programmes in other towns close to Toulouse. The notion spread rapidly and not only in France. Such was the take-up of the idea in other countries that an international body, known as the International Association of Universities of the Third Age (AIUTA) was established as early as 1980. By 1983 AIUTA had 31 members with programmes operating in 130 centres.

The British contacts were principally made in 1978. Peter Laslett, as part of his Elmgrant supported research, visited the Caen UTA, while Brian Groombridge, as a guest lecturer of the British Council, and Cynthia Wyld, Administrator of and funded by the Beth Johnson Foundation (another instance of that charity's valued assistance in these affairs) visited ParisX Nanterre, Grenoble and Lyon.

The enthusiasm of this intrepid trio for these new initiatives, to say nothing of their equal flair for spreading the word, galvanised the informal exchanges that were already ongoing among the nation's leading exponents of lifelong learning, particularly as it touched on the older echelons. Naturally enough, the French U3A example was emphasised in Peter Laslett's forthcoming publications, while, over the next three or four years, the contacts were maintained and built upon with some relish.

Brian Groombridge developed links with, among others, Helene Reboul of the Lyon UTA, Maximilienne Gautrat of the Paris X Nanterre UTA and Patricia Floriet of the Grenoble UTA.

Of especial benefit was the connection that evolved with Michel Philibert, Co-Director of the Centre Pluridisciplinaire de Gerontologie and based at Grenoble, home of a notable French UTA. World-famous for his sagacious scholarship, Michel Philibert has been shrewdly described by Brian Groombridge as 'Peter Laslett's philosophical opposite number'. With his astute grasp not only of the patent quantities of European Third Agers but also of the unique qualities, social and cultural, of the last generation to recall life before the 1939 watershed, his influence on British thinking is difficult to overestimate. Moreover, he was a ready sympathiser and pragmatic helpmeet in the British cause, for he lucidly spotted and applauded the essence of the self-help doctrine as a legitimate statement in older age citizenship.

There were more hands-on connections at a higher education level. With Peter Laslett at Cambridge; with Frank Glendenning at Keele; with Professor David James of the University of Surrey, the beginnings of a fruitful partnership with U3A, given his dextrous mix of sharp-mindedness and empathy; with Brian

Groombridge in London, accompanied by his colleague from the Department of Extra Mural Studies, that prince of adult education tutors, Peter Shea – with such luminaries as these, educative sparks began to fly. In 1979 students from the Grenoble, Lyon and Paris U3As visited London for study purposes with the London lecturers, while, in conjunction with the Beth Johnson Foundation, joint summer schools, with both French UTA and UK retired adult students participating, were satisfyingly organised on an annual basis from 1980.

It is well-known that the French model resembles in some ways the British extra-mural system, which obviously attracts some older students, and this was certainly a major reason why the United Kingdom universities responded less than strongly to this continental approach. They believed they were doing something of this already: the progressive thinkers in the extra-mural departments, such as Brian Groombridge, were seeking something more radical to engage older people in the United Kingdom.

It is only right to underline a further spanner in the works, for, as well as some university and other providers being critical of the U3A initiative, there were also queries raised by the unions representing college lecturers. Peter Shea, just as one illustration, recalls how he had 'a holiday break of mine clouded (by) a demand by the union that I present myself to explain why I was advocating an adult educational organisation that would not pay fees to its tutors.' That was not a lone instance. The first full U3A conference at the University of Keele in 1984 fielded a panel of adult and continuing education officers, some of whom were preoccupied with fears that the spread of U3As would find their colleagues queuing at the labour exchange. It reflects enormous credit on the several institutional insiders who stuck to their principled guns and welcomed the U3A incomers in what was sometimes an atmosphere of suspicion.

What had happened in France, with its relatively weak extramural tradition, was that a legislative decree had obliged the French authorities to consider provision for adults, and it was the genius of Pierre Vellas that had diverted some of the appropriate resources and organisation towards older adults. Soon a basic methodology of a committee of retired persons emerged at the participating universities. Each of these committees negotiated a contract with its university for the use of facilities and tuition. Although 'satellite' additions were devised for nearby townships, one drawback, already noted, of the French version was that, unless one resided within the immediate catchment area of a university, there was no opportunity to join a UTA. Moreover, what was offered was the traditional academic fare, and this at a time when British adult educators were hopeful of seeking broader curricula.

Those explicit criticisms should in no way be allowed to belittle the magnificence of the concept: the throwing open of higher educational amenities to an age-group and generation that had been more or less abandoned was, whatever else, a noble gesture and, for those many people who craved university teaching in a university setting, it was a precious boon. It is true that, towards the end of his life, Peter Laslett, his well-attuned nostrils ever ready to sniff out humbug, came to believe that, in some centres, the UTAs were being fobbed off with the less effective tutors, just as it used to be said in portions of the English education service that remedial pupils were stuck with the least able teachers. Nevertheless, he was always complimentary to the general conception. A retrospective judgement must be that, without the inspiration of the French model, the British version would certainly not have been designed.

There was, furthermore, an added stone for the foundation. An Anglo-French conference was held in the autumn of 1980 at the Wye College. It was supported by UNESCO, the British Council and the Department of Education and Science and it subject was 'Learning, Education and Later Life'. This led to a key document, *'The Wye Declaration'*, drafted by Brian Groombridge and published in *Adult Education*, the organ of the National Institute of Adult Education, with Michel Philibert's translation appearing in the French academic journal, *Gerontologie*. This concisely and challengingly established the rights of older people and the responsibilities of the public and voluntary agencies in regard of education, broadly defined.

What most intrigued Peter Laslett was the aspect of negotiation. Although, in order to attract governmental funding, many adult classes of all kinds in Britain had to satisfy the test of the market and register a sufficiency of students, there was little in the way of user deliberation and contractual consent. It was this aspect of agreed access that spurred him on to think in terms of retired Britons similarly bargaining for facilities and, beyond that, moving to a more complete self-determination. He spoke of 'a self-generated governing body of elderly and retired people' as the key to the U3A structure.

There was another piece in this educative jigsaw. The recurrent element, applied to older age, was important, but there was also the adjacent hypothesis of Community Education. This idea urged that the cloistered fashion of formal education was over-institutionalised and too remote from ordinary experience. It pressed the solution of education being woven much more seamlessly into the fabric of everyday existence, recognising the wholesome truth that, however the official system might primly protest, it was the community at large – the home, the neighbourhood, the workplace, the television – that formed the authentic educational power. Research in the 1960s suggested, in rounded terms, that the influence of home and neighbourhood out-gunned the school, for good or ill, in the ratio of four to one, so that there was considerable technical backing for the eminently sane social argument that the education system was divorced at its peril from its host community.

The ramifications of Community Education for older people were self-evident. American and British research emphasised the fact that older people themselves thought education was exclusively for younger people – in a 1970 survey for the Pre-retirement Association two-thirds of retired people supported this antiquated opinion. The attendant myth – that older people were ineffective learners – was a further contribution to this wholly negative attitude. The uniformly poor showing at this time of older people as attendees at official educational courses was partly explicable in terms of this cultural gap, whereby older people had been indoctrinated to believe that 'Learning' was not for them. The so-called University of Life had taught them to give actual universities and other like agencies a wide berth.

Eric Midwinter was noted as a leading Community Educator, for his efforts in downtown Liverpool and elsewhere had been of this mould, whilst Michael Young, the arch-proponent of community solutions and Founder-Director of the celebrated Institute of Community Studies in Bethnal Green, was a staunch supporter of such approaches in education, no less than in other social and civic fields. Eric Midwinter was a close associate of the energetic figure of John Rennie, the Founder-Director of the Community Education Development Centre (CEDC), based in Coventry, and John Rennie was to remain a faithful friend and encouraging counsellor to the nascent U3A movement. Community Education officers, in part under the influence of CEDC efforts, and as we shall later observe, were destined to play a very useful role in the establishment of many U3A groups nationwide.

At first sight paradoxically, the needs of pre-school children, a field in which both Michael Young and Eric Midwinter had been prominently engaged, serves to demonstrate some of these varied elements. In 1961 Belle Tutaev's wake-up letter to *the Guardian* led to the formation of what, by the end of the century, were 800,000 youngsters in 20,000 play-groups with 240,000 parents acting as helpers. The U3A founders did not hesitate to utilise this as an example, for it was Britain's most extensive exercise in social co-operation since World War II. The analogies will not be lost on U3A adherents: a democratic and federal structure; a self-help theme of local autonomy; an enlivened social life for the participants, and a demonstration of lay capacity (for the number of paid staff or of self-contained premises is negligible in the play-group movement). Reassured that mutual aid and education were by no means incompatible, the founders found both practical aid and conceptual enlightenment in this massively successful self-help movement.

This lengthy 'prequel' to the U3A story may possibly surprise some with its intricacies and *nuances*. It is a matter of some import for the inheritors of the British U3A tradition to sustain and transfer to their successors some grasp of this seminal thinking and activity. 'Three blokes brought French idea to Britain' is a glaring half-truth that does scant justice to the convergence of thoughts, to say nothing of the actions of other contributors, which combined to set the stage for the U3A drama.

Gradually, the cast, the scenery and the script were assembled. Now we reach the fateful years of 1981 and 1982, when the U3A was premiered for an unsuspecting and, initially, it must be admitted, largely indifferent British public. All in all, there was a sense both of unease that older people were not getting a fair shake out of the education service and that the time was propitious for radical experimentation. It was time for the curtain to be raised on Britain's first original national exercise in adult education since the establishment of the Open University in the 1960s. Thus, after the Chorus in *Henry V*, 'Turning th'accomplishment of many years/Into an hour-glass . . . prologue-like, your humble patience pray,/Gently to hear, kindly to judge our play.'

Three: THE EASTER OF '82

1982 and all that . . . 1982, in the U3A saga, is like 1066 in English history, what Sellar and Yeatman famously called a 'memorable date'. It is only fair to add that the impact was not quite so marked as that of the Conqueror's masterful strategy at Hastings. Nonetheless, 1982 was certainly the year of U3A's nativity.

There were preliminary *sorties* in 1981, just as, one presumes, William of Normandy spent some of 1065 resolving issues of support and *materiel.* In February 1981 Peter Laslett hosted a meeting in Cambridge, attended by several educationists and social scientists, including Michael Young, Eric Midwinter and Dianne Norton. This discussed and lent support to the notion of bringing the U3A ideal to Britain and it was quickly followed by a spring workshop, organised by Eric Midwinter, in his role as Director of the Centre for Policy on Ageing (CPA), held at the Nuffield Foundation, then the base for CPA's activities. FREE members were invited to this, along with others who had shown a particular interest in this new idea. John Rennie, of the Community Education Development Centre, was present, along with Brian Groombridge, at a time when 'Learning in Later Life' courses were being launched with his encouragement in London. Sidney Jones, with Help the Aged sponsorship, at the Polytechnic of North London and Stella Rosenak, at the Middlesex Polytechnic, were the tutors principally involved. The Nuffield Foundation get-together was a lively but practical affair, with minds now very much attuned to an acceptance of the principle and brains turned to how most efficiently to implement the idea.

These two meetings formed the basis for two important actions. One was an application for financial aid from the Nuffield Foundation, which was then the core funder of the Centre for Policy on Ageing and which had a special remit to offer charitable succour to projects involving older age. The Director of the Nuffield Foundation, the astute-minded political scientist, James Cornford, was himself highly sympathetic to positive steps being taken to engage older people more readily with their own services. Michael Young, ace drafter of such proposals, agreed to draw up an application. In the meanwhile, the momentous decision was made to hold a public meeting in Cambridge to advertise the concept of U3A in the UK. The night of Monday 20 July was selected and a press release was circulated to the nation's newspapers and assorted media.

There was no response. It was as if William the Conqueror had landed on the pebbly shores of Sussex and the local Anglo-Saxon peasantry had dismissed him as a passing yachtsman and placidly continued their domestic activities of ploughing and weaving. The chasm between the excitement of the tiny band of enthusiasts and the indifference of the huge multitude was distressingly wide. It was this vast disappointment that led Dianne Norton, framer and distributor of the doomed press release, to coin the wry phrase much chuckled over in early U3A circles to the effect that the British U3A was 'launched more times than a rubber boat in a high wind.'

This was a shift from academics mulling and musing over theory in the comforting privacy of Cambridge colleges and London charitable headquarters. This was a shift to the chillier world of reality and thus it was with some trepidation that the organisers assembled at the Guildhall, Cambridge on that fateful Monday evening. There was one advantage. The decision to hold the meeting in Cambridge meant that there was already a bevy of local talent whipped up by the energies of Peter Laslett and his associates, whereas, in, for instance, the more anonymous confines of

London, finding an audience might have been more difficult. To all-round relief, the stately Guildhall was satisfactorily filled for the occasion.

There were brief addresses by Peter Laslett and Eric Midwinter, followed by an inspirational speech from Michel Philibert, the evening's special guest, a philosopher who had travelled from Grenoble to add his benediction to Britain's attempt to emulate the French success, with which he was so notably associated. The Frenchman, black-bereted, wistfully smiling, leaning casually on his walking stick, was the perfect choice for the occasion. Liberal-minded, rational, piquant in his fluency, he enthralled his listeners with an appeal, not so much to the more mundane element of older people making up educationally for lost time and chances, but more to a nobler vision. He saw U3As as the agency whereby older people undertook 'the reinterpretation of their life', for their own sake and for that of others. Michel Philibert was the gifted advocate of older age as the repository of priceless experience and of U3A as the vehicle for its buoyant expression. The Third Ager, for him, was someone to be cherished as a vital human resource, not someone to be ushered passively to the sidelines of society. Michel Philibert was wont to quote his famed countryman, Montaigne: 'the shorter my possession of life, the deeper and fuller I must make it.'

The meeting was judged a success by the organisers. Many of those attending declared an interest in future action in Cambridge and practically all had found something of value in the discussion. The first-ever public debate on U3A in Britain had passed off gratifyingly. Nor apparently had all the seed of the press release fallen on stony ground. There was a request from the BBC Radio 4 consumer programme, *You and Yours*, for an interview. Eric Midwinter, whilst working with Michael Young at the National Consumer Council, had had some dealings with this very worthwhile series and, next morning at noon, Tuesday, 21 July 1981, there was another 'first' – asked to talk about the previous evening's happenings, Eric Midwinter was able to make the first broadcast petition on behalf of U3A.

The outcome was staggering. Almost 400 letters arrived in the next few days. Radio is sometimes regarded as a less efficient weapon for a reply than the printed word, where readers have an address static before their eyes. Radio, being more transient, depends on people snatching for pen and paper when something catches their fancy, so this enthusiastic 400 was rightly regarded as highly significant. It suggested that a public chord had been and could be touched. It was at this point that Eric Midwinter was enthused enough to exclaim publicly and prophetically that here was 'a show that would run and run', although, truth to tell, there were to be some tricky hurdles *en route*. It is worth pausing for a moment to recall some of the sentiments expressed in this correspondence, for the flavours indicate what would soon be recognised as the general U3A mood: 'your broadcast leads me to believe that you are suggesting something that I thought must one day develop, making learning accessible to those who realise its value for its own sake' . . . 'I have been trying to teach myself something of the arts and, although I find it stimulating to study, I know it would be beneficial to have some guidance and an opportunity to communicate with like-minded people' . . . 'I am quite convinced that such an establishment would discover a lot of talent otherwise going completely to waste' . . . 'I would like to start where I left off compulsory schooling at 11 years old' . . . 'I always wanted to be a teacher, bit late now, but I've never lost my desire for learning' . . .

One fondly hopes that at least some of these 400 correspondents joined U3As and realised their ambitions. Certainly there were some who were involved in the early discussions at national and local levels. Some letters from people in the London region were forwarded to Brian Groombridge, for there were welcome omens that his colleagues and he would be central in the establishment of a U3A in the capital, whereas Dianne Norton dealt with the vast remainder. They included letters from people anxious about the onset of a possibly boring retirement, or lonely and in search of invigorating company, or worried about their older relatives' lack of mental stimuli, or simply intrigued by this novel concept. They were sent a response that both clarified the meaning of the

Third Age and emphasised the keyword of 'negotiation', urging the formation of 'a self-generated governing body of elderly and retired people, whose primary task would be to negotiate for the use of whatever facilities and resources, including teachers, where necessary to the development of whatever educational activities they chose to pursue.'

It was at this stage that Peter Laslett was moved to compose *The Objects, Principles and Institutional Forms of the University of the Third Age*, a document that was first published in the August of 1981. Primarily intended for the Cambridge U3A and, by extension, as an embryonic constitution for all other U3As. It soon became the national basis of all subsequent statements as to the philosophic and administrative construct of U3A. It consisted of twenty objects and eight aims and, subsequently, it was summarised by Eric Midwinter and Dianne Norton, with Peter Laslett's encouragement, in a shorter document under the title of *All Our Futures.*

This breviate of eight objects and five guiding principles were as follows:

Objects

First, to educate British society at large in the facts of its present age constitution and of its permanent situation in respect of ageing.

Second, to assail the dogma of intellectual decline with age and make those in their later years aware of their intellectual and aesthetic potentialities.

Third, to provide from among those who have earned freedom from work the resources of development and intensification of their intellectual and cultural lives.

Fourth, to create an agency where there is no distinction between those who teach and those who learn, where as much as possible of the activity is voluntary, freely offered by members of the University to their fellows.

Fifth, so to organise this institution that learning is pursued, skills acquired, research openings pursued and intellectual interests developed for themselves alone, without reference to qualifications, awards, or personal advancement.

Sixth, to undertake investigation into the process of ageing in society, and especially on the condition of the elderly in Britain and the means of their improvement.

Seventh, to encourage the establishment of similar institutions in every part of the country and to collaborate with them.

Eighth, to help to mobilise the efforts to offer other elderly persons in Britain other opportunities of educational stimulation on as wide a basis as possible.

Guiding Principles

i. The University of the Third Age shall consist of a body of persons who undertake to learn and to help others to learn. Those who teach will be encouraged also to learn and those who learn shall also teach, or in other ways assist in the functioning of the institution – by, for instance, counselling other members, offering tuition to the housebound, bedridden and hospitalised, by assisting in research projects, by helping to provide intellectual stimulus for the mass of the elderly in Britain, by taking part in offers of manpower to educational and cultural institutions which may require this, such as art galleries, museums and libraries and so on. Secretarial, administrative and fund-raising assistance would be an important function for those wanting to help the institution.

ii. Joining the University shall be a question of personal choice. No qualification shall be required and no judgement made by the University of the Third Age as between applicants. The standards of the University should be those set by its individual classes and other activities, and the form taken by each individual pursuit shall be decided by the members collaborating for that purpose.

iii. Everyone joining the University shall pay a minimum fee, to be kept as low as possible, for its upkeep. No support from the funds of local or central government shall be expected or sought, but fund-raising shall become an integral part of the University's operation.

iv. No salary shall be paid any member of the University for teaching or otherwise helping other members, although it is accepted that, in pursuance of the interests of the members, arrangements will be maintained with all other providers of adult education programmes in the area and special arrangements sought with national bodies of a cultural and aesthetic nature.

v. The curriculum of the University of the Third Age shall be as wide as its human and financial resources permit, but the preference of members will be the only criterion of what is done. Strong emphasis will be laid on research projects, on practical skills, on physical and allied leisure pursuits as well as on intellectual and academic pursuits. Insistence on learning as an end in itself will guide the decisions as to what activities to undertake.

Thus was the charter unmistakeably laid out in Peter Laslett's ringing, uncompromising tones. It was – it is – an unalloyed, precise agreement, free from prevarication and happily short on provisos. One theme of this text will be, in later chapters, an attempt to gauge how close the British U3A has kept to those clear-cut founding principles.

First there was the word and then, fortunately, there was the money. Michael Young had attended the Cambridge meeting and immediately joined the nascent committee. Eric Midwinter and he began to seek funds. In October 1981 the Nuffield Foundation kindly agreed a grant of £9000 to the nascent U3A. The Centre for Policy on Ageing, with its charitable status, acted as a conduit for this money, until such time as U3A's position could be regularised, it being illegal for the Nuffield Foundation to make a subvention to any body than another charity. About the same time the Christian and Voluntary Service organisation made a similar grant for the proposed London U3A, this money being nurtured, in the same fashion and for the same reasons, by the Department of Extra-Mural Studies of the University of London,

where Brian Groombridge and Peter Shea were keeping a benevolent eye on proceedings.

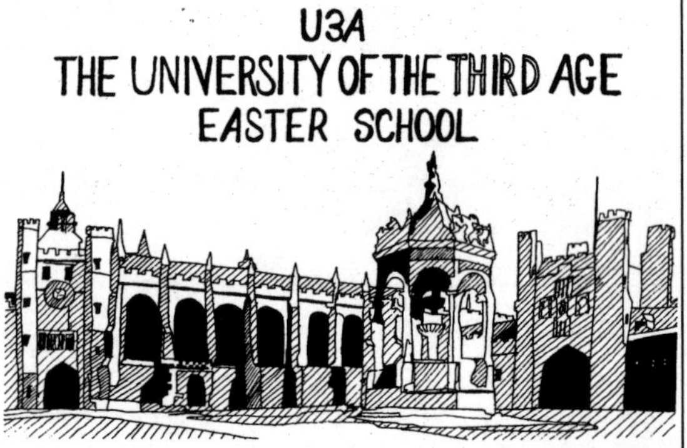

U3A
THE UNIVERSITY OF THE THIRD AGE
EASTER SCHOOL

James Norton

It was determined to mount an experimental Easter School at Cambridge in March 1982 and now thoughts turned to what was believed would be an event of extreme and fateful import. An *ad hoc* group of Cambridge insiders, chiefly associates of Peter Laslett, and metropolitan outsiders, such as Dianne Norton, assumed control of the planning, meeting occasionally in Peter Laslett's rooms in Trinity College so to proceed. Their programme foreshadowed the shape of the U3A pattern of what Peter Laslett graphically called 'intellectual democracy' that later emerged. They resolved to run several days of local classes, followed by a two day national colloquium, the former to try out the theories in practice and the latter to use that practice to sophisticate the theories. Lenin, with his shrewd *penchant* for adjusting the demands of concept to peremptory calls for action, and *vice versa*, would have been proud of them. Moreover, in so planning, they contrived to establish the precedent of local activity within the ambit of national overview. This was to prove crucial.

Easter of 1982 dawned brightly and cheerfully, the daffodils already crowding the Backs of the Cam in Wordsworthian splendour. St John's College, lofty and resplendent, was the base for the workshop and 75 people enrolled. Fifty of these were Cantabrigian, almost all of them Third Agers, ready and willing for the educative fray. The remainder were drawn thither via the national network that was already burgeoning. They embraced both adult educators who were keen to spread the new gospel and Third Agers from across the country, eager perhaps to learn lessons in order to do likewise in their own bailiwicks. The classes were mainly in traditional subjects, but with considerable scope allowed for discussion and allied participation. The end-of-school conference was highly pragmatic, with attendees focusing on mundane issues of everyday organisation as much as upon the intricacies of theoretical dialogue.

There was substantial optimism at parting. It was certain that a Cambridge U3A would be established with every chance of a successful outcome. Delegates learned the encouraging news that, just prior to the Easter School, the embryonic London U3A had convened a steering committee. Brian Groombridge had chaired a meeting attended both by fellow academics, such as Peter Shea, and by retired people, among them Pat Kisch and Jean Tait, who were both to play invigorating roles in the evolution of the London U3A. An Oxbridge-oriented U3A and one in the capital city was a heartening start, both of them vital in the political and promotional scheme of things. Just as important, it was clear that several others present at the workshop were determined to, in the words of Wilfred Pickles (a name familiar to all this generation of Third Agers) 'have a go'. The conservative view was that half a dozen U3As would soon be up and running.

The immediate administrative result of the Easter School was the formation of a four person National Committee. It was comprised of Michael Young as Chairman, Eric Midwinter as General Secretary and Peter Laslett as Philosopher-in-waiting, together with Dianne Norton, the one and only official, as Executive Secretary. Indeed, the legendary first meeting of this august body was held in Michael Young's antiquated jalopy, as it transported the quartet London-wards after the Easter School had ended. In spite of, maybe because of, its peripatetic mode, the National Committee made a momentous decision that was, one would like to think for better rather than for worse, to sculpt the contours of the new organisation.

The three male members of the grandiloquently titled National Committee each had long experience of helping to start voluntary bodies and the bitter element of that experience was uppermost in their minds. Michael Young, in particular, and perforce as his frequent amanuensis, Eric Midwinter, were very well aware of the competing claims of local and national agencies. They had sobering recollections of the disadvantages of either sort. They had presided over local projects that had gone swimmingly, but, when the time came to tell the world of such triumphs, there was no national frame of reference. They had installed central advisory or promotional points for this or that brilliant idea, but, when people asked where they could see schemes operating locally on the ground, answer came there none.

The three Founders seized the opportunity, often denied them for one reason or another in some of their previous enterprises, to establish a bipartite system that managed to enjoy the best of both worlds. They were determined to find a balance between local groups, operating freely and independently, and a national framework, operating supportively and innovatively. In fact, this resolve had been expressed as early as September 1981. There were, after all, key principles that all-comers might be expected to accept, while there was an obvious need for an agency to proselytise the new idea and propagate new U3As countrywide. Equally, there was as urgent a necessity to have models of what could be achieved, preferably strategically located across the nation. These were graphically to be described as 'windows' on the project, practical evidence that the British U3A notion was not pie in the academic sky, but pudding to be eaten as proof of its day-by-day viability.

At the same time, all three were avid decentralisers. The idea of a stern and detailed *diktat*, enforceable on everyone, was anathema to them. In any event, much of this was exploratory. If the U3As were to be the creations of their memberships, the national organisers were foresworn to cross their fingers and hope for happy outcomes. One did not know exactly what a U3A would look like or whether there might be a range of options. Flexibility and independence was the motto. The national control was, therefore, turned to a low setting. Would-be supplicants to this broadest of churches had to subscribe to three articles of doctrine only. The first was that the agency must be open to all Third Agers, as socially defined. The second was that the purpose of the agency must be educational in its widest sense, not forgetting the needs of leisure and social companionship. The third was that the agency must be democratically run, with the members in congregation being the sole arbiters of content, approach and style.

The National Committee immediately put its money where its mouth was. There could have been no more forceful demonstration of this yearning for national/local harmony than the car-bound decision to split the money two ways. There was, after the expenses of the Easter School and some peripheral activities had been accounted for, £6400 in the kitty. It was resolved to retain £3200 for a national base and to give £3200 to the emerging Cambridge U3A organisers, so that a prototype would be viewable. Indeed, few U3As have had such a healthy investment at the point of origin, as did Cambridge in 1982.

True to its homely beliefs, the actual headquarters of this great crusade was Dianne Norton's spare room in her Wimbledon abode. There the central office remained until the autumn of 1988, for, that is, almost a third of the British U3A's eventful existence. It is difficult to overestimate the value of that spare room and its valorous occupant. Without a national HQ it is probable that a few U3As would have started and the message would have spread a little and perhaps a few others would have begun business. As we shall have cause to note, however, the benefits of a national base were to be twofold: there was a small propagandist machine whirring away, trying to persuade others to start U3A groups; and there was a hub for keeping the growing number of groups in some form of meaningful contact.

Communication between centre and periphery was another item on the agenda in Michael Young's speeding motorcar on that shining March evening. The mobile National Committee could all recount atrocity tales of uncommunicative organisations and were keen to avoid that error, if at all possible. As early as the August of 1982 a newsletter was sent to all organisers who were known to the National Committee, reporting on progress thus far. There were now more mentions in the press and more inquiries flooding in, so that a standard response had to be printed for ease of answer.

Then in September of 1982 came yet another launch. The National Committee published a practical manual, with (aptly enough, given the venue of its first meeting) a motorcar on the cover, bearing the number plate *U3A DIY*. It was made available to individuals or groups interested in starting a U3A. It was divided into three sections. WHAT explained the definition and purpose of a U3A. HOW offered a step-by-step guide, with sample letters, a poster, a questionnaire for potential members, a record sheet, suggested topics for study-groups, advice on possible research and a page about contacts with the press and media. WHERE consisted of a series of pieces of counsel about where to turn for assistance, including leaflets from varied charities and other bodies concerned with old age or adult education. Several would-be organisers found this manual of practical use, so much so that it was eventually updated and republished.

Perhaps the prime duty of the Executive Secretary was to field the names and addresses that flowed in on every post and try to channel them to like-minded people in the same area, with the hope that these individuals would make contact and take up the challenge. Failing that, it was a matter of filing the names and awaiting signs of U3A life in the appropriate district and then forwarding them. Often the advice was the same as that proffered the writers of the original 400 *You and Yours* letters: as there was not as yet any U3A in your neighbourhood, perhaps you would consider starting one. Beyond that, there was a lot of networking to be done by Dianne Norton and, of course, she was in some demand to speak at public rallies or to initial steering group meetings. Her joint work with U3A and with FREE found the one complementary to the other: one way and another the networking extended rapidly.

All the National Committee undertook a range of responsibilities. Peter Laslett, as well as ensuring that the Cambridge model developed satisfactorily, remained active in raising the issues of older age and education in academic and other circles, with particular reference to the novel U3A. He hailed it as a premier example of new old age producing fresh institutions relevant to its new character and as proof that older people, far from being the pawns of the professional cadres, were clearly capable of organising their own services. Michael Young, that spawner of scores of voluntary organisations, pledged to legitimise the national U3A by negotiating its legal status, something he had done perhaps a hundred times for other agencies hitherto. Eric Midwinter's role as Director of the Centre for Policy on Ageing gave him a broad-ranging brief to speak and write about the positive aspects of Third Age life, of which U3A was already self-evidently a fine illustration. He embarked on a series of talks that ran the gamut from groups of professional educators and 'old age' professionals to inaugural meetings of potential U3As up and down the kingdom.

One issue was little discussed by the self-styled National Committee, and that was the title. This was not because it was regarded as a minor point, but because there was no disagreement that the French styling should be anglicised and adopted forthwith. Oddly, this decision was to cause more early dissension inside and outside the movement than most of the others. The protestants were of two denominations. There was self-righteous indignation among some university authorities that the organisers had presumed to deploy the word 'university' at all. The National Committee was accused of a form of institutional burglary. Because there were no premises, no salaried staff and no sanctioned degree courses, there was, *ipso* facto, no university. There were even occasional heavy hints that the U3A organisers, lacking the beatification of an official charter, were acting illegally.

The National Committee shared a sense of history, not least in the character of Peter Laslett, who was adamant that the new agencies could and might be purer versions of the original university concept than the modern distortions. The early medieval university had, at its best, conceived of bands of fellow-scholars gathered together for the selfless pursuit of truth. The spontaneous coming together of older people in dialogue and allied activity for its own sake was very easily defended against the modish, new-fangled universities, obsessed with often weird epistemological divisions and with a bizarre insistence on grading its clients in an atmosphere of false competitiveness. In short, the National Committee met this institutional assault head on, with a perky questioning as to whether the current universities themselves should be using the name.

The second problem was more intractable because it appeared to affect the very practice of U3A activity, so much so that vestiges of the issue are still discernible today. Given that the invention of new institutions for Third Agers was directed at those, in major part, who had found the existing system, universities and all, wanting, then it seemed to be piling Pelion upon Ossa to deploy 'university' in the new name. These critics urged that, in a word, it was off-putting to use 'university' in the title. It frightened off the very people that the organisers were keen to attract. Anecdotal evidence was produced to uphold this position, with cases cited of many older people who ran a mile when faced with a University of the Third Age and kept at a respectful distance.

Such was this concern that several fledgling bodies opted for alternative names. These ranged from Third Age Learning Circle and Learning in Later Life to Shared Interest Society and Leisure 50. Others stuck to U3A as a title, without elaborating what the acronym meant, just as there are many who might not be able to decipher ICI or UNICEF precisely but have the right idea about what those agencies do. Not the least of the negative imagery of older age resides in the nomenclature of its amenities. 'Home helps'; 'meals on wheels'; 'senior citizens'; 'day centres' – they each have some of that dulling worthiness and war-time sombreness, redolent of the 1940s. They scarcely enjoy the exhilarating ring of bustle and excitement.

It was part of the thinking that older people deserved better and that sights should be raised; hence 'university' was paraded without hesitation. The time was ripe for Third Agers to develop modern, positive approaches, dismissive of outmoded images. There were also a couple of practical points. Obviously, one could ride on the back of the existing French coinage, so that the public relations ordeal of launching a brand-new title was avoided. That apart, future negotiations with the international movement would have been very much hindered had an alternative title been adopted. Next, it must be said that no alternative of any weight really materialised. The concise nature of the acronym, with its appetising sandwich of letters round a number, was distinctive enough in all conscience and made promotional activity that much easier.

500 groups – and 140,000 members – later, there is scope for believing it was the proper decision.

There was a final reason. There was a tongue-in-the-cheek aspect. Faced with the grand citadels of the modern universities, all lavish expenditure and prestigious character, the U3A movement was embarked on a homespun adventure, whereby often small numbers of older people would meet, without the stress and strain of academic rivalry, in unostentatious places and with negligible resources. Thus there was an element of good-natured impudence in the stance of the National Committee and the other early U3A protagonists, a wholesome cocking of a snook at the bastions of established scholarship. What was being asserted was the right of every trueborn Briton to start a university in his or her sitting room or backyard, should that be so wished. One of the first rallying cries that rang out was (with due deference to the other nationalities and the other gender): 'an Englishman's home is his college.'

It had been a busy and, for the founding band, a slightly nerve-racking year. In social entrepreneurship, as on the stage, timing, what the old-time comedians called 'waiting', is crucial. A little late or a little early with the punch-line and its effect is lost. Was, then, 1982 the right occasion for U3A to be started in Britain? Three or four years later, when it appeared that progress was stalling, when it was all too apparent that funds were inadequate and when there were constitutional and structural problems of some consequence, there were critical voices. Among what had become the high-ranking hierarchy of U3A in the UK, there was a view expressed that the Founders should, like the experienced comedian, have 'waited'. It was argued that taking the 1982 plunge, with little money, little preparation and little support, had been mistaken. It was argued that the Founders should have patiently built a treasure-trove of funds, a network of local expertise, a host of prestigious academic and political backing and a modicum of public relations input. Only then ran this plausible case, should the U3A have been launched, with a watertight guarantee of national triumph.

At that juncture, this was a persuasive contention, as are many lines of reasoning blessed with the video replay tapes of retrospect. What was not clear was where might have sprung these hitherto unseen seams of gold and thus far invisible troops of adherents to the cause. It is true that the Open University, with which the names of Michael Young and Peter Laslett were initially associated, had received the massive boost of relatively heavy government investment. Most of the other ventures – the flourishing and potent Consumers' Association is one strong illustration – with which the founding trio had been involved had been started with peanuts rather than plenty. The spring and summer of 1982 produced, for them, normal conditions. There was a good idea, a few disciples and a bit of money – and that usually meant it was time to take a deep breath and a risky gamble.

All three had, in any case, grown very critical at the Open University's narrowly degree-oriented approach, its feverish anxiety to be deemed to be on parity with other universities on their terms and its dilatoriness in developing broad-based continuing education programmes. This they ascribed in main part to the Open University's serious reliance on public funds and a governmental policy that insisted on an intensified degree regimen in return. Peter Laslett, in particular and as the principles he enunciated confirm, was steadfastly opposed to the utilisation of state funding for U3A, partly on the grounds that its hands might be tied by subjection to state policy as the price paid. By extension, he remained suspicious of state-financed universities that might, by that default, find themselves unwilling or reluctant to permit of that openness of 'negotiation' with Third Agers that he felt was the prerequisite of U3As of the continental pattern. It is difficult to envisage from where else substantial finance might have arrived, other than from the state. It is also difficult to imagine that the governments of the day would have been willing to subscribe generously to an as yet non-existent body.

In the Founders' minds, therefore, was the sense of the time being propitious for pioneer experiment. It was simple enough to cry from the rooftops that people in the British Third Age should adopt the role of active burghers and organise their own educational agencies, or even that, given appropriate encouragement, they would thus act in the manner of citizens of a Greek city-state. What was on trial was a mesh of hypotheses of a social, political, cultural and demographic as well as of a directly educational nature. It was tacitly understood that the experiment might fail and that, if it did, not one but several concepts – among others, a fresh, positive image of older age; lifelong learning for its own sake; self-help as an organisational device; non-formal educational strategies – would be severely tarnished.

The United Kingdom was the test-bed. Its Third Age population was placed, all unconsciously, on stand-by. The question posed was whether the response would be active or passive. It was the 'memorable date' of 1982 and the U3A equivalent of the Conquest was in motion.

Four: THE FIRST FIFTEEN

Gradually, U3A groups were born in different parts of the country, each one the cause for much rejoicing. These embryonic groups developed along lines that were soon to become familiar to U3A *aficionados*. First, often a lone individual, or, more fortunately, two or three interested parties would float the idea as best they might. Sometimes the crusading founder would have institutional connections, usually with an academic agency, occasionally with an older age charity, and, in those cases, there might be aid with publicity and meeting rooms. Otherwise the intrepid organisers would find themselves forking out the initial expenditure for photocopying, telephone calls and postage. The National Committee was sometimes able to help with a very humble grant of a few pounds, but, in general, a local launch was a hand-to-mouth affair.

What these would-be administrators were advised to do was to surround themselves with an *ad hoc* committee, a small band of fellow-enthusiasts who would assist in spreading the word. This was normally done through local press and radio, plus posters in civic outlets, among which the public libraries proved to be by far the most helpful. The aim was to move as quickly as possible to some form of public gathering. Here the advice was to include as many representatives of other agencies, particularly in the adult education arena, as possible, not least in the hope of allaying fears and suspicions about the thrust of U3A endeavours. It was soon discovered that, where such bodies as the WEA, adult education colleges and university extension departments were not thus kept properly informed, it could lead to some defensiveness on the part of those excluded agencies. Where at all possible, the General Secretary or the Executive Secretary would attend this opening public meeting and address those foregathered.

The purpose of the meeting was twofold. First, it was an opportunity to discuss the new concept in some detail and describe how it might work locally. Second, it was ordinarily utilised to recruit a steering committee or working party, whose task it would be to formulate an operational plan for the new U3A group. It was not unknown for such dedicated people to take to the streets and button-hole shoppers and other pedestrians to ask them whether they were interested. The questionnaire provided in the U3A DIY kit, or a version of it, was also widely deployed. This asked for individual details, about experience and occupation, as well as what interests they had or, as importantly, were keen to take up. There was also a section that invited likely members to say how they might contribute, be it with giving lifts or otherwise helping with transport, with office and allied skills, with leading classes, with offering their homes for classes, and so forth.

One version of the questionnaire, rather than cold-bloodedly ask for direct information, was couched in a style for use at meetings where there might be subsequent discussion. This raised questions about people's favourite book or piece of music, rather than the more direct listing of literature or music as possible interest-groups. It was this device that led to what Eric Midwinter claimed to be U3A's first 'schoolboy howler', although the gender and age was at odds with this designation. Someone suggested her favourite film was *Tess of the Vaudevilles*, although whether this was, in fact, an acerbic comment on a not very outstanding film was never revealed.

It is time to examine some of the 'early bird' U3As and to pursue some of the often allied regional developments; time, too, to consider some of the early failures.

i. Early Birds . . . Yeovil . . . Bath . . . Somerset

Cambridge, with Vernon Futerman a most efficacious Director of Studies, had soon reached giddy heights, with a £20 annual fee, hundreds of members and scores of interest groups, while London, too, made immediate and steady headway with the same degree of achievement. London's fee was £4 a year, with Sidney Jones acting as organiser. Rather more surprising was the runaway success of the Huddersfield-based project, where the indefatigable Edith Bentley, who was also to serve on the U3A national committee, was instrumental in mounting a wide-ranging programme of social and academic groups. Edith Bentley was a retired nurse-tutor, who had already been involved with work in Huddersfield to improve the educational and leisure chances of older people. With what, for that time, was immense aid from the local authority, the Huddersfield U3A flew off to an amazing start, soon numbering several hundred adherents and – almost an emblem for the more homely focus of U3A – it organised a weekly dance as an occasion for all members to get together socially. The national organisers were, of course, more than content to watch three large examples of the U3A principle grow so swiftly in three such distinct areas; the capital city; one of the two leading academic arenas, and a sturdy northern working class bastion.

However, as well as the powerfully backed Cambridge, Huddersfield and London regimes, there were some much smaller outfits developing. Some pride of place must go to Yeovil. Second to affiliate, when matters were formalised in 1983, it is now head of the official list, dating its entry 22 October 1983. The Yeovil initiative began in a local college, where a 'new horizons' group had been formed. There had been a *Guardian* article about the nascent U3A movement, to which one of the speakers made reference. There was sufficient interest for a steering committee to be formed, with John Ashworth in the chair. As with several groups in those early years, there was some reluctance about the 'university' usage, and Yeovil Shared Interests Scheme, yielding the melodious acronym 'YSIS', was coined. Indeed, it was not until the year 2000 that Yeovil constitutionally adopted the U3A title.

YSIS began with classes that included discussion, hobbies, country dancing, drawing and painting, music, play-reading, needlecraft and books. It charged £5 a term or 50p a class. Having jogged along steadily with 60 or so members, Yeovil has recently passed the 100 mark; it runs some twenty activities, as well as monthly coffee mornings, with a

speaker, and a number of other events. But what is perhaps the most fascinating fact is that one of the present group is the daughter of a founder member. The generations wheel around very rapidly. We are reliant on Hilda Quick, currently the Secretary, for these facts and figures.

This was not, however, the lit fuse for explosive activity in Somerset, where chief development was later rather than earlier. Nonetheless, there was the astounding instance of the Bath U3A, the fiefdom of Audrey Cloet, who was to win many plaudits in her role as U3A's National Organiser. Established in 1986 and now with 1410 members, the Bath U3A, attracts – for Bath has a population of about 85,000 and an older age echelon of about 20,000 – one in fourteen of that city's Third Age clientele. The present chairman, Nancy Catchpole, records how a monthly lecture, open to the public, is arranged to sustain recruitment, with enquirers invited to the next monthly coffee morning for further induction – and there are three more such social occasions each year to welcome recently joined members. The Bath U3A newsletter has ten issues a year and there are many other facets to what is a large but well-oiled piece of human machinery.

How did it all begin? Audrey Cloet and Jean-Vernon Bosly were strangers brought together by the cupid-like darts of Harry Muscutt, one of the first two U3A National Organisers. They were the two people in Bath who had made enquiries about U3A and, as always, the advice was 'contact each other and launch a group.' This was August 1985. Audrey Cloet contacted J-V Bosly, with the suggestion, 'let's meet him and tell him we don't think it will take off in Bath.' Plainly lacking in prophetic gifts, Audrey Cloet and her new-found colleague gathered around them a few more people: 'it was a great experiment', wrote Audrey Cloet, 'we were trying to lay the foundations of a group where every member could take an active role.' Come December 1985, and there was a real launch, with Harry Muscutt addressing 28 potential members who reacted kindly to 'our casual request to them to throw in a fiver.' Wisely, a steering committee was appointed to work gradually 'towards a more formal structure, as we thought it a mistake to settle on people and ideas too early in the life of the organisation.'

Slowly, the issue of self-directed learning was teased out, as J-V Bosly posed the purpose as a question: 'can the business of setting up a U3A in Bath itself be undertaken as a learning project to be enjoyed.' Self-evidently, the process was both enjoyable and effective. 'We had 50 members, pioneers in mutual aid learning'; then came affiliation to the national body; next, with Pamela Haber's encouragement, came the evolution of study groups; Kate Owen guided the U3A over the rocky road to a formal constitution, and by the following Christmas there were a hundred members. Now there are fifteen times that number – and it is gratifying to see how one of the U3As Harry Muscutt helped spawn was the home of Audrey Cloet, his highly distinguished successor.

The massive extension of actual U3A groups in Somerset lay ahead in the 1990s, so much so that, currently, the county has no less than 21 U3As of many shapes and sizes. Taunton, of 1985 vintage, but affiliated in 1991, and now with 236 members and 29 groups, offers a representative Somerset example. Pat Halliwell, its Information Secretary and, because 'U3A is the major activity in my life', an honorary Lifetime Member, has forwarded some personal glimpses of a gestating U3A. Marion Harvey was the culprit. Jean Frost writes, ' 'Come to the meeting in the municipal hall', said Marion Harvey as we walked together out of church, taking it for granted that I had seen her article in the church magazine. I had not, and asked what it was about. 'I want to start a University of the Third Age', she said, 'three o'clock next Tuesday'. I told my husband; he said, 'go and see what it's all about, if you don't like it, don't go again.' I did go. I liked it. I went again and have been going for the last 15 years.' Doris Argile, Taunton's long-serving first Secretary, tells how, at that meeting, a steering committee was appointed and four groups were mooted. 34 of the originals still remain on the Taunton roster.

ii. Early Birds . . . Harpenden . . . Stevenage . . . Hertfordshire

Of practical interest at U3A's point of genesis was Harpenden, in Hertfordshire, where the General Secretary persuaded a neighbour, Reg Davis, to form a U3A. Reg Davis not only effectively did so, but went diligently on to evangelise regionally, and even as far afield as Dublin, in those early years. After a faltering beginning, a group foregathered and laid some claim, in 1982, to be the first U3A actually to undertake a piece of learning activity. It met in the local Trust Hall on a weekly basis, cheerfully accommodating itself to a guinea pig role, as Eric Midwinter used many such sessions experimentally, trying out varied possibilities.

At that juncture it was difficult to know what would and would not suit this new educational mechanism. Thus one week this group of twenty or so, but slowly increasing in numbers, would be a reminiscence circle; the next a poetry appreciation group, with members reading their chosen verse and explaining their choice; similarly with a selection of records; another time they would be transmuted into a drama workshop, or a mime demonstration; or choral speaking . . . or choral singing . . . and so on. The accent was properly on participation: there were, for instance, 'coincidence' or 'why I' *motifs*, aimed at ensuring everyone contributed, while, interspersed with sessions led by individual members, there was a scheme of ten minute mini-talks, an induction into the skills of public speaking. The attempt was then made to feed some of the results, both good and bad, into the U3A communications system, again a tiny example of how necessary it was, and is, to maintain a central/local balance. Nearly 22 years later the Harpenden U3A valorously sustains that weekly general programme, the downside of that initial impetus being that it was slower than most to develop an interest-group list, given that its members were wedded to their more generalised weekly slot.

Nonetheless, it was considered vital to explore the possibilities of such participatory learning, just as Bath so carefully and thoughtfully undertook the project of determining how a self-directed learning organism should proceed. It became quickly apparent that the interest-group was to be the essential cell of the U3A experience. Given that degree of significance, it was of crucial import that the interest-group reflected the basic philosophy of the movement. As with the local U3A group, as with, as soon transpired, the national framework, the emphasis was on the democratic.

Just as the local U3A group members were the sole arbiters of what activities should be undertaken, so, in its turn, was the interest-group to enjoy similar demotic control. As with Michael Young's 'brain train' groups, the distinction between tutor and tutored was diluted and the divisive labels of 'teacher' and 'student' shunned. All were members – and, as the founding principles urged, the aspiration was that all would both give and receive. The person who led the French conversation group today might be the novice in the philosophy group tomorrow. Terms like 'group leader' or 'convenor' were introduced. This was partly to encourage the practice of people organising groups in which they might, from the knowledge viewpoint, be on a par with their colleagues. The concept of learning together was pressed, with the task of the convenor one of stewardship rather than lecturing. An early example in the London U3A was the French specialist who, bored with a lifetime of teaching foreign languages, preferred to run a poetry appreciation group, where she was as eager as anyone to begin at the beginning but happy to offer some organisational oversight.

The other reason for the infiltration of this sort of nomenclature into U3A methods was, in any event, to maintain a high level of group participation. One emerging standard practice, even where the group leader was an expert in the relevant subject, was to invite group members to undertake study into some aspect of the theme and take it in turns to offer the lead presentation to the group. All this was in line with Michael Young's fundamentally democratic view of how human activities should be arranged, with lay persons given full opportunity to make good their talents, most preferably in unpretentious situations of human size. The self-mobilised, highly participative U3A interest-group was a model for Michael Young's overarching vision.

Peter Laslett's take on this was uncompromising, for one of the 'objects' he had formulated spoke of the importance of eschewing the distinction between those who taught and those who learned. Schooled in the formalistic structures of an ancient university, but sharply and unsentimentally alive to its foibles and drawbacks, he would trenchantly announce that education was people who did know telling those who didn't, but he would never allow anyone to assume that he or she fell exclusively into one camp or the other. The very idea of people seeking and sharing knowledge in unison was, for him, the founding principle of the true university. Moreover, his urgent ambition to see older people regarded as providers not recipients in social exchanges encouraged him to applaud the development of the involved participatory group.

It was, however, at this level of the basic learning U3A organism, that the tenets of Community Education came into their own. The likes of John Rennie, and his colleagues at the Community Education Development Centre, constantly decried the implication of 'compensatory' education, with its inference that children and adults had 'deficits', holes that had to be patronisingly filled with previously prepared educational ballast. Their warmer and more humane opinion was that, according to personal experience and background, everybody brought something, some talent, some gift, to the educational party and it was the task of the educator to draw out and build on this. Often the most productive setting for such exercises was in the conversational mode of a not oversized group in undaunting surrounds. The Community Education method was thus eclectic about curriculum, refusing to accept the starchy rigidity of official epistemology, and believing that the benefits of educational development might be found in a much wider gamut of topics. As for teaching, a brief descriptor might be that the Community Educator was one who had been re-professionalised from didact to facilitator, while the effort was made to professionalise the lay person, adult or child, that he or she might become, in sensible part, a self-teacher. Or, to complete the workings of this educative theorem, the purpose was to narrow the distinction between teaching and taught . . .

Eric Midwinter was wont to tell the tale of washing up after a U3A meeting, feeling perhaps the need for practice prior to his homeward sojourn. He asked his companion if he could wash, the childish delights of the bubbles affording him more innocent pleasure than the tedium of drying. She willingly assented, stating that she had to avoid plunging her hands into detergent-affected water. He wondered aloud why this was, suspecting it might be some skin allergy. The answer was much more exotic. Here was a recently retired aromatherapist, knowledgeable in the soothing oils prepared for the Pharaohs and exactly where to apply them. He asked her if 'they', with a backward nod towards the members in the main hall, were aware of her mystic arts. She laughed. 'Aromatherapy's not education', she smiled, 'education is about physics and geography'. Eric Midwinter shopped her to the committee. She thereafter ran interesting sessions on this engaging topic with considerable audience participation.

Of course, it would be folly to pretend that every U3A interest-group incorporated all these pure traits of educational collectivity. Sometimes either the teachers, because of their nature, or the taught, because of their right, insisted on a more tutor-led, less contributory path, while some subjects seemed to be less open to the participative approach than others. Nonetheless, many aspired, in part or whole, to the ideal. It is important to give prominence to this the fundamental unit of U3A activity, not least because, for many members, it was their inaugural and even sole linkage with the movement. It is important, too, to acknowledge the deep thought given to the dynamic character of the interest-group. The Founders were very clear in their minds about this. They were not in the business of providing a cut-price, second-rate service to the old folk at home. They believed with enormous conviction that this was the superior way of making available educational provision.

Turning back to more illustrations of pioneer U3A groups, Stevenage was another of the early starters in pursuit of persons attending the seminal Cambridge Easter School. In September 1982 Iris Newbold and Lise Addison started what was known as the 'discussion group', under the auspices of Stevenage Leisure 50 and held in the town's museum. First a dozen and then a couple of dozen people attended and, with Iris Newbold arranging the programme, as she does so commendably to this day, and Lise Addison acting as administrator, growth was steady. 25p a week, if you attended, was the hospitable sum charged. Joan Catteau joined them and inaugurated what was to be a feature of the Stevenage activities – a participatory musical element. What a brainwave it was to launch a 'Can't Sing' choir . . . it was hard to evade recruitment. Similarly she courageously announced she would start a band for anyone and any instrument – and the first afternoon found her with a lady with a violin and a gentleman who had learned to play the mouth organ in a prisoner of war camp. Joan Catteau boldly built a sizeable combined choir and band of some virtuosity. One particularly recalls a concert they gave in St Albans, during which a duet from *Don Giovanni* was performed by a man who had been singing since the 1920s and a woman who had been singing seriously for three months. Here was U3A in a harmonious nutshell: the one keeping going an interest of long standing; the other finding a chance to develop an interest that had perhaps lain dormant for years because of

'Second Age' pressures. Stevenage runs some twelve interest groups and has a membership today of 195.

The presence and model of the Stevenage and Harpenden models from very early times meant that Hertfordshire had what geographers call 'the momentum of a start'. It was a chief, if by no means the only reason, why several other U3As were soon created in that county, without the benefit of anything resembling a regional network. It exemplifies a phenomenon that, in those years, was identified among U3A *aficionados*, as 'contagion'. U3A was catching. Sometimes people would hear of a local U3A happening and possibly attend it, before trying to emulate it on their own neighbouring patch. Sometimes another kind of initiative worked well, in part because the U3A notion was thus in the air; its character was beginning to be understood in the wider area and prospective customers responded the more readily. Sometimes it is the simple fact of U3As being conveniently placed to offer prompt and germane advice. This element of infection was to be repeated countrywide, although the converse – where some areas seemed in virtual quarantine and easily able to resist the benign virus – was, at that time, as worrying as the contagious quality was satisfying.

Hertfordshire now has fifteen U3As, offering good cover of that fertile territory, and the total Hertfordshire membership is roughly 6000. They range in time from the likes of St Albans, which, as chairman Cliff Crellin recalls, began in the 1980s through the efforts of a retired dental worker who had been a U3A member elsewhere, to the recently formed Borehamwood and Elstree group, a 2002 entrant, but already running 17 interest-groups. Lea Valley was another 1980s runner, the result of a suggestion by Janet Eade of Broxbourne Council, and with an input from Audrey Cloet, by this time the vigorously energetic National Organiser. Lea Valley, the home base of Len Street, later to be a celebrated U3A worthy, was so successful that Broxbourne U3A, already enjoying similar success, was its Millennium baby.

Among several largish groups in Hertfordshire are Dacorum and Hertford. Judy Baldwin, the Dacorum secretary, tells of how the council's Leisure Officer mooted the idea and advertised a meeting. Expecting a couple of dozen, a hundred assembled, and the Dacorum U3A, covering a very large area around Hemel Hempstead, Tring, Berkhamsted and the surrounding villages, leapt to life. Now there are over 900 members, with 60 activity groups and, such is the extent of its writ, this well-organised unit arranges three monthly general meeting, one in each of its main districts. Dacorum has also helped with the formation of the Luton and Chiltern U3As.

Hertford and District U3A has published the story of its first ten years and a merry yarn it makes. Audrey Carotti was out walking with her husband when they happened across three ladies in distress. 'You've heard of three old ladies locked in the lavatory',they explained, 'well, we're three old ladies locked out of our car.' Help was sought, and, in subsequent conversation, the three automatively excluded women described how they had met in a U3A arts group. Appetite whetted, Audrey Carotti appealed to her neighbour, Irene Manley, for help. A steering committee was formed, useful aid was tendered by the Welwyn/Hatfield and Bishops Stortford U3As and a public meeting advertised. Cathy Henderson, another neighbour, was roped in – she is now Vice-chairman – and takes up the story: '. . . we expected perhaps 25 or 50 people. So we bought a pint of milk and some tea-bags . . . in the event between 70 and 80 people turned up, queuing in the street and crowding in the entrance

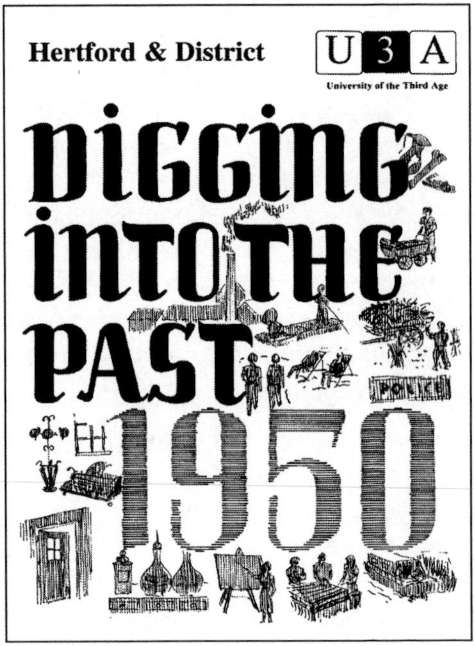

lobby. Those of us who had initiated all this felt a surge of panic (not to say a shortage of biscuits) but we had obviously discovered a real need.' Cathy Henderson 'dashed out for more milk' and, ten years on, helps preside over 116 interest-groups, serving over a thousand members. 'No, we are not capping', exclaims Jennifer Thomas, the current Secretary, in a defiant refutation of the dreary waiting list mentality.

One sees in those few examples both the workings of cheerful happenstance and the value of the nearby U3As as providers of assistance. A final Herts illustration shows how that evolutionary chain works. Harrow, just over the county border and officially in Greater London, has had a breath-taking history. Pam Gonsal, now its Secretary, reports how Audrey Cloet, in partnership with a local friend, Alan Klein, with help from Dianne Norton, and under the able chairmanship of Robert Clarkson, began with 60 members in 1991. It swept along at lightning speed and now has 76 interest-groups, roughly divided into eight categories, and an amazing 1300 membership. In 1997 five members of the Harrow U3A met with 38 members of the public in Watford and inaugurated the U3A there. Robin Burgess reports that sixteen of those are still members, including the Harrow member, Reg Cooke, who chaired that initial gathering and is now Watford's President. Watford run 42 groups and has 340 members. The next link in the chain was in 2001, when, as the Watford U3A grew, a number of its members decided to establish a U3A in neighbouring Ricksmanworth, which already has 365 members on its register and 30 groups in its brochure. Nearby South West Herts, started in 2002, has another 248 members. In a dozen years, therefore, this busy patch of the north-west home counties has generated a composite U3A membership of over 2000.

iii. Early Birds . . . Saffron Walden . . . Essex

Returning to the most ancient of U3A's history, Joyce MacElroy was another attender at the productive Cambridge seminar of 1982. Formerly a nurse, a physical training instructor and a youth play leader, she was enthused enough to become the mainstay of the Saffron Walden U3A, a group whose early history was, happily, recorded at the time. She persuaded friends to join her in a meeting at the local library of this ancient Essex market town and, although the reception was mixed, there was sufficient support to continue, so much so that at a second meeting, with some Cambridge U3A colleagues giving assistance, a frame of ten or more activities was developed. Saffron Walden U3A was launched in the January of 1983 with over fifty members, with an annual enrolment fee of just £1 and with help from the Essex LEA, the local library, the local youth and adult centre and, as the chief advertiser with explanatory posters, from local shopkeepers. Joyce MacElroy acted as progress-chaser, attending all the interest-groups in turn, arranging accommodation and so forth.

The combine of a monthly general meeting with a variety of groups, ranging from the history of ancient religions and modern languages to bridge and scrabble, were to become something of a norm, but there were two points of interests. John Jones, a retired deputy head teacher and expert in the history of ballet, led a research group, a reminder that original research had figured in Peter Laslett's vision and, indeed, his advice was sought by this team. Next, Saffron Walden may well have been one of the first U3As to be televised. There had already been some televised discussions of the possibilities of U3A, both on BBC and ITV, for instance during the Granada *Chalkface* series in 1982, programmes about education for the laity, with which Eric Midwinter was much involved. However, the Channel Four series, *Years Ahead*, one of the first such attempts to capture on TV the more positive aspects of older age and for which Eric Midwinter acted as consultant, included a major item on Saffron Walden's activities. This was broadcast in the autumn of 1983 and a video was presented to the Saffron Walden film starlets. Like all other U3As, Saffron Walden introduced a strong social programme. As John Jones tellingly wrote at the time, 'the students' union is every bit as important to the students as research is to the university.' Saffron Walden currently has a solid membership of 290.

Talk of Saffron Walden serves as an opportunity to observe the rise of U3A in Essex at large. Today there are eighteen U3A groups in the county. Progress in Essex demonstrates the chain-reaction that was occurring in several parts of the nation. Southend was an early entrant, dating from 1987, now attracting 138 members and running fifteen groups. Colchester was even earlier, for it held its first meeting in 1985, when a retired doctor, Geoffrey Smerdon, with the continuing support of the University of Essex and with advice from the Cambridge U3A, called a meeting. That very day a steering committee, comprising Geoffrey Smerdon, two ex-engineers, a retired adult education centre principal and a housewife, met and things began to happen. Now there are 300 members and 37 groups.

In 1989 two recently retired women – one of them, Marian Allen, is our correspondent – sought help from the both the Southend and Colchester U3As, as well as from the national office, and thereby launched the Basildon and Billericay U3A in slightly wobbly fashion with eight people attending the first meeting, at which three study groups were tentatively mooted. Success beckoned. Within three years the membership was such that those living in the Brentwood area decided to start their own U3A, whilst, later still, the Thurrock U3A, another district abutting Basildon, was formed. Here Jean Curtin, Vice-chairman of Havering U3A, picks up the baton of this organisational relay race. She describes events succinctly: 'Eric Wade helped Marian Allen set up the Basildon and Billericay U3A, being its first Chairman. In 1990 it seemed appropriate for him to set up a U3A Havering.' Which he did to no uncertain degree, such that Havering now has 244 members and arranges 28 group activities.

Chelmsford, established in 1993, is much the same strength and style as Havering, and, in 1993, it attracted the attention of Beryl McDonell of Maldon, who, having read about U3A, had prudently stored that tit-bit in her memory pending retirement. She went to the Chelmsford group and enjoyed it, but wondered 'why can't Maldon have its own U3A?' She answered this rhetorical question in the grand manner and started one. The Maldon Council of Voluntary Service helped and, something of a rarity, the Maldon Council offers continuous support. The Chelmsford U3A was encouraging and put Beryl McDonell in touch with a Chelmsford member who, another link in the lengthening chain, was busily prompting the creation of the Witham and Braintree U3A. Margaret Nicholls, Secretary of Barking and Dagenham U3A, explains how, in this case, the influence was transoceanic. Ron George read a leaflet about Australian U3As and, with the backing of Pat Cooney, head of the local college where Ron George had read the leaflet, a U3A was duly launched.

Paula Russell, its Chairman, explains how Redbridge U3A was a 'splinter group' (a phrase much in evidence in these potted histories) from the Epping U3A, formed in 1990 and now with some 600 members. People in the Redbridge, Gants Hill and Woodford districts were finding the travel to Epping sufficiently bothersome to warrant starting their very own group in 1995. Beginning with 50 members, there are now 700 members, the biggest list in Essex – and now there are as many study groups as originally there were members.

A final sample of U3A life in Essex comes from Tendring. Here there was a Huddersfield interconnection, for Ken Hiller and his wife were enthused by a couple they knew who found much pleasure in the Huddersfield U3A. The linkages are poignant: Ken Hiller and his Huddersfield pal had flown in the same Stirling aircrew in World War II. After a month or so of activity, Ken Hiller organised a pub lunch for his twenty members: 'I pointed to one lady member whom I knew to be a competent shorthand typist (and who lives opposite us, so was very handy) and said 'you are now secretary'.' Having chosen the rest of the committee in that peremptory fashion, 'I was hoist by my own petard, because they democratically pointed at me and said 'and you are chairman'. Now, for all his tremendous endeavours, he has been elected Life President 'and it is all done quite formally and correctly now.'

iv. Early Birds . . . Barnstaple . . . Devon

Another pioneer venture was in North Devon, and Margaret Walker, the present secretary of Barnstaple U3A, has provided a lucid account of its origins. It had an initial link with a scheme in South Devon, one well documented at the time, with which Michael Young was very involved. His youth and later career had been heavily influenced by his connections with the Dartington ideology of education, arts and crafts and, of course, he would later adopt 'Dartington' as his title when elevated to a life peerage. The European Social Fund and the Nuffield Foundation had funded a scheme, based on Totnes, close to Dartington, to encourage self-reliance among the mature unemployed and retired people. During the late 1970s the problems of late redundancy and early retirement had become something of a social quandary in South Devon. Many people had taken up work in the area as a prelude to a sunny retirement; the scourge of unemployment late in career left them peculiarly forlorn and rootless.

It was first called the New Horizons Project for Mature Redundant Workers and Early Retired Persons. This was scarcely typical of the Youngian litany of succinct labels. Not only did he persuade the management committee to change that to Third Age Project (TAP: they jibbed at 'University', as their writ encompassed training for re-employment, transport, volunteering and so on), but he also encouraged them to adopt something of the U3A philosophy of self-help. Thus, under the benignant directorship of Frank Watson, a former naval officer, several of the groups that emerged included – arts and crafts, local history, French conversation, gardening, creative writing, for example - educational classes. South Devon TAP did affiliate with U3A in 1984, but, from an official U3A viewpoint, did not last long.

Turning more specifically to North Devon, a small proportion of this South Devon grant was allocated to look into the similar need of its northern neighbours. David Davies, Director of the newly-formed North Devon Trust, established an agency called 'Liaison' to encourage retired people to recycle their skills, majoring on the provision of pre-retirement courses. In the autumn of 1983 Dr Davies suggested to the 'Liaison' personnel that it was high time a U3A was formed. Michael Young attended and spoke at this meeting and events moved quickly. By the end of the year a committee of ten had been appointed and the draft constitution prepared by the national body had been adopted. Dianne Norton spoke at the first of the new U3A's monthly lunchtime meetings, stressing the need to broaden personal interests for greater enjoyment of retirement and to use social occasions as the base for educational activity. 'This is, indeed,' writes Margaret Walker, 'how things worked out, for the monthly lunch attracted people who were then encouraged to start study groups and activities'. This North Devon group soon transmuted into the Barnstaple U3A, with a present day membership of 195.

It was to play a leading role in the establishment of other U3As in the region, not least because of the lively amount of interest in the surrounding region and the pressure on Barnstaple's resources. Barnstaple was one of the first U3As consciously to strive to create fellow agencies. Torridge, North Devon Coast, Braunton, South Molton and Barnstaple/Taw all appeared, almost as Barnstaple satellites and almost all before the end of the 1980s. South Molton commenced activity in the convivial rooms of the 'Goose and

Gander' hotel in 1987: 'so many people bless the day they became members of this fast growing organisation', is their current and equally convivial verdict. In 1991 Barnstaple Taw U3A began operations, describing themselves as a 'splinter group', siphoning off many who could not be accommodated at the Barnstaple monthly luncheon meeting and naming themselves after the nearby river. Dee Harding, one of the founder members, has described how amazed they were at the response, with people at the inaugural meeting standing in the corridor, with the allocated room over-crowded. All follow the Barnstaple pattern of a monthly lunch with a speaker, plus a modicum of varied group activities.

Devon, all in all, has rational coverage in U3A terms. It currently has 18 U3As. Among later entrants were, in 1992, West Dartmoor, another Audrey Cloet special, albeit after someone had spotted a U3A clip on television, now running some 30 interest-groups in the environs of Tavistock and deploying an interesting construct of full and associate membership; in 1995, in Exeter, where Audrey Cloet again, this time with Eric Midwinter, were the instigators in a town where there had been, inexplicably, two false starts, but where, thankfully, a 134 strong group does well; and, in 1998, in Plymouth, where, with assistance from the local university, other U3As and the national office, this relatively new U3A, as its Minute Secretary, Veronica Dey reports, has sped to a membership of 250 in quick time.

v. Early Birds . . . Merton . . . London . . . Greater London

Merton was the first London borough to join London in representing U3A in the metropolitan area. It was, in fact, a London U3A member, Douglas Norman-Smith, who was to the fore in pressing for a Merton U3A. With aid from the local College of Adult Education, this was accomplished, via a steering committee in 1983 and a launch in 1984. Merton currently runs 33 groups and activities for its 280 members. It is superfluous to remark that, for complete national identification, it was crucial for the U3A movement to gain ground in the Greater London area. The response was gradual but pronounced, as first one and then another borough adopted the U3A formula, with, all the time, the marvellous London U3A, demonstrating always that largeness need not be the foe of creativity, growing in strength and imaginative force.

Now it has some 1500 members, and Marian Bieber, a highly talented former international administrator and journalist and throughout its history one of its several impressive leaders, reports there are now 113 interest-groups. There is much else besides. A weekly Monday lecture is positively maintained, with a taped version available to home-bound members; there is a two or three day Easter conference, always fully booked, around a theme such as 'France', with interdisciplinary input, along the lines of history, art, music, architecture and so on, and these, too, are taped for the use of members. London U3A is especially to be congratulated for this kind of service for home-based members: there are also telephone-linked literature and poetry groups. There are summer events and there are publications, for instance, two books by Ralph Blumenau based on his London U3A courses.

Given the widespread geographical spread of its membership, London U3A has found it more convenient to centralise its activities into its own premises at the old Hampstead Town Hall, where there are also to be found administrative offices and the audio-visual and IT equipment: 'we have frequently had fundraising events to top up the budget and have never gone to outside sources of funding. These self-run events have been concerts, book sales etc. We have always stuck to the self-help principle.'

Amongst what are now 23 Greater London U3As, there is Ealing, which began in 1988 on the initiative of a local education adviser. Its founder member, Hilary Smith, together with Ron Stent, an Ealing resident, and a London U3A member, John Roamer, helped to launch the Ealing U3A, now with 158 members and fifteen groups, plus, like London, a weekly lecture, always an exacting chore to sustain. Christine Edwards, the present Chairman, has exciting plans for broadening both the base of the course programme and the width of the U3A's catchment area.

Bexley U3A, founded in 1991, also had some local adult education support at the outset. Patricia Kay, its Chairman, tells of how it was all something of an instant success, soon shooting upwards to over 500 members, with over 50 activities to entrance them. A 'Meet and Greet' team in the vestibule of the hall where the monthly meeting is held has been 'enormously helpful', and, a delectable touch, on the U3A's tenth birthday the loyalist survivors from the first meeting were given a special newsletter and a celebratory mug. Bexley has also been instrumental in helping to form the Sidcup, Dartford and Abbeywood Thamesmead U3As in the immediate vicinity. Sidcup, for example, was started in 1993 and operates a busy programme of 39 activities, including the mysterious 'Rummikub' (a tiled version of rummy, apparently) for its fortunate members. Frances Hobden, its Secretary, tells us about the rise of Waltham Forest, itself a consequence of the saturation of the nearby Epping Forest U3A, which advised on what course to take. Six people met at the first meeting and promptly formed a steering committee six strong: now there are over 200 members for whom 25 groups are available.

Thus to the mammoth Bromley U3A, with 1400 plus members and a range of a hundred and more interest groups. Its President, Leslie Stacey, writes forthrightly of its birth: 'discovering on retirement that no U3A existed in Bromley, I set about rectifying the omission.' With a vengeance . . . he called a meeting at the central library and 'the 200-seater hall was packed to overflowing'. Bromley LEA gave a starter grant of £500, and has since made an annual donation, while, in 1999, a Millennium Festival Awards for All award of £5000 was received. When, in the late 1990s, membership peaked at 1700, Bromley, like Bexley and in a pattern that would increasingly be observed across the country, decided to open new U3As in Orpington and Beckenham. This means that, today, there are well over 2000 U3A members in the Bromley area.

Another London borough with a burgeoning U3A is Sutton, where the group, formed in 1986, now has over 300 members, with more than 30 activities, some of them so popular that civic and other premises have had to be sought. As Bob Taverner and Ted Berg report, Sutton illustrates the virtues and vices, as nationally perceived at that time, of local institutional response. There was a small council grant and the library nominated one of its staff as contact and adviser; the local liberal arts college 'was reluctant to make contact and seemed to see us as something of a threat', although, happily, it has become more enlightened as the years have drawn on. That dichotomy of friendly libraries and unfriendly colleges was played out up and down the country in the 1980s.

vi. Fallen Sparrows . . . Manchester

These many examples, from Barnstaple to Merton, demonstrate how widely the U3A writ already ran, both geographically and socially, from the earliest part of its history. It also demonstrates how success bred success, notably in the manner in which local U3As begat neighbouring U3As. However, although it has been said that history is about winners, this history must perforce recognise that there are also losers. Sadly, there were several attempts at U3A-ship that failed, often despite considerable endeavour. A case-study of the collapse of the Manchester initiative has been kindly provided by Derek Legge, now 87, but then Head of the Department of Adult Education of the University of Manchester. His file shows how Leslie Jones, of this department, worked hard to convene a number of meetings to discuss the U3A possibility, the first of them in the May of 1982. These included further gatherings in the north and south of the city. A newsletter was started and the papers include the names and addresses of about a hundred interested parties, although some of them were from well outside the immediate Manchester area. Tutors made attempts to set up learning exchanges and other classes such as local history, computers and art.

A year and a half passed. By the end of 1983 Leslie Jones was forced to concede that 'the venture in this area has drawn a blank' and the so-called *ad hoc* committee, now a meagre six in number where once it had been thirty, was disbanded.

The Mancunian group was composed chiefly of adult educators. Their debates, as the papers demonstrate, were full of reviews of the substantial range of adult educational opportunities available in an environment well known for its progressive attitudes to continuing education. They were obviously bothered not to deter from the endeavours being made by these agencies to attract mature students and they present a face, not uncommon in those pioneer times, of anxiety about the effect of self-mobilised action on the professional offerings. The longish period of the Manchester experiment had been sustained by what Leslie Jones called 'hidden subsidies', in the form of gratis use of public rooms and administrative mechanisms. 'This cannot go on', wrote Leslie Jones forcibly, 'and it **should** not go on. When all public spending is being cut drastically by government and institutions are having to spend more of their resources watching every penny that is spent, there can be little justification for spending on free riders.' He added, 'But most of the people U3A ought to be serving haven't got the money themselves. The ones who have the money don't need U3A in this area.'

Writing further on this point in the 1984 winter edition of the embryonic U3A newspaper, Leslie Jones said, 'one consideration that weighed with most of us . . . was the fear that our provision of adult education free of charge might lend support to those who are set on cutting back more and more the public funding of this important activity. This would be highly undesirable in our view'. In the abrasive climate of the 1980s, such worries were understandable. They were certainly reflective of a genuine concern, to which reference has already been made, among some professional educationists at this time that the U3A precept was bad for business and might lead to the loss of jobs. In the outcome, there has been little solid evidence that U3A has had much effect on the funding of state provision, although there were to be occasional reports that higher charges for publically funded courses in some places led to an exodus of some customers from the Egypt of local authority evening classes to the Promised Land of U3A. Notwithstanding that, the reality of anxiety cannot be denied; the U3A movement had bridges to build with the rest of the continuing and adult education services.

More pertinently, Leslie Jones drew attention to the sprawling nature of Manchester, with its mean radius of twelve miles from the city centre. Transport could be difficult and, as he had previously noted, a quarter of the Manchester inquirers were not apparently on the telephone, another barrier to communication. Even when meetings were tried in different parts, they had not been fruitful. 'The 'north of Manchester', wrote Leslie Jones, 'is not a recognisable community neighbourhood such as U3A seems to demand.' It was noticeable that, the special case of the metropolis apart, U3A was flourishing in compact areas, in the Stevenages and Saffron Waldens of this British world. The U3A editorial comment on the Manchester problem readily accepted this analysis with a call for U3As to be formed in the districts and suburbs of Greater Manchester, in, so to say, the 'villages' that made up that large conurbation.

Looking ahead, one finds that this is precisely what happened. Greater Manchester now has ten U3As, although none of them is strictly close to the city centre as such, with the oldest established being Stockport, which commenced official business in 1986. Stockport, far from being nurtured by the professional cadres, arose from someone reading a newspaper article about U3As. The present Membership Secretary, Marian Cunliffe, reports on how the national office funded two public meetings and the first committee meeting was convened in the February of 1986, when 33 members were already enrolled. Stockport now has 200 members and organises 23 groups, including the intriguing 'John's Outings', the John in question being a prominent member and official, John Hayes. There is also Bolton, where our correspondent is Colin Harding of the U3A committee, and where, in early 1990, a mature student of health education undertook a project concerned with the general health of older people that inexorably led to a noting of U3A as a useful social antidote to some health problems. Alerted to this, the then Principal of Bolton College of Adult Education convened a public meeting, at which a steering committee was formed and a programme arranged. Other help came from other public bodies, colleges, libraries, museums and the like. A decade had passed and many statutory institutes were keen to help. Bolton now has eleven mainline groups and eighty members.

A final example from Greater Manchester is Sale, which began, like many others, through the initiative of local individuals and with some help from a neighbouring U3A. It started, as its Secretary, Josie Anderson explains, with 15 members and is now 290 strong and growing, with some 24 groups on its brochure, and it is further distinguished by holding most of its meetings in the community centre where Eric Midwinter changed for football matches, when, it is otiose to add, he was still sunk in the jejeune throes of the First Age.

vii. Fallen Sparrows . . . An Analysis

However, in part because of those experiences in Manchester and elsewhere, it very quickly became a much-repeated tale of U3A lore that U3A was a phenomenon fitted to the sort of locality that approximated to the average market town and less suited to the big multi-centred city – or, for that matter, extensive rural area. Another failure was recorded in Mid-Wales. Roger Palmer, armed with a £1000 grant from the Manpower Services Commission's 'Opportunities for Volunteering in Wales' scheme, embarked on a U3A venture based on Montgomery but covering a wide tract of Mid-Wales. He dispatched mail-shots in profusion and pasted up 500 posters, bearing the inspiriting message of 'This Life is the Great Schoolmaster', and was received in silence. He, too, decided that the local approach might be more beneficial, for, in this one respect of attracting custom, the issue of transportation in the remote countryside was not unlike that to be found in the straggling streets of the city.

Manchester is the best documented but not the only instance of disappointment. Liverpool, Norwich and Leicester were three other cities where worthy efforts to start U3As ended in collapse. One must be grateful to Leslie Jones and his Mancunian colleagues for detailing their terminal route in such stoical detail –

and, to be fair to Manchester, at least the attempt had been made: some other mighty conurbations, among them Merseyside, Tyneside, Clydeside, Leeds, gave negligible hints of any interest whatsoever at this stage. Of the pioneer starters, only Nottingham and Bristol were drawn from the ranks of the provincial industrial cities, although even those examples demonstrated that the organisers were not quite dealing with impossibilities.

In retrospect, another factor may be worth considering. London, Cambridge and Huddersfield had the advantage, in personnel, funds or kind, of reasonable material assistance. This enabled them to plan confidently and make progress quickly. Most of the other experimental groups began and survived on impoverished budgets, begging and borrowing rooms, stationery and whatever else was required. In either case, one characteristic of these successful ventures was the immediacy of their attack. Like their bigger compatriots, those that began in a small way, often launched from someone's sitting room, were quickly on the front foot. They moved swiftly from winning friends and influencing people to cobbling together some form of steering committee to actually forming groups and allied activities, often within a week or so of the opening initiative.

It is a commonplace of community development, where one is looking to mobilise *ad hoc* lay involvement, that delay is perilous, usually fatal. Impetus is rapidly lost. The lesson was the same as had been witnessed nationally; that is, in the Founders' determination to jump in before all the funds and legalities and rules and concepts had been agreed. During the years of the Liverpool Educational Priority Area Project and its aftermath, Eric Midwinter and his team had adopted the phrase 'blood on the snow' to highlight this essential need to cut the cackle and act colourfully, even cavalierly. It was explicitly agreed that an overt clue – 'blood on the snow' – was very soon required to convince people of the earnest of action. Michael Young was himself a lifelong adherent to this cheerful aquatic school of taking the sociological plunge. He knew full well that overmuch debate could lead to social atrophy and the unhappy ending of the lost chance. Thus were many who contacted the national office urged to do something practical, like starting a U3A in their own kitchen. Most of the initial U3A successes occurred where there had been some 'blood on the snow' from the onset. How Michael Young would have rejoiced in Marion Harvey's purposeful statement in Taunton: 'I want to start a local University of the Third Age, three o'clock next Tuesday.'

There is some evidence that failed ventures were associated with over-lengthy gestation periods. Sometimes these occurred where professional adult educators forgathered and, following the orderly conduct and process to which, in their local governmental and other institutional posts, they had grown accustomed, they sought to mull over the issues and advance sedately, considering the constitutional options and academic niceties, and, all in all, moving forward cautiously, if at all.

The Manchester committee endured for eighteen months. That may be not be a long period when one is planning carefully structured academic programmes. When one is trying to persuade laypeople to take up the cudgels of community development, in education or in any other field, it is an inordinately lengthy and lethal time. Something of the same problem blighted the troubled Leicester experiment. Meetings were held, and the General Secretary and Executive Secretary danced attendance at these, only to find that, rather than grasping the nettle of action, the prudent decision would be ceremoniously arrived at to hold another meeting. Leicester mark one endured as a registered U3A from only June to October of 1984. In fact, it was not only the cities and with the professional providers that this occurred. There were one or two places, including a memorable incident on the Sussex coast, where individuals, having offered to take a lead, sat in costive deliberation, refusing to act decisively themselves and halting others from taking action, until delay led to petrifaction. The South East Sussex U3A was in official being from only 1984 to 1986.

Happily, Leicester enjoyed new beginnings crowned with success. But it was 1994/95 before, as the current chairman, John Cook, reports, a husband and wife duo, Joy and Derek Sharpe invited friends to their home and simply began a U3A. Over against the agonies of protracted discussion, we discover that, in John Cook's concise phrases, 'the group was started by a wife who realised that when her husband retired he would need some help.' Its launch followed quickly in August 1995 and national affiliation was sought six months later. Now Leicester has a membership of about a hundred and offers twelve activities.

Fast-forwarding a little, Leicestershire at large has quite suddenly a healthy U3A climate, fielding some thirteen U3As, although they range from six with less a hundred members to the likes of Market Harborough, Charnwood and Melton with over 300 members apiece. One of the later arrivals is Oadby & Wigston U3A, situated to the south of Leicester and affiliated in 2001. Eileen Holly, its Secretary, is chair of the local Age Concern Trustees, and, in this case, the originating idea came from one of the Age Concern officers. Hinckley U3A, on the other hand, was the brainchild of a community centre worker, Carla Clarke, who, with John O'Callaghan and one or two others, began this group in the early 1990s; it is now building on a steady platform, and mentions among its notables its first Secretary, Denis, a former police inspector; possibly the oft-spoken line of Ernest the Policeman in S G Hulme-Beaman's admirable *Toytown* series – 'I'm afraid I'll have to take your name and address' – came in useful in Denis's U3A capacity.

There has been quite a flurry of 21st century action in Leicestershire. Such was the growth of the Market Harborough U3A that, as Liz Thake its Secretary explains, the South Leicestershire U3A was formed in 2000 and already has over 400 members and nearly 40 activity groups, also in the Market Harborough area. But the development continues. In turn, the South Leicestershire U3A have been instrumental in assisting in the establishment of the Great Glen, Lutterworth and Kettering U3As, in 2001, 2002 and 2003 respectively, all in the same southern tracts of Leicestershire. For example, Great Glen was formed 'on the initiative of its present Chairman, Mary Lawson, with help from Pauline Cameron of the South Leicestershire U3A'. It now has over a hundred members. This recent development has made for heavy saturation indeed in these parts of Leicestershire.

Norwich also had to wait awhile and then, in 1990, it sprang to vigorous life, one of the several fruits of the social horticulture of Audrey Cloet, of which rather more anon. A steering committee was soon formed, including among its number Doreen Tallett, a long-time supporter of U3A, who retired in 2003 after a long stint as the Norwich chairman. The inaugural meeting was in September 1991 when 55 members enrolled. Now there are a hundred groups and 612 members, a highly commendable outcome. There are eight more U3As in the rest of Norfolk, most of them of a later vintage. The only other one of appreciable size is North Norfolk, based on the town of Holt and started in 1990 with fifteen members when its founder chairman moved to the district. Now its has about 400 members and runs 43 interest-groups.

To round off this East Anglian part of the saga, nearby Suffolk has today nine U3As, among them East Suffolk, where Derek Barbanell, who had previously served on the Colchester U3A committee, has been, from its beginnings in 1988, a chief protagonist. East Suffolk, incidentally, by a short head from Burgess Hill U3A, was the first U3A to respond to the call for local data for this study. It covers a wide area incorporating Ipswich, Felixstowe and other Suffolk districts, with its northern realm around the Saxmundham locality having a separate programme of monthly meetings, whilst remaining part of the larger body. Hadleigh U3A arrived on the scene in 2000. The national office advised Joan Pitcher on advertising and forwarded relevant materials: she was slightly taken aback by the response, but gallantly booked a room and, with the aid of officers from the Sudbury U3A, soon had fourteen groups up and running. 'This is the story of Hadleigh U3A', she writes, 'and what an enjoyable experience it has been'.

viii. Early Central Action

So many of those launches reflect the courage, some would say the foolhardiness, of individuals, who simply went out and started U3As practically on their doorsteps, in a fashion that would and did alarm seasoned administrators, hedged in by all kinds of bureaucratic restraints. That factor of the tension between, at the extremes, procrastination and impetuosity was to surface at the national level and, indeed, at the regional level in subsequent years. Without being unduly portentous, one might borrow from Matthew Arnold's *Culture and Anarchy*, published in 1869, in which he wrote of the clash of the two traditions of Hellenic 'spontaneity of consciousness' and Hebraic 'strictness of conscience'. As any institution grows, there is often some conflict between allowing the dynamism and energy that creates this growth to be left free, and a countervailing pressure to consolidate the gains and, by formal procedures, preserve them. Too much of the one risks confusion and incoherence; too much of the other threatens over-earnest inertia.

The central core of the new organisation was yet to face that sort of crisis, of a nature being played out in towns and cities across the country. The central core remained, in any pragmatic vein, that Wimbledon spare room, with Dianne Norton running the changes, as she answered the now persistently ringing phone and the piling stacks of mail, on job specifications that included posts in a non-existent accounts department and an ethereal publicity office. Optimistic and inexhaustibly willing, U3A's first administrator, combining roles that ranged from office clerk, via editor, to leading spokesperson, provided that central core. The steps towards legitimacy were taken when Michael Young ensured that the national body, under its legal title of The Third Age Trust, was registered as a Company Limited by Guarantee in October 1983 and as a Charity in the same month.

The two priorities were feeding information to possible new disciples and maintaining contact with the old apostles. A newsletter had been forwarded to local organisers since the summer of 1982, but it was already felt by the committee that there should be some form of communication with individual members. In September 1983 a run of 5000 newspapers was published. Listening naively to the assured advice of an experienced media expert that older people had a quirky sense of humour, the officers christened their baby, *The Last Post*. The experienced media expert was in grievous error. There was a minor outcry. The only chilly comfort in this exercise was that U3A won its first national prize as a consequence. This witty masthead won the *Health and Fitness* magazine 'Lead Balloon Award for 1983'.

The next attempt was equally blighted. In February 1984 *Late Extra* was launched, the second edition of the membership newsletter. This was not savaged by the readership, but it struck a violent chord in a Yorkshire college, which claimed the title for its own. Their saucy imagination subdued by these setbacks, the officers settled for the more prosaic *Third Age* for the next newspaper in the summer of 1984 and for many more to come, until, finally, *Third Age News* was adopted.

The other important event of 1983 was a second seminar, held on 29 June, at the Nuffield Foundation, also then the home of the Centre for Policy on Ageing, in London. James Cornford and Anthony Tomei of the Nuffield Foundation were present, along with the four members of the National Committee. There were 23 delegates from the localities, covering 22 places where U3As had either started or were under consideration.

It was tantamount to an annual national conference. With the Third Age Trust on the verge of legitimacy, the concept of confederation was confidently asserted, with the benefits of group autonomy, in balance with the advantages of a licit national framework, lauded. Local U3As were now invited to become formal members of the national body and a *pukka* national conference was earmarked for the summer of 1984. As an interim measure prior to that occasion, three of the activists present were elected to the National Committee. These were Sidney Jones, who was busily ensuring the bright future of the London U3A; Angela Black, who was devilling away in the South Yorkshire region, and Leslie Jones, who was grappling with the awkward Manchester situation.

Also present at this productive and lively workshop were Professor Boris Ford, the noted intellectual and critic, and Editor of *Universities Quarterly*, and Richard Bourne, onetime *doyen* of the educational press corps when the *Guardian* educational correspondent and now Director of the Royal Commonwealth Institute. It was a cocky feather in the U3A cap. Boris Ford had imaginatively decided to devote the larger portion of the January 1984 edition of his journal to the University of the Third Age, chiefly composed of articles by Eric Midwinter and Richard Bourne, who visited U3As, such as Harpenden, as part of his task. It was a further step in the right direction of putting the issues clearly to the academic audience, many of whom were still suspicious of this new creature, were they even conscious of its existence.

Centrally and locally, there were, then, ups and downs in the game, as some would-be U3As triumphantly climbed the ladders and some would-be U3As disastrously slid down the snakes. Eight U3As were officially registered with the national office by the end of 1983. There were to be many, many more additions, just as there were to be losses, through disbandment or, more notably, through disaffiliation. Some commenced, soldiered on but were either late in making the decision to affiliate or failed ever to join the national brigade. There were cases of U3As having to disaffiliate almost as soon as they had signed the dotted line, usually because of the difficulty in finding a committee. Edinburgh sought affiliation in 1984 but very soon was dissolved. Green Norton and Gosport/Farnham registered with the Third Age Trust in 1984; both finished in 1988. Incidentally, there was some semantic objections to 'affiliation' and 'disaffiliation. in U3A circles, but the words strictly describe the status, whereas 'membership' tends to confuse the issue with its other usage of individual membership.

It was exciting; it was volatile, but, in day-by-day practice, it was no more than maybe a score of actual or potential hobby-horses in a tiny whirligig swirling around someone's backroom in London SW19. Yet it was a real beginning: possibly this is the correct spot to herald the U3As who enlisted with the U3A national colours in that opening year October 1983 to October 1984 and who have bravely stayed on the regimental strength over the ensuing 20 years.

In sequence, they are Yeovil; Nottingham; Oxford; Barnstaple; London; Wakefield; Tynedale; Merton; Bradford; Harpenden; Bristol; Stevenage; Saffron Walden and Abergavenny, plus the multicellular West Midlands grouping, now registered under various districts. They boldly form the first fifteen.

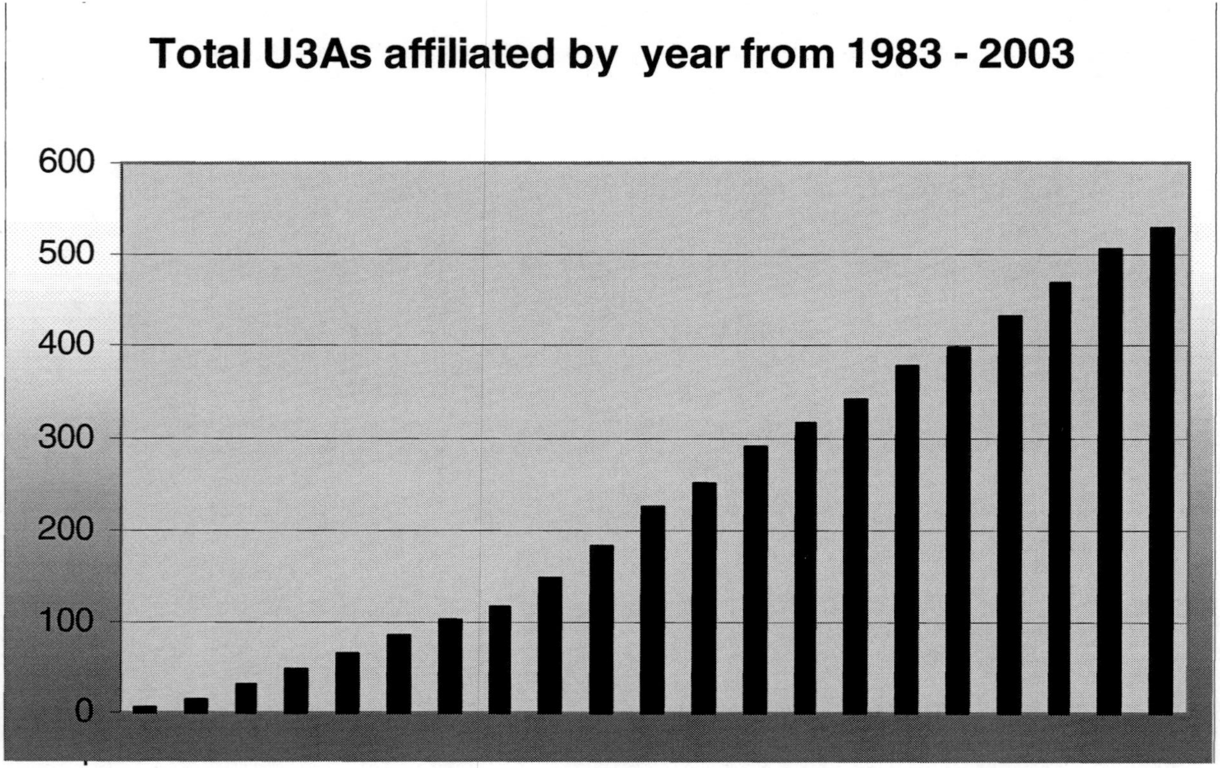
Total U3As affiliated by year from 1983 - 2003
600
500
400
300
200
100
0

Five: HUNDRED UP

Money was a problem. Both the local groups, with one or two fortunate exceptions, and the national agency were operating on threadbare shoestrings of budgets. The Calouste Gulbenkian Foundation, whose mercurial Director, Peter Brinson, had been an expansive supporter of Eric Midwinter's work both in Liverpool and at the Centre for Policy on Ageing, made a grant of £4300, while the National Extension College, one of Michael Young's foundations, offered £2400 in grant-aid. This funding came in 1983 and helped considerably with publications, small subventions for 'start-up' purposes and other organisational uses. This enabled the central activity to survive another couple of years, which was manifestly a vital reprieve, but what was lacking was some wherewithal to spread the gospel more extensively. The reliance on individuals hearing by chance of the U3A concept, and having the wit and natural resource to do something about it, was, it was felt, an insufficient device for the nascent movement.

---

i. The National Organisers . . . The West Midlands

Michael Young and Eric Midwinter decided on one further appeal to their old friends at the Nuffield Foundation. Perhaps encouraged by what they had heard at the recent national seminar at Nuffield Lodge, Regent's Park, the Director, James Cornford, and the Assistant Director with responsibility for education (and now, deservedly, the Director), Anthony Tomei, were sympathetic. The Nuffield Trustees smiled benignly on the application and £5000 was granted to support a National Organiser for a two years period, his or her remit the encouragement of new U3A groups.

The officers were astounded by the wealth and range of the response to their advertisement of this post. There seemed to be many who were keen to try their hand. When the Chairman, General Secretary and Executive Secretary interviewed candidates, they were even more impressed by the richness of the quality, so much so that two people were asked to share the job. They were, sprightly and alert, Jenny Betts, and, unflappable and open-minded, Harry Muscutt. They fitted the bill in remarkably similar ways. Both had adult educational experience (Harry Muscutt had been head of a School of Art and Design); both had recently edged into the Third Age; both were already involved in U3A enterprises; both came from populous regions – Jenny Betts from Preston in the north-west; Harry Muscutt, whom, of course, we have already encountered at work in Bath, from Sutton Coldfield in the West Midlands – both involved themselves in intricate patterns of regional networking; both were very effective in the role. The precedent was established of deploying Third Agers in these kinds of appointments and that, in itself, was deemed of much import.

Harry Muscutt's prime target was his home ground around Birmingham and his associates and he devised a strategy of regional oversight. The West Midlands U3A group evolved as a honeycomb of several cells, each linked indirectly to the national body through that West Midlands. Harry Muscutt was ably supported by John Aitken, of the Extramural Department of Birmingham University, who had earlier met and had been influenced by Dianne Norton in the spring of 1982. From the earliest of times, an annual university-based study day was thereby arranged for the West Midlands members. This was exactly the sort of contribution Peter Laslett had hoped the British universities would tender and, happily, there were to be other examples.

A 1983 newsletter – 'A Positive Approach to Retirement' is its merry banner heading – gives some flavour of this network. Active programmes are reported for Birmingham, chiefly with classes for Handsworth, Hall Green and Harborne, for Solihull, for Sutton Coldfield – about the last of which Marie Smith has written vividly to the author of being recruited by Harry Muscutt when he descended on the 'Pleasant Retirement' course she was attending in 1982. There were also exploratory moves in Walsall, the Wolverhampton/Stourbridge districts and, later, Kidderminster. Some of these proved futile, but, for instance, Bromsgrove joined the fold. So the system developed. Six newsletters a year were produced, the radical idea being to acquaint all members with what was being offered everywhere with a view to encouraging across-the-board engagement. One consequence of this mechanism was perhaps a lowness of numbers in each cell, but, given the experience in Manchester and some other conurbations, this progressive plan seemed to be a ready answer to the 'city' question.

Gerald Marsh, another who acknowledges a debt to Dianne Norton, has written graphically of how he found himself – the genuine teacher having been called away to nurse his ailing mother – conducting a poetry appreciation group in what had been a dance hall in the 1930s. Ray Lee appeared out of the blue; he was in the Birmingham Central group, but wished for something nearer home; Gerald Marsh agreed to transmute his poetry group into the embryo for the Hall Green U3A, which, with its 75 members and seven interest-groups, continues to this day. Today's chairman, Patricia Morton, tells how the whole group still sustains a weekly get-together to discuss an annually decided theme, 'where we feel the light bonds of acquaintance are strengthened almost imperceptibly into friendship', a lovely encapsulation of the U3A ethic.

This intriguing pattern endured for ten years in this style. During this time one or two grew sufficiently strong to leave the nest and become independent members of the Third Age Trust. Sutton Coldfield, now a sizeable body of 420, gained independent status in 1988, while Solihull seceded from the West Midlands group and sought national affiliation in 1992; it now has 145 members and arranges 17 interest-groups. Three of its active members attended the inaugural meeting in 1983. Solihull has assisted in the formation of three other U3As – Shirley, Arden and Blossomfield – in what has proved to be a flourishing location for the movement.

There were financial pressures on the network and, as has often happened with a regional exercise, concerns were expressed about an additional bureaucratic tier. Not without regret, the West Midlands group, with Gerald Marsh in the chair and Harry Muscutt still its diligent secretary, decided to dissolve itself in 1993. Ceding its own affiliation, it advised its constituent bodies to affiliate directly with the national body. The West Midlands group must be credited with two splendid decisions. It started when it was necessary to have such an organisation; it stopped when that organisation was no longer required, although a less formal 'liaison link' was left in place. It was said at the general meeting at which dissolution was agreed that this was now the best course for the propagation of U3A life in the West Midlands, but people are often loath to yield up something that has worked so well for them. Ceasing was as bravely honourable an act as beginning.

The West Midlands now has fourteen U3As, including outposts in the previously unfruitful Kingswinford district of Stourbridge and in Wolverhampton. Of the seven units remaining in the West Midlands group in 1993, Halesowen, Dorridge, Hall Green and Yardley opted immediately for individual affiliation. Yardley, as its secretary, Roy Kibble, relates, arose when Mike Byrne, the local community librarian, was asked if he could help by a local band of U3A enthusiasts: the neighbouring Acocks Green U3A group was floundering rather, and, in effect, the Yardley group, having begun its activities, was joined by some remaining Acocks Green members when that unit closed for good. Unusually, Yardley does not run special interest groups as such, but draws up a rolling six months programme, founded on the ideas and suggestions of members. There are other continuities. Harborne & Edgsbaston, with some 70 members since its recent inception in 1999, is chaired by Mary Knox, who, with her late husband as chairman, had started the former Birmingham Central group as part of the West Midlands confederacy. They had heard of U3A while on a leisurely tour of France in 1982 and reacted positively to mention of the idea in a local newspaper soon after their return to England. Bromsgrove also became a national affiliate in 1993, although, by strict geographical location, it appears in the national register under Worcestershire's roster of seven U3As.

Of course, some of the West Midlands U3As discovered a different route to U3A-hood. Coventry, for example, has a longish history, dating from November 1985. With help from the Third Age Trust, from the Cambridge U3A and from the local technical college, where meetings were held, a committee, that included a retired head teacher, a civil servant, an anaesthetist and a shipping executive, moved quickly to organise matters. Now Coventry, chaired by Joan Warner, the provider of this information, runs over twenty groups, among them DIY advice for women who live alone, and has 375 members. In another characteristic shift, it has assisted in the formation of two other U3As in the Coventry area, namely, Coventry Spires, based in the Styvechale district, and Coventry Sherbourne. Then there is nearby Rugby, one of seven Warwickshire U3As, completing a rational array of some 28 U3As in central England. It was, according to its secretary, Kath Pierce, one of those U3As whose formation resulted from a nap hand of local individuals, local college, friendly neighbouring U3A, the national office and a grant from the local council. Its 150 members now enjoy the choice of 14 interest-groups.

ii. The National Organisers . . . The North West

In Lancashire, Jenny Betts became heavily involved with another upbeat model of networking, this one based on Preston Polytechnic, now the University of Central Lancashire. There had been a very early experiment instigated by Keith Percy, head of the relatively new – it had been formed in 1979 – Extra-mural Studies at Lancaster University. Small but busy, this agency had pioneered the notion of Open Lectures, based on the undergraduate programme, free of charge for members of the public, among them many older citizens. In this respect, it had some similarities with the French U3A operation. Keith Percy and his associates volunteered to establish a U3A in the Morecambe and Lancaster area in 1982 and, not without attracting some controversy among professional providers resentful of what they regarded as '*parvenu* amateur' competition, they soon enrolled over a hundred members. Although unaffiliated until 1989, it now has 154 members.

It was, however, the Preston Polytechnic, latterly the University of Central Lancashire, that was to take the northwest by the scruff of its lifelong learning neck. Enter the indomitable character of the doughty Jim Soulsby. Then a relatively young lecturer of great thoughtfulness and resource, and now transferred to work his spells at the National Institute of Adult and Continuing Education in Leicester, he grafted, often in concert with Jenny Betts, to establish self-mobilised groups, using the college as a highly valued base. Frequently seeking partnerships with local bodies and operating in the several rural districts as well as the more industrialised locales, an amazing array of groups were founded, amazing as to both style and geography. By 1994 there were as many as 45 of these groups, some of which began autonomously and then affiliated to this overall programme. The university supports the network with administrative help, with the production of an interesting intergroup newsletter, and with the organisation of the annual Bessie Wade memorial lecture on later life issues, an event that honours the memory of a woman who gave much to the early development of these groups. The inaugural lecture was delivered by Eric Midwinter.

As with the West Midlands pattern, here were the makings of regional governance. Indeed, since 1988 the northwest U3As have organised an annual conference, varying the venue around Southport, Heatons Reddish, Wythenshawe, Salford and Preston among other locations. As with the West Midlands, the slight downside to this was the ambivalent attitude towards the national identity. Few love bureaucracy. The small Lancashire groups were happy enough with their regional back-up in Preston and, especially with the advent of fees for national membership, were reluctant recruits. Principally through the bustling good offices of Harold Potts, U3A's first national treasurer and a stalwart of the Chorley U3A, not only have links been maintained with the Life Long Learning groups (LLLs), but also several LLLs did agree to accept national status. Jim Soulsby's sanguine conclusion is that, without the input of the University (which modesty forbids him from identifying with himself) there would have been many fewer groups in the northwest, but that those few would probably all have been Third Age Trust members. Nonetheless, the evangelism of Harold Potts and others has been quite well rewarded.

The modern county of Lancashire, much smaller, of course, than the ancient Palatine shire, currently boasts nine U3As, all of which also appear in the Central Lancaster University LLL brochure, together with a couple of Cumbrian groups, Ambleside and South Lakes, plus another ten from Greater Manchester, and six from Merseyside, Cheshire and Derbyshire. Those figures serve to demonstrate the range of the Preston project and, more pertinently, show that, of the present 47 LLL-type listings, the goodly sum of 27 are now affiliated to the central body as *bona fide* U3As. Even allowing for the quartet who signed on and thereafter signed off, it is a most creditable outcome.

This represents a reasonable coverage of the whole region. To take one or two disparate examples, the South Lakes U3A, based on Kendal, illustrates the LLL practice admirably, as its Secretary, Kathy Webster, has explained. People on holiday in France and noticing the U3A car stickers; a *Guardian* article describing the U3A concept – not for the first or last time were these the motivators. However, the nearest U3As were in Scotland or South Lancashire. Thus there was some response to a *Westmoreland Gazette* advertisement from the Central Lancashire University in 1991 inviting local folk to form an LLL. Once established, the group was told that affiliation was an option and that it was down to the membership to decide; almost immediately, in the spring of 1992, South Lakes voted affirmatively; it runs 29 interest-groups and, from ten at that inaugural meeting, now has a membership of 383, 'and without exception', writes Kathy Webster, '. . . we consider U3A one of the most wonderful organisations there is.'

On the other hand, Macclesfield Rural U3A was more home-grown, beginning in 1997 on the initiative of Lucinda Hodges of the local teachers' centre and founder member Audrey O'Neill. The national office was to the fore, in the commonsensical shape of Roy Wilson, by this time the National Development Coordinator, together with assistance from the Buxton and Sale U3As. Beginning with five groups, Macclesfield now has 30 and a thriving membership of 286. Clitheroe U3A, too, was 'the inspiration', recalls its Secretary, Jean Duck, 'of one person, who had knowledge of the workings of a neighbouring group': this was in 1998 and there are some 300 members in Clitheroe. As well as group activities and short courses, they have introduced 'An Afternoon with . . . ' sessions at which a member talks about a specific topic that might not warrant a course as such. Then there is Cockermouth, which opened for business in 1998. One of nine Cumbrian U3As, it is already over 350 strong. 'Towards the end of August', wrote its first Secretary, Mary Wandless, 'I received a mystery phone call from a strange man who had a proposition to make.' It was Trevor Roberts, proposing to bring U3A-dom to Cockermouth; 'since then the U3A simply exploded – it did not need a gestation period – it simply came into being . . . enthusiasm was infectious. We knew that Cockermouth was ready for this new, exciting event.'

Carlisle and District U3A, established in 1991, is about the biggest of the north western groups, with some 600 Third Agers and running 45 interest-groups. Their summer newsletter for 2003 says it all. Under the headline, 'Lifetime Membership Awarded to John and Barbara Eden', it describes how this couple made 'a truly unique contribution...with their foresight and drive in the early days' and who have variously been Chairman, Secretary, Membership Secretary and group leaders, as well as John Eden's efforts in obtaining two large grants for the U3A's IT centre.

All over the nation, as the twenty or more years of U3A history ensued, the many individuals who had worked to create a U3A for their Third Age fellows were being recognised, like Barbara and John Eden, for what they had brought to the life of their district.

Finally, it is in the foundations of Chorley U3A that one may witness the combination of these varied strands both of personal endeavour and institutional backing. Credit must be bestowed on: local people who responded to a press advertisement; to Jenny Betts, in her lively coordinator role; to Jim Soulsby and his energetic colleague, Kathy McGowan, from the then Preston Polytechnic; to Dianne Norton burrowing away in what was rather ostentatiously referred to as 'the national office'; to Age Concern Chorley; and to Chorley Library and other local institutions, to say nothing of later grants from BT and the National Lottery for the setting up of electronic wizardry and computerised magic. Interest-group listings have sprung from 3 to 24; the membership stands at 286, while Chorley U3A, in prime U3A entrepreneurial style, seems to have persuaded the world and his wife to rush to support its doings.

iii. Regional Developments . . . Cornwall

While on the subject of regional foci, it might be appropriate to describe at this juncture the Cornish experience, for it was not dissimilar from that of the West Midlands and the Northwest and, in any event, some of the early gleanings of U3A life happened in the late 1980s. We are much indebted to Ian Searle, the hard-working Secretary of the Carrick U3A and now happily co-opted to help national sub-committees, for his careful log of this south-western saga, which, like the tales of the West Midlands and the region covered by the Preston-oriented LLLs, is instructive on the pros and cons of regional structure.

Wadebridge U3A had been formed in the mid-1980s, the first glimmering of U3A in Cornwall, when, in 1989, three members of the co-operative movement raised the question of whether U3As might be sponsored. It was scarcely an idle request, for the co-op had a long and laudable history of adult educational action. Michael Young, a long-while admirer of the co-op, would certainly have cheered on that approach; he regarded the old-style co-op as very much a model for the U3A. This led to Mary

McArthur, of Cornwall's Educational Guidance Service in Truro, consulting with the likes of Peter Laslett and with Edith Bentley of the Huddersfield U3A, and, with the joint help of the co-op and the Third Age Trust, meetings were convened and very soon seven U3As were in operation. This magnificent seven composed an heptarchy known as the Cornish U3A forum, which acted as a regional help-meet but which had no contact with the Third Age Trust. To complicate matters, one or two other Cornish U3As, notably Launceston, Hayle-Penwith and Gunnislake, were independently formed, with affiliation to the central body.

In a most courteous letter to Eric Midwinter in 1995, when he was researching the development of U3As nationally, Barbara Scammell, then the Chairman of the Cornish Forum, explained the reasons for this non-allegiance. The remoteness of Cornwall and its relative impoverishment, not only economically, but also educationally – there was still no university in Cornwall – had made progress difficult, leaving the balance of cost and benefit of national membership regarded as unfavourable. At this point there were eight members of the Forum, with a membership of about a thousand.

Ian Searle picks up the story: 'the strange result of this kind of heretical organisation was mutual distrust, members of the CUF not wanting to owe any kind of allegiance nor to pay their capitation fees to a remote central body. The Third Age Trust, on the other hand, saw themselves as the legitimate line from which the bastard Cornish U3As had deviated.' The Forum, through arranging insurance and other protection as well as through organising joint activities, acted as a valuable regional overseer, although, of course, it had no official powers. However, there was a degree of apathy over nominations for official posts in the Forum and, in 1999, it was duly wound up, with a recommendation, as happened in the West Midlands, that constituent members should seek the shelter of the national umbrella.

The debate continued acrimoniously. The Cornish U3As found the national approach unappealing. The national case was that the concept, as witness the involvement of no less an advisor than

Peter Laslett, and some initial funding had been of national provenance and that there was a moral onus on U3As to share in and contribute toward the national movement. It took two extraordinary general meetings, in 1999 and 2002, of the Carrick U3A, by far the largest of the Cornish groups, to shift towards and ratify affiliation. There was the distressing mix of rancour and resignations that too often attends such passionate considerations. Ian Searle has since been prominent in encouraging Carrick's engagement with both regional and national affairs.

There is cautious optimism about the future, as the regional network has been considerably strengthened and the regional and national lines of communication have been sophisticated. These strategies have included an annual Cornwall conference and the division of this shire where there are many transport and allied difficulties into 'neighbourhoods' for more localised participation within the regional banding. As Ian Searle concludes, 'pride and allegiance to one's own U3A are enhanced by an awareness that we belong to a bigger movement than that.' Only three 'forum' U3As have not registered with the central office, while there have been six additions. Cornwall now boasts 14 orthodox U3As with a total membership of over 1500.

Among them Carrick, with 527 members and over 30 interest-groups, flourishes in the Truro and Falmouth districts. Other Cornish examples include Gunnislake, where a Womens' Institute Book Circle decided to spread its wings, U3A style, in 1996, and did so successfully, with local help and with national support from Roy Wilson, then overseeing national development. With 84 members and 18 or so activities, their recruitment cleverly deploys the local estate agent to leaflet incomers. John Newcombe, the Gunnislake chairman, was busily active on the regional front. He served on the NEC from 1999 to 2002 and he very sensibly took on the role of initial chairman of the Devon and Cornwall region in 1998 and through its opening years. Bude, where, as its chairman Mary Dobson, explains, the chief initiator and her predecessor in the chair, Carol Harriott, had moved from Looe where she had been a U3A member. There were press adverts, meetings and support from the Launceston and

Wadebridge U3As and from the regional network. A relative newcomer, Bude U3A is 92 strong and arranges eleven interest-groups.

Looe has two U3As, arising in chief part, from that predicament facing many U3As of having too many members to fit into the available hall for general meetings. Queenie Shearman, a former member of Colchester U3A, started the Looe and District group in 1991 when she moved there. After careful planning a start was made as part of the 'forum' evolution. There are now 150 members and 23 interest-groups and a recent donation has been received from the Cornwall and Isles of Scilly Health Authority, in recognition of the well-being infused by U3A activity. The partner group, Looe Valley, operates, according to Tony Eaton, one of its officers, as an 'afternoon', as opposed to the District 'morning' body, but its 83 members, as well as enjoying their eight afternoon activities, have access to the morning ones as well, a felicitous arrangement.

iv. Regional Developments . . . Oxfordshire

Oxfordshire was another county that gained from a form of regional impetus, with many U3As being spins-off from the original shire-wide Association of Students of the Third Age (ASTA). Barbara Bond, Witney U3A's Development Officer, has contributed some valuable insights into that movement. It had ambitious designs to maintain links with the county public authorities; it held regular branch meetings from 1984 to 1990, and, for example, it organised an annual local history costume drama competition, the plays written and performed by members, which – here Barbara Bond elects for veracity above modesty – Witney won several times. Some of the ASTA branches signed on as U3As, often finding that the business of coping with growing activity impeded liaison with other ASTA branches, so much so that, by 1990, the actual network was more or less moribund.

Witney, affiliated in 1985, has, for example, jumped from a basic membership of 50 to a fruitful group of over 200, with 17 activity groups – 'many thanks to the founder members and long may it flourish' is Barbara Bond's final heartfelt cry. Jessie Maclachlan, writing from the Headington U3A, explains that ASTA was too close to ASDA for operational comfort; hence the willing change to U3A. She had been an Oxford ASTA member and an attender at U3A national conferences prior to launching the Headington group on the outskirts of Oxford, with the deliberate aim of running a smaller equivalent, with its blessing, of the sizable Oxford U3A. Several Oxfordshire U3As retain ASTA within their titles. ASTA in Henley is one of these: it began in 1982, after what the current Secretary, Valerie Alasia, calls 'fact-finding trips to the Oxford branch of ASTA' and then, primarily under Hilton Nawell's guidance, built up to a dozen or so study groups at the present time. As interest built up, further U3As were established. Oxford's success, for example, led to Myrddin Davies gathering together some friends and neighbours and starting the West Oxford U3A in 1995 and it now has 195 members.

Oxfordshire now has seventeen registered U3As catering for some 2500 Third Agers, but what is interesting is that no less than eleven of them were up and running by 1989, largely a tribute to the ASTA influence. It is safe to say that Oxfordshire was thus the first county of any material size to enjoy, district by district, fairly comprehensive U3A coverage. There are few Third Age persons in Oxfordshire who do not live within a few miles of a U3A locus. It was – it is – a notable achievement.

v. Regional Developments . . . Guildford . . . Surrey

In 1983 the University of Surrey, on the initiative of the percipient David James, Professor in the Educational Studies Department there and a person already mentioned in these annals in connection with old age and education, was instrumental in establishing an organisation called 'Activities and Interests for Mature Students', yielding up the attractive acronym of AIMS. The purpose was to set up U3A-style bodies in the university's catchment area, which, given the indifference and occasional hostility of some higher education facilities at that time, was most heartening. After some protracted discussions, three groups were launched. These were Banstead, Wonersh and Guildford.

All three affiliated to the national organisation, although, as its Chairman, Leslie Warner, explained, in the case of Wonersh, this was not until 1994. Wonersh, based on a complex of villages, was, apparently, deterred by the costs of affiliation, but now, with its 20 or so activities and 320 members, it is a fully-fledged U3A, although – 'sentiment dies hard', says Leslie Warner – it still refers to itself as 'Wonersh U3A (AIMS)'. Banstead, on the other hand, almost immediately signed up with U3A nationally, doing so in 1985. It now runs 37 groups and has over 300 members. Very soon the familiar U3A ripple effect occurred. In Elmbridge two friends, Margaret Lewandowski and Peggy Briggs, began to make enquiries about the U3A concept and were put in touch with 'a brilliant speaker' from the Banstead U3A, one Len Lamerton, whose persuasiveness was potent enough for these two friends to form a committee. A general meeting was advertised: 'at 2.50 pm the committee was assembled facing a sea of empty chairs – save for two staunch, but doubting friends of the two Margarets. Embarrassment began to mount, but Len Lamerton whispered a confident 'don't worry; they'll come. And they did. Just before 3.00 pm a flood of people began entering the hall. More and more they came until extra chairs had to be fetched.' Today Elmbridge U3A has 377 members.

Guildford U3A was set fair to become the centrepiece of the Surrey U3A map and not only because it was hard by the supportive University of Surrey. The founder of Guildford U3A in 1985 was Margot Clegg, destined to become one of several legendary figures in the local development of U3As. Sprightly in mind and alert in intellect, she quickly grasped the inner meanings of the U3A conception and, with the wholesale backing of her highly practical and equally dedicated husband, Philip Clegg, she created one of the first of what came to be called 'the large U3As.' A self- declared and unrepentant 'disciple' of U3A theory, her zeal was such that Guildford U3A membership soon zoomed over the thousand mark. In simple terms, its membership is now over 1200; its interest-groups number more than a hundred; a loose-bound 'faculty' system has evolved to help manage this sizable growth, and a series of lively social events is programmed to ensure that sociability in so big a group is sustained. In the mid 1990s the striking rate had become astonishing and indicated the benefits of size in terms of a wide spread of activities. On average, each member attended between three and four groups. By the 1990s, there were Guildford members who were attending as many as nine different sessions a week. That is practically full-time; there are many tutors in conventional colleges who would ruefully envy an education institution with that element of magnetism.

A significant aspect of the mercurial Margot Clegg's heritage – she is now President of the Guildford U3A – was her total belief in what she has described as 'rapid growth through an 'open door' policy, making it a management responsibility to cope.' Not for Margot Clegg the sombre shadow of the waiting list. She unreservedly accepted that part of the U3A objectives that called for assistance to be given to other groups and to all willing Third Agers. This was the precise converse of U3As who pleaded administrative pressures as grounds for restrictions on entry.

A gloss on this was support for new U3As in the county, although some of this missionary work strayed over the boundary into Hampshire. Two examples are Farnham and Woking. Woking Council, as its Secretary, Tom Allen, relates, was keen to emulate Guildford success and were to provide facilities and other help. With Guildford U3A assistance, Woking U3A was up and running by 1992 and now has over a thousand members. In Farnham, Guildford members, among them Tony Collyer, were to the fore as a U3A was started there in 1990; now there are close on 800 members. And the ripple has rippled on. Tony Price, writing from the Farnham U3A, reckons that, Farnham, sometimes with the aid of the Guildford and Farnborough U3As, has assisted in the formation of no less than eleven U3As within a ten miles radius of Farnham.

There are 22 U3As in Surrey and that is very comprehensive indeed. What, however, is impressive is the strength of these U3As, for sixteen of them have 300 or more on the register. Two other examples are Spelthorne, where there was some local authority backing at commencement in the 1995/96 period, and where over 500 members enjoy a very varied programme of 45 interest-groups in the Ashford, Staines and Sudbury area; and Reigate and Redhill, dating its affiliation in 1987, where its first Chairman, Ray Jackson, was another who had heard of U3A on the very fruitful *You and Yours* radio show and where, as Joy Krill, the current Secretary, reports, there are well over 400 members and 54 activities covering 33 subjects are arranged.

The U3A striking rate in Surrey is formidable. Such has been the barnstorming expansion in the county that, as of 2003, there were approximately 9500 U3A members in Surrey. In 1995, when these ratios were first calculated, Surrey had 3781 U3A members, that is, roughly 1:50 of its estimated U3A population. On the basis of the national figures then, it was suggested that Surrey's potential take-up was 5000 U3Aers. Surrey has not only passed that but has, by now, probably doubled it. It changes the perspective of what is possible. Surrey has raised the ante. The ratio is now 1:20. It is quite astounding. U3A penetration is deeper in Surrey than in any other local authority area. To put that into perspective, were those proportions to be achieved nationally, U3A membership would be 600,000, not far short of five times what it is presently.

In the later part of this study, we shall return to the social and cultural variables of recruitment. Whenever one does begin that analysis, the Surrey example shines brightly and challengingly.

vi. Regional Developments . . . Sussex

Perambulating down through Surrey to Sussex by the sea, one finds another piece of embryonic pattern-making of a regional character. Sussex was a county that very much benefited from having a number of U3As that were formed in the 1980s. This sprinkling of U3As, after the fashion of U3As in other places, gave rise to other U3As, which, with the help of sundry Sussex educational institutes, all led to the Sussex U3A Network.

The Sussex U3A Network, for instance, organise as many as twelve Study Days a year, with themes ranging from 'Manufacturing News; should we trust the media?' to 'Mozart's *Figaro* – the perfect Opera'. Let us watch how some of the contributory U3A groups sprang to life, often with assistance from their neighbours.

It being a small world, Lewes U3A was started in 1985 by Stella Claydon, who was Acting Head of Sidney's Jones' Department when he was seconded on London U3A duty, who was on the London U3A founding committee and who had launched a much-respected course in 'Learning in Later Life' at the then North London Polytechnic. With such a profound intellectual inheritance, success was assured and Lewes now has 275 members. Its interest-groups range from the eclectic – 'Members' Interests' – to the scholastic – 'Classical Greek', while an interesting initiative was the early foundation of the 'Lewes Lectures', 'open to the public as a mark of our thanks for support in the town for our work' and delivered, free of fee, by high-level university staff and other local eminent citizens. Lewes has also been helpful in backing other Sussex U3A starts, among them Seaford.

Another was Ringmer U3A, where, as one of the originators, David Smith, recalls, Jack Gray, a Sussex University lecturer, instigated proceedings in 1989 with a meeting in Ringmer secondary school's dining room. Soon, with intellectual appetites whetted, they forsook this site and built up 'modest but steadily growing enrolment' in this Sussex village. Arun Valley, in the Pulborough area, is another Sussex example of a U3A of pleasingly humble proportions – it has about 140 members and 16 groups – with a lively programme, nicely adapted to the needs of a more rurally based body, meeting in members' homes in various parts of the district.

'Crawley U3A is proud of the fact that it was one of the early groups to affiliate': this was as early as 1985 – yet Crawley U3A has an even longer prehistory. In 1979 a London-bound commuter contacted the West Sussex LEA about the needs of her mother, for whom she was the carer, and this led to the launch of the 'Learning in Later Years' (LILY) organisation, strongly linked with local bodies, such as the Community College and the Council for Voluntary Service. LILY pricked up her ears when the U3A idea was floated and contacted Dianne Norton, who visited Crawley to explore possibilities. Crawley LILY became Crawley U3A and soon expanded, as its Secretary, Beryl Sinclair, has explained, from about 50 people to a membership of 448, with some 22 groups on its advertised programme.

Eastbourne Central U3A began at much the same time, affiliating in 1985, and it still has two of its eight originals *in situ*. Now one of three U3As in Eastbourne, its approaching 200 members enjoy a very wide range of 26 activities. Then there is Hastings and Rother U3A, where Mike Williams, editor of the highly influential U3A *Sources* publication, is vice chairman, and where, from a start in 1989, some 250 members are engaged in some 33 activities of varied brand. Another successful launch was that of Burgess Hill U3A, a little later in 1993, very much on the individual initiative of the late Mimi Goldman. With help from the town council, and a stall in the market place, she gallantly established what is now a huge concern, with over 800 members with a wide gamut of study group among which they might choose.

In 1983 Ted and Edna Wright (as Edna Wright, now its President, recollects) travelled from Shoreham to Brighton and Hove U3A, only to be subjected to 'weekly pressure' from Graham Woodman, who served a valued term as national Chairman, to start a group in Southwick and Shoreham. This they shortly did and, as well as helping Graham Woodman with setting up the Worthing U3A, the Southwick and Shoreham U3A joined the Brighton, Lewes and other U3As in promoting the Sussex Network around the University of Sussex Centre for Continuing Education.

The Haywards Heath U3A was launched with a phrase that would have appealed to Michael Young. According to Judy Chapman, who became Chairman, seventeen people met to discuss the matter, boosted by the presence of Winifred Goad, Secretary of what is now known as the Sussex U3A Network and self-evidently no stranger to the 'blood on the snow' school of philosophy. 'At last' Winifred said, 'no more shilly shallying; you must form a committee.' Honor Jacomb-Hood went into the kitchen with two men and returned with a Chairman and a Treasurer'. This puts something of a gloss on the term ‘kitchen cabinet’, but order prevailed. Edwina Gunner was one of the seventeen, leaving home with her husband’s warning of ‘don’t take on anything’ ringing in her ears and arriving back home – ‘I realise now that the note-book was a mistake’ – as Secretary, reassuring her husband, ‘don’t worry; it’s a good idea, but I don’t think it will catch on in Haywards Heath.’ Of course, it did. With help from the Seaford, Crawley and Brighton U3As, it was soon under way and now has over 600 members.

Colin Simpson was recruited as a group leader: ‘I felt someone tapping my shoulder and a sultry feminine voice came from behind me; ‘I’ve got an offer you can’t refuse’, the lady said. ‘Ay, ay’, I thought to myself, ‘I didn’t know this sort of thing went on in Haywards Heath’ . . . ‘I want you’, she said, which raised my hopes - for them to be immediately dashed when she continued, ‘I want you . . . to take over the Art Appreciation group of the U3A.’ It was Judy Chapman; and Colin Simpson, having agreed to take five meetings, was still in charge of the Art Appreciation group over ten years later.

In toto, there are 25 U3A groups in Sussex, almost equally divided between the East and West administrative divisions of the old shire. With approximately 6500 members in sum in the county, this represents a comprehensive and fully-fledged response to the self-learning needs of Third Agers in Sussex.

vii. Regional Developments . . . Hampshire

Although it is convenient to address the rise of U3As in local authority packages (especially if one is comparing population and other statistics, which are often cited by local government ambits) the U3A principle is no respecter of such arbitrary borders, so that, for example, Sussex was to have some influence on Hampshire. By way of illustration, the Petersfield U3A was another that owed something to the help of Professor James of the University of Surrey. A retired higher education lecturer, John McCormack, and a retired university administrator, Len Kail, the U3A’s

Secretary and the teller of the tale, were its founders, way back in 1985, when there was such a bustle of activity in Surrey. Petersfield now has 450 members and 37 interest-groups. Again, it was Tony Collyer, of Farnham U3A in Surrey who helped put Old Basing on the U3A map. This was, as Membership Secretary, Dorothy Pender recounts, 1998 and now there are over 200 members.

Solent U3A was set up by a historian, George Watts, in 1986, and, as Olive Obin, the Secretary, reports, he still makes an annual appearance to run the Christmas quiz. Fleet is of later vintage, having registered nationally in 1994, but it has grown rapidly to be almost 900 strong, with a programme of 30 groups. Then there is a fine example of chain reaction. Chandlers Ford U3A was established in 1998 with the assistance of Winchester U3A. It grew quickly to its present status of 268 members and 35 groups and soon took the initiative in founding the neighbouring U3A of Monks Brook, which was started in 2003 and shot rapidly to 170 plus members.

Hampshire presently has no less than seventeen U3As, with a total membership of well over 6000, another highly commendable example of regional coverage and penetration. By far the largest of these U3As, with over 1200 members, is the long-running and redoubtable Farnborough U3A. Apparently the first hint came from a community worker attached to the local education authority and six people met in January 1989. Dianne Norton addressed the first open meeting in April and soon 190 Third Agers had signed on for a September start. There was an early alarm when the education centre, where groups met, was closed – 'a valuable lesson – don't put all your eggs in one basket', we are warned in the Farnborough briefing. Now there are about a hundred interest-groups, plus a development committee purely appointed for 'constantly monitoring the progress of existing groups and investigating the possibilities of starting new ones.' It is Farnbrough's proud claim that 'we do not have waiting lists for membership or groups'.

It is an inspiriting story. In personal terms, it is the fable of a composed, sedate woman taking the town of Farnborough not so much by fiercesome storm as by peaceful stealth. In another show of cross-border cooperation, Mina Lewis had had connections with the Guildford U3A before becoming the Chairman and virtual organiser of Farnborough U3A. A firm believer in the Laslettian precept of 'negotiation', she toiled hard to win the confidence and thus the highly practical assistance of local institutions, so that the U3A has gone from strength to strength. Were U3A action to be presented in terms of J B Priestley's *The Good Companions*, Mina Lewis would be cast as Miss Trant, calm, quiet, very, very determined, not as Suzie Dean, brash, volatile and nervy.

It is said of great cricketers that one should not judge them by their statistics alone but by the subtleties of their style. In Farnborough's case, however, the figures are as compelling as the fashioning. The Third Age population of the Farnborough area is about 11,000, although, of course, there will be some who travel from outside these limits to enjoy the delights on offer. Allowing for this and making a conservative calculation, this suggests that one in ten of the potential clientele are registered as U3A members and the ratio is possibly closer to one in nine. The intensity of this recruitment is quite staggering and few districts in the United Kingdom come near to emulating it. In the very unlikely event of these proportions being recreated across the nation, it would produce a gross total in U3A membership of 1.3m.

These tales from seven different areas, all of them with fresh beginnings in the early years, do demonstrate the extraordinary variety of U3A origin, extension and sponsorship. They suggest that those early roots, deeply planted and carefully nourished, led to a rich harvest. There were, of course, similar developments in a number of other districts. Conversely, there were to be localities that did not have the advantage of early momentum where the U3A idea struggled to implant itself and blossom.

In more or less degree, all of the areas analysed here had some budding regional oversight. Thus, just as pertinently, these several illustrations also underline the complexities of a subject that was to prove a permanent as well as a perplexing issue. This was the notion of regional structure. There were to be those who wished to impose it unilaterally; there were to be those who argued that its evolution should be entirely left to local happenstance. At first sight, these examples tended to favour the latter school of thought, for the endings of the stories have been good and, if not everyone, the majority have lived happily ever after. Yet, at the same time, they also indicate how quite potent regional leadership runs the risk of incommoding national authority or even, conversely, being swamped by the increasing power of its constituent bodies, something of an argument for those who would have a more formal regional infrastructure.

Let the jury be hung temporarily on that matter, for there is much else to consider from those few years of consolidation that followed the opening spell of U3A's history, particularly as the central U3A organism took something of a battering from the slings and arrows of outrageous fortune.

Nevertheless, it was a moment for rejoicing, for the less than a score of U3As of the first year or so had leapt to a healthy hundred or so by the end of 1989. By the happy chance of signings on and signings off, Farnborough U3A now stands exactly as the hundredth affiliated U3A in date-order. In 1996 Eric Midwinter wrote of a speaking engagement at Farnborough in these words:

> *'Behind me on the platform was hoisted a gorgeous square-shaped banner. Beautifully designed and delicately embroidered, the craft members had each undertaken to produce a shield emblematic of each interest-group. There were then some fifty shields. Like the trades unions, the friendly societies and the church groups, like the Mothers Union, of an older tradition, the banner presented a proud and colourful token of some 600 Third Agers' dedication to the cause. It was a fitting example of the message and the messenger being at one. May the number of shields increase; may the banners grow in size and in number; may the membership in procession behind the banners fructify; and may the U3A in the UK pursue its happy march with a pleasing mix of flair and expedition, and in wholesome comradeship.'*

Six: CRISES

Now the exhilarating image of Farnborough's heraldry must yield to the sterner stuff of the challenges faced by the central officers in the lists of national U3A politics during the later years of the 1980s.

---

i. Crisis – the Age-limit Question

Just as the first Trade Union Congress was a minor and unassuming affair in Manchester in 1868, followed by a major and imposing gathering a year later, so did the London quasi-conference of 1983 precede the first official National Conference of 1984. This was held at the University of Keele, with fifteen U3As represented. A main event was the first Third Age lecture, delivered by Sir Roy Shaw, Chairman of the Arts Council. It was an address highly sympathetic to the issues of learning in later life and it was well received. On the administrative front at the AGM, Michael Young and Eric Midwinter were affirmed in their roles as Chairman and General Secretary, other committee members were elected and the discussions were orderly and useful.

There was one controversial note only. There were U3As that properly included members, sufferers from early retirement or late redundancy, who were under 55 but who were licitly in the Third Age. Some U3As found this uncomfortable. Moreover, there were those who, succumbing to the easy rigidity of the bureaucrat, found the definition of Third Age too complex and preferred the false simplicity of discrimination by age alone. There was a motion, moved by the Huddersfield and Bradford U3As, to insist on a lower age limitation of 50. The founding trio was distraught at the prospect, with Peter Laslett showing signs of incipient apoplexy. The absolute point of the Third Age designation was that it refused to bow to the arbitrary whim of the artificial birthday, rather recognising the social determinants of each individual.

It is impossible to overestimate the crucial nature of this moment. It was as if the first Pentecostal gathering of apostles had denied the existence of the Redeemer or the first Bolshevik Internationale had declared itself in favour of the sanctity of private property. Luckily, an alarmed and indignant platform carried the day with, in the end, some comfort. In the scale of things it was an incident that passed over in a few minutes, but, had the vote gone against the Committee, U3A might just have become another old-style pensioners' club, thereby failing in its primary cultural role, that is, as a positive expression of a modern view of older age. Small in itself, it was to be the first of several critical junctures for the national office in the late 1980s.

Harry Muscutt and Jenny Betts continued their organisational labours, while Dianne Norton kept the home fires burning in U3A's domestic depot. 1985 saw the appearance of the first 'travel pages' in the national newspaper, a portent of what would become a massive element in U3A activity, where the quest for learning through group travel has been always well supported. In 1987 there would be the significant journey to Paris of U3A art-lovers. This was the very first national U3A excursion, an historic date to savour. In that same year the Third Age newspaper printed its first *Literary Supplement*, 'loved by some and hated by others', while these years of the middle 1980s witnessed the first formalised Regional Networks in Oxfordshire and East Sussex and the first conference of Northern U3As.

1984 had been marked by the publication of *Mutual Aid Universities*, edited by Eric Midwinter. It was published by Croom Helm in its 'Radical Forum on Adult Education' series. The series' editor, Jo Campling, who had a keen eye for emerging educational experiments, had approached Eric Midwinter almost as soon as the U3A movement had shown signs of regular life. Described as 'the first account of the ideas and development' of U3A in the UK, Asa Briggs, in his biography, *Michael Young; Social Entrepreneur*, published in 2001, referred to the book as 'this interesting volume'.

The contributors, among them Peter Laslett, Michael Young, Michel Philibert, Dianne Norton and John Rennie, have already appeared in these pages and their relevant thoughts expressed. It would be repetitious to revisit the text too heavily. There was a contextual account of the international situation by David Radcliffe, of the University of Western Ontario, Canada, but the global condition of U3A will be analysed in a later chapter. However, there was one other essay in the collection that is worthy of recall, for it touched on a subject not yet fully explored. Thus far the concept of mutual learning groups has been chiefly justified in social and civic terms, with the vast experience of U3A members and with the right of lay people to organise their own affairs to the fore. Paula Allman, of the University of Nottingham, now produced a paper, 'Self-help Learning and its Relevance for Learning and Development in Later Life' that added a substantial psychological gloss to this topic.

In a densely argued essay, Paula Allman confronted the conventional mode of teaching – the **pedagocic** – with its emphasis on the acquiring of skills and information, with her preference for the **andragocic** approach, much more concerned with the process of dialectic thought, with the marriage of reasoned thinking and experience and the raising of questions rather than the consumption of answers. 'An andragocic approach to adult learning', wrote Paula Allman, 'recognises that by virtue of being adults both teachers and learners have the potential for further development. Therefore learning is a process wherein adults come together to think, to question and reflect on what they know . . . and then to test this against and within experience.' She went on to contrast 'pedagogy', where 'the teacher is always controlling the learning experience' with 'andragogy', where the accent was on 'collective exploration'.

Furthermore, Paula Allman pressed the point that 'the learning process is primarily a group rather than an individual one' and she urged the precedence of 'dialogue' over 'monologue' as its essential style: 'not only does the peer learning group share the decision making process with regard to the content and method of learning, but they also share the responsibility for managing the group processes'. In other words, both the 'learning process' and 'the group dynamics' are the joint responsibility of the group members. She insisted that 'we can only realise the full promise of the experience (of self-help learning) if we challenge the accepted relationships of teacher and taught and the relationship of both these to knowledge'.

This scholarly rationale for the 'learning circle' approach was timely. It is true that what the military call the exigencies of the service had a hand in U3A interest-group development. With lean resources, the habit of smallish groups, often meeting in people's houses, quickly grew, irrespective of advanced psychological theory. Nonetheless, there was here a cogent design. The learning circle comes together to think, reflect, act and practise, according to the themes being pursued, with all ideally contributing both as teachers and learners. It calls upon everyone to share with others in mutual respect, the undeniable text of the self-help *credo*, and, in so doing, it elevates the 'dialogical' approach above the 'monological', follow-me-leader approach that is so dourly typical of much of traditional educational practice.

Michael Young and Eric Midwinter, fully versed in and accepting of the Plowden-style creed of child-centred as opposed to subject-oriented schooling, were very alive to these possibilities and were entirely enthusiastic about the 'dialogic' approach. Peter Laslett, with his imperishable vision of communes of scholars and his belief in 'negotiation' as the key to adult learning, was equally ready to plead the cause of collaborative learning. What Paula Allman's synthesis of modern research into the styles of thinking and reasoning provided was another and complementary dimension. It demonstrated the case for the self-help learning group being an improved kind of education.

This sat well with the Founders' own argument. It cannot be underlined too heavily that all three believed with urgent conviction that what they were proposing and developing was not some second-best alternative. This was not some form of educational Red Cross, bringing emergency relief to the old folk, until such time as the sophisticated professional machinery could be involved. This was the preferred alternative. They thought that what they were supplying was the superior model.

ii. Crisis – the Financial Question

Belief was stimulating, but it did not pay the bills. The central funds were in some disarray and were a source of some anxiety to the Committee. The Committee was still meeting, with apple pie, courtesy of the hosts, a constant on the lunch menu, at the Centre for Policy on Ageing and did so until 1988. It is interesting to note that the CPA staff commented on these meetings being the most boisterous of all those held there, ringing laughter frequently disturbing their professional labours. Whether the merriment resulted from the adrenaline flow associated with the rush of creative juices or from the hysteria consequent on examining the accounts is a moot point. An appeal was made to local U3As for funds to run the National Office.

Beset themselves with money problems, the local U3As stumped up a sorrowful and derisory £142.

Serious consideration obviously was required. This question dominated the business portion of the 1985 National Conference, held at Ruskin Hall, Oxford. 33 U3As were represented on this occasion, the first, self-evidently, at which an annual report was presented. The conference featured the second Third Age lecture, in which the brilliant community physician, John Muir Grey, endorsed the idea that a healthy mind boosts a healthy body. He examined his clinical tenet of 'the Fitness Gap', the chasm that increases with age between what one does and what one can do: it has mental and societal as well as physical attributes and one of its causes is cultural; that is, the propensity of older people to play out the role ascribed to them, to slow down and otherwise give up active life.

Not the least of the issues discussed under the financial flag was the strict precept declared by Peter Laslett that 'no support from the funds of local or central government shall be expected or sought but fund-raising shall become an integral part of the university's operation.' Peter Laslett, on his own unabashed admission, had existed in the lotus-flowered shelters of privilege for the whole of his professional career. Where he had enjoyed the luxury of opulently state-sponsored theatre, his colleagues, Michael Young and Eric Midwinter, had spent their lives ducking and diving for pennies and shillings to stage knock-about shows and keep them precipitously on the road. That said, they fully understood Peter Laslett's fear of public finance. He was anxious less the piper pick the tune. He was worried that, were the local and central authorities to be involved financially, they would pervert the course of U3As for their own purposes, such as insisting on certain courses or on the recruitment of certain clientele in exchange for their gold. As Peter Laslett was wont to remark of meetings, 'he who controls the agenda controls the world.'

It was a well-reasoned if stern adjunction. Michael Young found the distinction between public and private money slightly pedantic. On the one hand, commercial and even charitable funding might come with unwanted conditions. On the other hand, it was precisely public monies, which, so long as they were provided unconditionally, properly belonged to the people and should be made available to them. In any event, several U3As were already in receipt of help, in kind or cash, from local authorities and some would perhaps have never started or might cease to function were that denied them. There were also twilit areas in between. Was help from a college or university, each in receipt of public funding, an indirect tweaking of the absolute denial of state assistance?

Another instance of this more puritanical zeal arose over membership numbers. Eric Midwinter, egged on by Michael Young, was obsessed, and remains obsessed, with quantity, on the grounds that, given the value of the U3A experience, U3A had some responsibility to evangelise and offer the opportunity of this particular brand of educational salvation to as many as possible. Peter Laslett initially wondered whether just a few shining lights of small bands of dedicated older scholars, with high levels of research and, in fact, political commitment, might provide the world at large with a more telling message about the possibilities of post-work life. It was like the choice between the monastic orders and the baptised laity, but, as we shall see, Peter Laslett did revise his concerns somewhat on this subject and was always concerned that U3As would 'provide intellectual stimulus for the mass of the elderly in Britain'.

Michael Young would occasionally tell Peter Laslett that he was being over-theoretical and unrealistic and that sometimes one had to sup with the devil with spoon of whatever length was at hand. This was, of course, highly relative. Several times over the sixty-odd years of his incredibly creative adult life Michael Young was asked at meetings, in those hoity-toity tones adopted by neo-realists, 'don't you think you're being a bit idealistic?' 'Oh, I do hope so', he would deprecatingly murmur.

Although, as chapter two explained, the combined beliefs of the three men were held in common, their peculiar skills and traits did mean that, in these early years of activity, they contributed differing characteristics. Peter Laslett was the conscience – and his abiding memory remains rightly the conscience of the movement. Michael Young personalised the idea, the notion of mutuality, with knowledge of the springs of how it might be advanced. Eric Midwinter was the proselytiser and campaigner, with, as Executive Secretary, Dianne Norton still excelling as publicist and administrator.

But what Peter Laslett did recognise was that, in his own metaphor, the U3A principles were Platonic rather than Aristotelian, that is, they were closer to the high standards set in the *Republic* than the more pragmatic descriptors included in *Politics*. It was our duty to subscribe to them and to do all we could to preserve them. Occasionally, for human reasons, we might have to sin and break the code, the chief excuse always being the risk of institutional collapse. The overarching principle was the preservation of U3A itself.

It was with this *apologia* in mind and with Peter Laslett's grudging benison, that, in 1986, Eric Midwinter and Dianne Norton went cap in hand to the then Department of Education and Science and asked for help. The officials were adamant that they could not add U3A to the lengthy roster of organisations that received an annual subvention; indeed, they spoke despairingly of organisations that had been on for years and that it was near impossible to excise from the list. They were, however, impressed by the concept, by the demonstration of its early success and by the degree of self-help involved in local financing. The argument submitted was that U3A nationally needed a grant that would tide them over the rocky introductory years, until such time as the movement would be strong enough to provide a little more than £142 for the upkeep of a central agency.

The response was generous. An award of £14,900 (just over a hundred times the sad collection from the local U3As) spread over three and a half years, was agreed. It was a decent enough compromise. We were a self-help movement and we did not wish, nor were we invited, to join the dismal rota of departmental pensioners who were fobbed off annually with a measure of financial relief, often paid against stringent safeguards as to its use. U3A, nationally, were pleased to agree that the money would be spent in three ways: for the maintenance of the National Office; as subsidy for the newspaper, and towards the development of new U3As. The hope was politely expressed by the DES that some of this development would be related to districts as yet untouched, with older people in socially distressed areas and among the ethnic minorities mentioned, and the Committee was not unhappy with that injunction. The grants that had supported the first two National Organisers were now exhausted, but Harry Muscutt agreed to act further as development officer under the third of those aims.

There was general relief, tempered by the knowledge that some more permanent solution, founded in the principle of self-support, must soon be revealed. The 1986 Conference and AGM were held at Sheffield. Michael Young stepped down as Chairman. It had been, for him, a longish stint. His reputation was that of a social entrepreneur who established new bodies, hurrying quickly on from one to the next, like some kind of organisational midwife, only stopping to ensure that the new-born babe was alive and breathing before rushing off to the next institutional confinement. He would sometimes mutter, in gently jocose mood, that there were very few organisations he had started, which had not deteriorated when he was no longer the sole member. However, he never lost his strong interest in U3A and always regarded it fondly, for, after all, it was one of his most impressive success stories.

Frank Pedley, a sitting Committee member, was elected Chairman in his stead. He had, then, risen from the ranks, but the credentials of his officer material were glittering. He came from a background of, first, adult education, and, second, educational administration. His spell as Chief Education Officer of Rochdale, where his radical stance, for instance, on Community Education, had marked him off as one of the stars of the educational firmament. He was already engaged with the esoteric world of Michael Young's acronymic organisations – he was for many years Vice-chairman of the Advisory Centre for Education (ACE) – and he was a close friend both of Michael Young and Eric Midwinter. Tall, craggy and imposing, he was to bestride the U3A national scene with some authority, albeit lightened by a mordant humour. For example, he had, from the outset, impressed everyone with his insistence, despite (perhaps because of) his long involvement with the education service, that new U3As should turn for succour, not to inflexible local education authorities, but to the more user-friendly local libraries. There was always the hazard that strings might be attached to local as to national education grants.

The short histories of local U3As are profusely littered with evidence of the sagacity of that advice.

The important decision was reached to levy a membership fee on local U3As. It was determined that this should be categorised according to size, ranging from £15 to £50. An annual associate membership fee of £5 was also agreed for supporters of U3A who, for various reasons, did not belong to any particular local group. In 1987, the National Conference moved to Bath, following a pattern of trying to visit differing parts of the country, in part to balance up the varying travel costs, year on year, for U3As, in part, to seek the services of local U3As to help with the arrangements. On this occasion it was affirmed that the membership fees should be £50 for U3As with more than a hundred members; £25 for those with 50 to 99; and £15 for those with less than 50 members.

However, there was a significant switch in attitudes at this gathering. Against a canvas of the national U3A mechanism being palpably under-funded and with some major sense that a top rating of £50 for U3As that had upwards of a thousand members smacked of unfairness, there was a move to introduce a *per capita* fee based on the estimated expenditure of the following year. It was pressed that individual members all received the quarterly newspaper, almost a justification in itself of the cost, although the reply that it was not necessarily welcomed nor enjoyed was a salutary one. However, there was, apart from its sense of natural justice, a general feeling that personal membership of the national body was an appropriate device. Every member should feel a specific part of this burgeoning national adventure. After considerable debate, this was agreed.

In 1988, when the Conference had gravitated north to Lancaster, the die was cast. The National Executive Committee, as it was now coming to be titled, had, after some close wrangling over the budget, arrived at the conservative figure of £1 a head for the levied fee. The debate was heated and rancorous. The Huddersfield U3A, with a large membership and, because of its local authority support, low costs, was agitated by the suggestion. Its delegate proposed an amendment that a ceiling of £500 be imposed, irrespective of size. Its founder, Edith Bentley, who had served so assiduously on the National Committee and who had worked so hard to help other U3As, was anxious not to lose contact with the mainstream, despite her members' reluctance to fork out for the national regime. This was her bold bid to find a happy medium.

The logic of this suggested compromise was not readily conceded. It was pointed out that a group of a hundred raising £100 faced much the same problem as a group of a thousand raising £1000. Self-evidently, human psychology was at work. Raising £1000 just seemed a tougher proposition and, of course, in the case of Huddersfield, the new rule meant an astronomic leap from £50 to approaching £2000, and from members who were paying very little, if anything, for their activities in the first place.

One of the Huddersfield problems was that members were, in effect, being asked to subscribe in general terms for the first time.

The decision to adopt a *per capita* fee was to have incalculable consequences.

iii. Crisis – the Constitutional Question

Before examining the fall-out from the momentous resolution to proceed with individual membership, it may be timely to discuss the other major challenge facing the U3A movement nationally, namely, the construction of a thorough-going constitution. It is timely so to do because, in terms of malign effects, it was the combined weight of both the financial and the constitutional settlements that led to the defection of leading U3As from the national consensus.

The constitutional histories of voluntary bodies follow a similar pattern. There is the heady beginning, free-wheeling, a trifle haphazard, some cocking of a snook at the niceties of administrative rectitude, with the accent on lively action. Then there is the realisation that this might be hazardous, making the agency susceptible to *subfusc* criticism. Pressure grows to constrain the action within the legal bounds of constitutional respectability. The innocents become aware of their legalistic nudity and cover themselves in the fig-leaves of corporate propriety.

This is a necessary step for any organisation. It is the genuine token of an institution's coming of age. Growth, at a certain but not always overt point, makes it needful to build in structural features for the better management of the organisation, where, beforehand, most matters could be dealt with better at a personal and immediate level. The handling of money and the rational implementation of democratic procedures make it, sooner or later, essential. It is the judgement about the timing of the change that calls for some *finesse*. The emotional tempo of the one is different to that of the other. It is as difficult for the more puritanical committee construction to sustain unbridled creativity, as it is for the more cavalier originators to cope with the rightful demands of formal oversight. Sometimes it is not unlike Sir John Fairfax' famous verdict on the English Civil War, delivered as he sat on a drum around a campfire during that internecine conflict: 'all the Publicans and Sinners are on one side and all the Scribes and Pharisees are on the other.'

Maybe the U3A case was not so bad as that. Nevertheless, the emphasis had been on creative action, with the spread of the idea being uppermost in the organisers' minds and with a tiny group of activists (a mechanism, of course, mirrored small at scores of local U3As) taking the revolutionary lead. The early conferences, for example, free from the restraint of undue 'committeeitis', were enlivening, even entertaining, get-togethers, full of jovial argument about the U3A activity, rather than how it should be controlled. Apart from the troublesome interlude about the age-limit, a vote was rarely taken or required. Naturally, the mood was one of excitement, as those present realised dimly that they were engaged in the beginnings of a growing social phenomenon.

It is sometimes hard for the child suddenly to become the adult. Too early – and some of childhood's delights, that is, the impetus of the imaginative impulse, are lost; too late – and some of the juvenile romps become embarrassingly gauche and inane. Curiously, two of the protagonists, as recent correspondence reveals, both think their contrary estimates were slightly askew. Frank Pedley, from his appointment to the Committee in 1985, had realised that a movement growing with such momentum would soon require a more formal democratic structure, rather than the existing cabal. As Chairman, he put his views on paper to the Committee and to the pre-conference meeting at Bath in 1987, but received little support. It was this that caused him not to allow his name to go forward for re-nomination as Chairman, believing that his approach was not representative of the movement at large. Eric Dyke, an early Chairman of the Oxford ASTA/U3A and with a meritorious career in adult education – he had been Principal Education Officer for Further and Higher Education and Associate Tutor at an FE Staff College - satisfactorily behind him, was elected Chairman.

Frank Pedley now thinks he introduced these matters 'prematurely'. Conversely, Eric Midwinter, reluctant to swathe the gusto of that early momentum in the wrappings of cautious governance, now believes, as General Secretary, he left the switch too long, for the size of the movement was already becoming top-heavy for what might be called the Che Gueverra approach. In any event, the national U3A was catapulted into predicament, symbolically enough, by administrative blunder or misfortune.

There was, naturally, a pile-up of organisational chores as the movement expanded and one item that suffered was financial management. It was Michael Young's practice to ask his accountant at the Community Studies Institute, where he was Founder and Director, to handle the accounts of his several fledgling bodies, until such time as they were of a size and prominence to control their own finances. Thus from 1983, when Michael Young had registered the Third Age Trust as a company limited by guarantee and as a charity, the accounts had been overseen in this fashion. Unfortunately, the long illness and then death of this hard-pressed officer left the accounts in a confused condition. When submission of the balanced accounts was to be made in 1987, Dianne Norton, as Executive Secretary, wrote to the Department of Trade and Industry three times, seeking advice on how most effectively to complete the necessary forms, in the light of her information from U3A's accountant being presented in a different form. Answer came there none. Time elapsed, and, with it, the automatic suspension of the Third Age Trust from the Companies' Register.

It was a mild enough error and, in 1988, the Trust was simply restored to the Register without penalties, there being a tacit recognition that some of the fault lay on the side of the registering authority, which had, to say the least, been tardy in its responses. At the same time, it was a definite error, for which the General Secretary, Eric Midwinter, could not but accept main responsibility, his only defence being that, along with other officers, his priorities had lain in the active pursuit of launching new U3A groups, when perhaps he should have been keeping a more watchful eye on the rather more boring business of accounting procedures.

It was a blow to those who wished to maintain a freer rein for a little longer, for, and there was no denial of this, it revealed a fearful rent in the body politic of the U3A. There was a loud outcry. In particular, the bad news had come to the ears of Margaret Hollis, of the Bradford U3A, to serve creditably as first elected Secretary of the National Committee for one year. She was, by discipline, a physiotherapist of high repute, having been the first Principal of the Bradford School of Physiotherapy and a leading published authority in this field. Margaret Hollis was sufficiently incensed by this dereliction of duty on the part of the U3A officers to take prompt action. Prior to the Lancaster annual conference of 1988, the Bradford U3A called a meeting of what they believed to be dissident groups, with a view to proposing, at the Lancaster AGM, that the existing national agency should be forthwith closed and a new and looser federation established under fresh management.

Frank Pedley, on whose recollection we rely for this stirring tale of political adventuring, heard word of this meeting. He was the prop and stave of the nearby Keighley U3A and rang up Margaret Hollis with a request that he might attend: 'reluctantly she agreed' (he writes) 'The atmosphere was very ugly, and it was with some difficulty that I persuaded them to abandon the resolution they had framed, on the understanding that there would be a radical overhaul of the organisation.'

A deal was struck. At the subsequent AGM, Eric Dyke, who was to prove such a shrewd and dedicated Chairman, announced the appointment, under Frank Pedley's stewardship, of a constitutional committee to review the current arrangements and draw up a draft schedule for discussion at an extraordinary general meeting. In practice, it was the task of this working party to rejig the Memorandum and Articles of Association, so that they were more relevant to the activities of a body now much larger than the original. The meeting at Lancaster vented some wrath on the officers, notably the General Secretary and Executive Secretary, for their imprudent acts in respect of these fiscal and legal matters and, in truth, substantial hot air was dispelled over a problem that was already halfway to remedy.

It was a master-stroke to appoint Frank Pedley as Chairman of this body, for, with his notable good sense and his reputation of being someone who had already flagged up the perils of being well nigh constitution-less, he enjoyed much confidence among the member U3As. Among the others serving with him were Graham Woodman, of the Brighton U3A, later to zoom to stardom as an effective national Chairman, and Harold Potts, of Chorley U3A, who would become Treasurer of the Third Age Trust in the new dispensation and serve faithfully in that office for several years.

The constitutional committee worked with a will and the special meeting was summoned to meet at Birmingham in June, 1989. There was a strong turn-out of representatives for this occasion, and, perhaps typically of such occasions, no less than 77 amendments had been tabled. There was a vigorous if at times pedantic debate, but the Pedley plan was negotiated and approved with its essentials intact. At base, it restructured and enlarged the National Committee, created a set of leading posts, such as Secretary and Treasurer, that were subject to election at the AGM rather than, as had been the practice, by the Committee, and detailed the number of representatives, according to size of membership, that each local U3A might field for voting purposes at the annual conference and AGM.

It was a thoughtful piece of drafting. Like the wisest legislation, it was founded in broad principles and simple reasoning, and, after that fashion, has graciously withstood the test of time. The chief objectives were made very clear and the means of achieving them were left sufficiently open, so as not to preclude alterations and re-interpretations as time passed and factors changed. As Frank Pedley was well aware, and as the activists feared, the drawing up of a constitution, indeed, the very sniff of clauses and subsections, attracts a certain mentality, a host of amateur constitutional sea-lawyers and hair-splitting, logic-chopping anoraks. There was some pressure, possibly stimulated by the fall from the Companies' Register, itself the catalyst for the discussion, to cross every 't' and dot every 'i' and to ensure that no contingency, however unlikely or bizarre, was not insured against with its requisite paragraphs, sub-heads and riders. That grand climateric of 77 amendments was awful proof of this. It is precisely that form of constipated statute that inhibits fast reaction on the part of officers and others eager to make practical progress.

Courageously, the Pedley charter steered a moderate course with decorous efficacy. It fundamentally defined the national U3A in its proper character *apropos* political science as a Confederation. It was not a federation of branches under central supervision; it was a confederacy of autonomous groups. It was an association wherein the constituent groups retained their independence, whilst, at the same time, they agreed to maintain an umbrella organism that would, by its very existence, strengthen each and every subscribing unit. The grounds for membership of the larger body – notably, the provision of educational opportunities to those in the Third Age through the practice of democratic mutualism – were still kept at a minimal, if elemental, level. It was the broadest of churches. When, in the late 1990s, another working party met to examine and, where necessary revise, the constitution, it was found that very little repair work was required, itself a mark of homage to the original drafters.

The hand of Frank Pedley on the U3A tiller as these troubled waters were navigated was a steadying one. He presided over the national councils as the precarious shift was made to individual membership, with its hope of some semblance of financial safety. He saved the national U3A from the peril of schism and possible collapse. He oversaw the restructure of the whole U3A on rational constitutional principles. Locally, he had been chiefly responsible for the establishment of the Keighley U3A and, when, latterly, he moved to Settle, he set about launching a U3A there. Since leaving the Committee, he became something of an elder statesman to the organisation and has barely missed attendance at the yearly national conferences.

In decent acknowledgment of this magnificent contribution to the welfare of the U3A in the UK, Frank Pedley was made an Honorary Life Member of the Third Age Trust in 2001 at the Manchester conference. It must have been a very proud moment for him, but perhaps not more so than when, a year earlier, at Norwich, Michael Young spoke on receipt of his Founder Member Emeritus award. Michael Young understood more than most the intricacies of keeping voluntary organisations upright and mobile and his estimate of Frank Pedley's input was acute: 'he is', said Michael Young, 'responsible more than any other individual member for the movement's success.'

iv. Crisis – Damage and Damage Limitation

The all-important point is that 102 U3As, affiliated in or before 1989 remained in national membership. Much was made and there is much to be said about the handful of U3As that resigned from the Third Age Trust – but the really memorable historical fact is that 102 gamely stayed.

In the years 1988 and 1989 there were nine U3As who disaffiliated themselves, although several of these were down to internal collapse rather than external disagreement. The four who caught the eye and left out of disagreement with the national consensus were Cambridge, Huddersfield, Dewsbury and, as early as October 1988, Halifax. The national officers watched the mail with some trepidation as these events unfolded. Basically, the movement remained constant. 'Only four', was the relieved conclusion.

Nonetheless, it was highly damaging. Although Halifax and Dewsbury were not sizeable groups, Cambridge and Huddersfield were, along with London, the biggest in the country. The first shock was financial. The carefully nurtured budget, aligned to an income based on £1 a head, was immediately in tatters. With a national membership of some 12,000, the four defections robbed the exchequer of a third of its membership and a third of its potential income.

The Third Age Trust was extremely fortunate to have Eric Dyke in the chair at this stage. Here again there was some personal aggravation, for the Oxford U3A, his home base, were not over keen on the *per capita* fee and, in practice, disowned him; neighbouring Abingdon offered him the solace of their official backing. Eric Dyke thereafter successfully set himself the task of soliciting varied corporate bodies and charitable foundations – Trustee Savings Bank; ICI; NatWest; Barclays Bank; Marks and Spencer, for instance – for funds. So competent was this diligent man in this regard that, by the turn of the decade, the Third Age Trust was for the first time financially sound. Eric Dyke was one of those who had castigated the Founders for not waiting until there were ample funds before launching the U3A movement. Whatever the pros and cons of that argument, Eric Dyke certainly dominated the high ground, in that, by his sterling efforts in balancing the U3A accounts, he had roundly won the right to criticise anyone on monetary matters.

Moreover, he was insistent on a valued distinction in the styling of revenue and expenditure. He earmarked the 'outside' funds – they had quickly reached what, for that day and in that circumstance, was the very handy sum of £8750 - for development and expansion work and the 'inside' funds, namely, the *per capita* membership fees, for the expenses of the national office and for services, such as the newspaper, to existing local U3As. It was a judicious dissection. Foundations were and are notoriously diffident about paying out grants for staple core expenditure as opposed to developmental projects; local U3As did, whatever their affection for the national body, want to see something for their money. From a financial angle, Eric Dyke's chairmanship was as rewarding as it was opportune.

The collateral damage was more lasting. The mammoth success of the Cambridge and Huddersfield U3As had been a huge boost to U3A publicity. The cultural polarity –the ancient academic site; the sturdy industrial township – obviously added to the pigmentation of the colours in which U3A in the UK could be painted. The two U3As had featured in press and media accounts of U3A life and activity. Both, to their enormous credit, had been helpful in support of nascent U3As – and not only in their immediate vicinity; we have already learned, for example, of Edith Bentley's missionary labours in the south west of England.

Through the blessed lenses of hindsight, it might be said that, frankly, the two models were more inspirational than practical. Cambridge U3A was a luminous *tour de force*, creating a dazzling array of activities for hundreds of eager people with immaculate efficiency and *panache*. Huddersfield, with its strong municipal backing, had built, with amazing potency, an equally wide-ranging if differing gamut of activities for its numerous clientele. Although this was not known at the beginning – and an aspect of the excitement was this sheer ignorance of quite what would happen – the more typical model for U3A, as the previous chapters have already demonstrated, was that of one or two individuals, meeting in someone's sitting room, calling a meeting in a local church hall and, with friends and neighbours, literally starting a U3A on the streets of their locality.

The three dissident Yorkshire U3As were most concerned about the money. The Halifax group even suggested to Frank Pedley, when he attended one of their committee meetings to parley with them on this question, that they might consider paying every second year. They wished to be an affiliated member once every two years, advancing and retreating annually, as in some ballroom manoeuvre purloined from a Jane Austen novel. This, of course, was tantamount to an adult trying to get into a football match through the half-price gate and was not accepted. Incidentally, this led to a constitutional *addendum* that obliged U3As that resigned and then rejoined to pay, at the committee's discretion, the missed interim fees.

At its simplest, this Yorkshire trio did not feel it would be getting value for brass. At this stage, and apart from the newspaper, the national body was not in a position to offer the existing U3As very much in material terms, although, as many realised, the exchange of ideas engendered by national togetherness, both countrywide and, increasingly, at local and regional levels, was a decided benefit.

The national role was to extend the remit of U3A to more and more places and people. We have already noted how often contact with the national office, the receipt of a small grant and publicity materials or the intercession of one of the national officers or organisers enabled new U3As to spring to life. In this sense, it was, financially speaking, like hire purchase. The local U3A received gratis what assistance could be made available – and then, once settled, it was trusted that they would repay by instalments. The Third Age Trust, at this point, might have done worse than choose for its motto the title of the 1962 British film, *Live Now, Pay Later*.

It was distressing to find that there were just a few U3As – and there is evidence that there have been others since who have gone through the same deliberations – which argued that they had no need of a central body, they could cope perfectly well without it and thus they refused to subscribe to it. What in actual fact they were saying was that, once they had heard of the U3A idea and started a U3A themselves, they no longer had need of a central body. They neglected to recall that, without that central starting-point, there would have been no U3As at all. Without the concept, there would have been nothing. The vision of Peter Laslett, the idea of Michael Young and the belief of Eric Midwinter, embodied in that Wimbledon spare bedroom, had little to count by way of resources, but, had they not joined in promulgating the notion, there would have been no U3As to contemplate leaving or remaining in the national collective. Worse, the bootlegging U3As were implicitly proposing that, having heard of it themselves and perhaps taken advantage of that knowledge, it did not matter a damn if no one else did in the future. It was a bit like those Greek tragedies, with Freudian undertows, where the children slay their parents. On a more homely note, a slightly earlier British film, the 1959 *I'm Alright Jack*, springs to mind.

The case of Cambridge was somewhat different, for the constitutional question was possibly as pertinent for them as the financial issue. The strength of a confederation – its balance of local autonomy with central encouragement – has the reverse image: the weakness of local independence threatened by central authority and central unity imperilled by local awkwardness. That tension is probably unavoidable: there must be dozens of central/local voluntary systems where the local units are fulminating against central *diktat*, while the central body grieves over the ungrateful intransigence of its constituent parts.

The shift to a formal constitution, plus the composition of affiliation fees that would make it financially secure, worried some U3As, anxious less their self-sufficiency be undermined. The Cambridge U3A was a prosperous and, in relative terms, luxurious U3A, a Rolls Royce to the dilapidated old banger of the Third Age Trust. It ran with great effectiveness; it employed administrative staff; it was a major player. Although some attempts were made to reflect relative strengths in the voting procedures at U3A national AGMs, it was the local U3A itself that was the natural unit of membership. For instance, there had been little support for the equivalent of the trade union card vote, with all the complications of checking membership lists and so forth, which might have given the two or three big U3As more sway.

It was in this respect that the different character, already referred to, of the 'official' as opposed to the 'activist' slant came into play; it is, if you will, the difference we encountered in chapter four when we witnessed the failure of Manchester and the success of, say, Taunton. As the national U3A edged towards constitutional probity, there was an accompanying tendency for the officious nit-pickers to come out of the musty woodwork, replete with smug archaisms remembered from long-gone meetings of yore. Some of it was excruciating. Jean Davis, a colleague of Eric Midwinter when he was at the National Consumer Council, used to talk of her first induction into committee work, a warning tale of how off-putting that experience could be to those who were keen to reach some quite ordinary and practical goal. She claimed the very first words she heard were spoken by a man who fussily declared, 'I want to move a motion through the chair'.

Sometimes, in such circumstances, one feels that procedure is designed to halt rather than accelerate action. Eric Midwinter was seated with the Cambridge delegation at one such national meeting in 1988. They were responsible for a smart, smooth, flourishing organisation. They listened aghast to some of the tortuous interventions and leaden circumlocutions. They shook their heads sadly. Were they really expected, one could read in their faces, to risk placing their wonderfully successful U3A in the hands of some who could barely be trusted with the proverbial whelk-stall – and, into the bargain, shell out £1500 for the privilege? Eric Midwinter's halting advice – 'stay and improve things' – was scarcely heeded and one suspects it is no accident that the Cambridge resignation came in the July of 1989, just one month after the constitutional debate at Birmingham.

In the fullness of time, one may demonstrate how the Pedley constitution astutely found the correct balance between the need for some formal barriers and the absence of others and how, by retaining a native simplicity, some of the small-minded wrangling that arrests the reasonable progress of business was avoided. It was to be a constitution that breathed life rather than suffocated but, by then, the Cambridge U3A had gone.

The apostasy of Cambridge, whatever the cogency of its leaders' rationale, was a hammer-blow to the Founders. They found it disappointing, irksome, even offensive. Revisiting the origins of U3A in the UK, a deal had been struck whereby the available funds had been evenly split between the central lobbying group and one single local group. Neither partner had, of course, real legal identity at this primitive stage, but, in any event, there was no thought of drawing up a contract to protect the investment or the idea and its logo. That would come later, a necessary corollary to constitutional reform, but, at the primordial stage, the last thing in anyone's mind was that the agreement would be reneged upon.

It is worth comparing the investments. The national office had, with its £3200, procured, by 1989, over a hundred U3As. The Cambridge £3200 was money down the drain: the official U3A had nothing to show for it. Initially, new U3As were lucky to get a £30 start-up grant, later munificently enlarged to £50, later £75; even now it is just £100. Someone quickly calculated that, had the U3A founding committee kept the lot, another hundred U3As might have been started.

At a personal level, it meant split loyalties for Peter Laslett. Wryly, and in a typical spirit of *camaraderie*, he had also become a member (although, of course, this had not cost him any money) of the Huddersfield U3A. He continued to act pragmatically on all sides. Although, like Eric Midwinter, he left the National Committee soon after, as the electoral process rightly took over, he was always ready with advice and was to be involved in several specific projects. But, as he confided occasionally to Eric Midwinter, he found the Cambridge withdrawal acutely embarrassing until the day he died.

Yet a hundred remained within the body of the kirk: that number must be emphasised again, and, at the risk of invidiousness, one U3A deserves a special mention in despatches. If an institution may be a hero, it was the London U3A. The London U3A could have made the same case as Huddersfield or Cambridge with even greater force and clarity. If anyone could manage without an umbrella, safe from the storms of administrative problems, it was this flourishing and very effectively run organisation. Alongside this humming mill of activity, the national office was, as yet, a single and often quiescent loom. Had London also opted out, both money and prestige would have been lost in some terrible abundance. It seems, too, that pressure was brought to bear on the London U3A to join the others in self-imposed exile.

Nobly, and to their eternal credit, the leaders of the London U3A stood firmly by the founding objects and principles: the phrases are explicit enough; 'to encourage the establishment of similar institutions in every part of the country and to collaborate with them' – 'to help to mobilise the efforts to offer other elderly persons in Britain other opportunities of educational stimulus on as wide a basis as possible'. Not for the London U3A the route that might have also removed them outside the pale of such cooperation and into inward-looking reclusiveness. It is right to hail London's moral valour at this crucial juncture in U3A's history.

v. Crisis – a Final Round-up

It is strange how large a part was played by Yorkshire U3As – among them Huddersfield, Keighley and Bradford, which last U3A, it must be emphasised, their officers having combatively raised the question of the inefficiencies of the central office, remained firmly loyal to the national banner – in these troubled dramas. The broad acres had enjoyed a few good starts from a U3A viewpoint, although the withdrawal of three U3As in prominent towns was something of a blow. It left nine U3As in this large area, among them the highly developed Craven and York groups, which were building very extensive memberships. One of the oldest Yorkshire U3As was the lively Whitby Whaler outfit, launched in 1987, with 34 people and six groups and an acronym that stood for 'Whitby Activities, Learning and Education in Retirement'. It now has over 500 members and organises over 20 interest-groups and 'has become a leading and integral part of the life of the town.'

Currently, there are 27 U3As in Yorkshire, several of them of a rather later date. They include Harrogate U3A, an elegant cameo in that elegant town, started in 1991 with aid from the national office and now with nearly 400 members; Ryedale U3A established in 1994 on the initiative of local individuals and now with some 300 and more members enjoying the benefits of a programme of 30 activities; Hessle U3A, which, as Liz Skipsey, its Secretary retails, 'originated from a chance conversation of three ladies' in 1991, when local adult provision was threatened with cut-backs – it now has 132 members and, in proportion, a fine total of 20 interest-groups; and, in turn, three individuals started the Swanland U3A in 1996, with Hessle's hearty assistance when the older group became over-crowded, and now has 400 plus members.

In 1994 a television piece about the York U3A evoked a response in Doncaster. Christine Ward, the Doncaster U3A Secretary, describes how Audrey Smith and colleagues received help from the national office, including a visit from Peter Laslett, and were soon up and running. Some Barnsley enthusiasts had the good sense to seek help from the Sheffield U3A in 1996 and the good sense, according to Beryl Toplis, the Barnsley U3A Development Officer, to hold their first meeting – 'a good start', apparently - at lunch-time in a pub. Now it has 315 members and 25 activities. Easingwold and District U3A did not begin until late in 2001, when, as Ann Roberts, its Secretary explains, representatives of the Thirsk and York U3As made presentations to Easingwold Over 50s Forum. Such was the rapid response that, with Mike Long, by now the U3A National Development Officer, and Joyce McKay of Northallerton U3A as guest speakers, a public meeting was quickly held and 'we have made tremendous progress.'

If, however, one were looking for some counterweight to the defection of the massive Huddersfield group, then the saga of the mighty Sheffield U3A falls neatly onto the historical scales. In both York and Sheffield there had been moribund attempts to start U3As, but now both triumphed at a second endeavour. The Sheffield tale is beautifully told in its very own history, published in 2002, and encouragingly titled *The Story So Far*. In 1986 Jenny Betts, with Sheffield names trickling through to her Preston fastness, called a meeting in Sheffield and barely a week later a steering committee was formed. Next 45 people met and adopted the title of SU3A and, at a 'market place' gathering, with people holding up cards denoting their interests, groups were quickly in place.

Space forbids the inclusion of the plentiful evolutionary detail. Suffice it to say that, Topsy-like, SU3A grew and grew, negotiating briskly and always looking ahead, never dependent, for instance, on any single source, such as the local authority. In this, too, it showed a different attitude to that of the Huddersfield U3A. With over 2000 members and 122 activity groups, it is the biggest official U3A in the land. At one fell swoop, it put the lie to the U3A lore that it was difficult to promote the activity with any resonance in a large industrial city. It is an exhilarating story and well worth the reading and it would be invidious to mention one or two out of the numerous active individuals who have contributed to this astounding triumph.

Some of the statistics demonstrate the intensity of this elaborate construct. 43 groups meet in private houses and 27 outdoors, including the 22 walking groups and the yachting group, while 46 other groups meet at 26 locations across the city. There are 23.6 members on average per group, with a range of 5 to 93, a splendid example how, unlike the formal educational services, U3A is able to cater for all tastes and in all shapes and sizes. The breadth of subjects that a large group is able to offer is well exemplified. On a wondrous visit to Sheffield in 1992, where he had been invited to speak at the AGM, Eric Midwinter met a member who was in a walking group, a painting group and a philosophy group. What a Renaissance style illustration of roundedness, in that combine of the physical, the artistic and the intellectual! What, from the national stance, a prodigious *riposte* this was to the renegade Yorkshire U3As!

Turning to Cambridgeshire, and aside from the *refusnik* lot in the university city, U3A lay rather more dormant. However, there was good news just around the corner, for, in 1992, the impressive Peterborough U3A was established. Its origins lay, as was becoming increasingly the case, in the much more flexible attitudes of adult and community education officers. Much of its success may be ascribed to the doughty and perceptive work of its Founder-Chairman, the redoubtable John Knight, a highly experienced adult and community educator, who wove together the eagerness of his newfound adherents and the willingness of local resource holders in so certain a fashion, that, within ten years, there were a thousand members with 65 activities from which to choose. As with Sheffield, so with Peterborough: its modernistic method looked to be more in tune with the 21st century and its whole tone was, for instance, quite different to that of the Cambridge U3A.

A couple of years later Melbourn and District was formed in Cambridgeshire, where there are now five U3As, all thriving in admirable manner. 'We began', reports Joe Mutty somewhat ambivalently, 'with a strong suggestion from the doctor's wife to the adult tutor at the Village College'. It worked. In Cambridgeshire, where years before the visionary educational administrator, Henry Morris, had built his open-access Village Colleges in contradistinction to what he saw as the 'insulated' provision of the ancient regime, the U3A concept was again vindicated. Amazingly, this 330 strong group with its 26 activities, serves a rural tract of about thirty villages and townships.

From the bustling city of Sheffield to the sparsely populated fenlands around Melbourn, U3A was and is in healthy fettle. The fraught days had been safely negotiated. Chiefly through the diligence of Eric Dyke, the treasury looked, if not overflowing, then stable. The constitutional and allied questions had been answered satisfactorily, with Frank Pedley the consummate *maestro*, and the mournful losses of old friends had been bravely borne. The movement had rallied. From a now more solid and tested foundation, there would be years of swift and resplendent growth.

Part Two

THE BUSTLING 1990S

Seven: THE TWO HUNDRED AND FIFTY MARK

The door opened and in swept a feisty, bright-eyed woman who proceeded to fire off combative answers to the interviewing panel's questions, adding, by way of variation, combative answers to questions that had not been posed, to say nothing of pressing a few searching questions of her own, to which she provided combative answers. Suddenly, the other candidates for the U3A Rank Fellowship, the remit of which was to act as National Development Officer for three years, looked staid, heavy-booted, ham-fisted and ponderously unfluent. Audrey Cloet had entered the national lists of U3A.

i. The Audrey Cloet Years

As sometimes happened, Eric Midwinter had been approached for advice in his role as Director of the Centre for Policy on Ageing by a funding body anxious to make some grants in the field of older age. This time it was the charitable arm of the famous Rank Organisation. He happened to know exactly the right pouch for such largess and submitted an application expeditiously. Some years before, while working in Liverpool, he had persuaded John Moores Junior, scion of the affluent Moores family of Littlewoods grandeur, to create a Fellowship for pre-schoolwork in downtown Liverpool, an annual subvention that endured many, many years. The argument had been that 'Fellowships' need not exclusively be linked with traditional universities and might be equally applicable to the normalcy of life in the real world. Deploying this argument again, and even more aptly, in U3A terms, the proposal, with a grant of £30,000 riding on it, was agreed, and Audrey Cloet became the U3A Rank Fellow.

Her credentials were impeccable. She had been chiefly responsible, as we have already observed, for the blaze-away triumphs of the Bath U3A, and, like the earlier appointments of Jenny Betts and Harry Muscutt, it was widely appreciated in the U3A movement at large when, as they say in the New York Police Department, 'one of our own' seized an opportunity such as this. And it was a major opportunity at an opportune time. With a hundred or so U3As up and running and with, in consequence, a reasonable degree of awareness nationwide, it was an apposite moment to step up the natural process and work at the creation of as many new groups as possible. Operating with gusto and a necessary pragmatism, but intrinsically imbued with the pure essence of U3A principles, Audrey Cloet descended on the kingdom and made a royal progress across it, leaving an abundant trail of U3As in her energetic wake.

Appointed in the autumn to begin her three year stint in January 1990, Audrey Cloet enjoyed three productive years, during which time the number of U3As doubled, so that, as of the end of 1992, the national total of affiliates was almost 200, with several more in train for early registration in 1993. Audrey Cloet would not, of course, claim responsibility for all of these, but her determination and vim were certainly major elements in the making of many of them. She reported at the end of 1992 and the agreed target of another hundred groups had, happily, been reached.

The Rank Fellowship rubric ran thus: 'to promote and develop localised and autonomous U3A groups throughout Great Britain, within the framework of reference provided by the constitution of the U3A movement nationally.' In other words, the Rank Fellow's primary role was to respond, for and on behalf of the national office, to the pleas of those wishing to start new groups. Three subsidiary elements were added. One was to help repair the ravages of existing groups that were suffering some form of crisis. One was to have an awareness of the patchiness of U3A growth and consider the arduous possibility of 'cold starts'. One was to utilise the experience to do some practical analysis about the size, shape and viability of U3As in varying types of social and geographical habitats – and much of the final report was dedicated to that third issue.

At the onset Audrey Cloet examined the twelve offers on file in the national office to start a U3A group. She was surprised, given that this was a self-help movement, that only four were from individuals, the others being from education, leisure and other organisational enquirers, but she surmised that this showed a gathering awareness in such agencies of the needs of older people and of the attractions of a low-cost initiative in a chilly economic climate. In parenthesis, it might be added that, frequently, the enquiry from a college or department was itself 'individual', in the sense of some right-thinking officer who believed in the self-help precept and wished to encourage it.

Audrey Cloet also analysed the general letters of enquiry and set up a method of monitoring incoming mail, all with a view to generating support for existing or potential U3As, together with a series of tactics for approaching individuals and organisations, area by area, with the formation of a new U3A in mind. It was also necessary to overhaul the resources that the national office could make available. The general leaflet was revised to include mention of the Rank Fellowship; the Third Age newspaper 'not only proved a valuable source of information for potential organiser but, with a regular feature on the Rank development work, stimulated interest in starting new groups . . . '; the DIY pack was again revisited and updated, and, all in all, the advice and materials made available from the centre were rationalised.

The ever-pragmatic Audrey Cloet spotted that, apart from saving would-be advisers time and trouble and enabling them to step off with a shining image, the provision of national materials, with the U3A logo and titles, instilled in the doubting mind a likely preference for the all-British usage. In fact, only one U3A of all those dozens registered during the period of the Fellowship opted for an alternative: this was 'the College of the Third Age', based on the college at Newcastle-under-Lyme. Moreover, there was further support by way of workshops for new U3As, with such features as 'intermediate technology', aimed at the production of attractive newsletters and the like, included.

The report for the first time offered some statistical evidence about the provenance of U3A groups, with a breakdown of 75 U3As included. Of these 30 were started by individuals, that is, either singly, or a small band of no more than four; 24 were started by organisations, be it Age Concern groups or adult or community education institutes (although even in these cases the vigour of one individual was usually the crux of success); seventeen were started by neighbouring U3As, and only four were what in the chilly argot of U3A development circles came to be known as 'cold starts'. These last were tantamount to virginal conceptions in districts where no interest at all had been evinced but where officers felt there was a likelihood of some headway. These were inevitably more time-consuming and painstaking in due process. If that arithmetic held good for the national network of U3As in 1992, it meant that, very roughly, 80 had been established by individuals, 64 by organisations, 46 by nearby U3As, with just a mere *soupçon* of 'cold starts.' The record of local U3As already described in these pages illustrates, in approximate terms, something of that balance of individual, organisational and, so to say, familial origins.

Audrey Cloet included as an appendix in her report a diagrammatic sequence of stages of fruitful development. It demonstrated again how powerfully useful was the Third Age Trust at the point of departure. Apart from the possibility of a small start-up grant and the presence of Audrey Cloet and maybe national officers or members of neighbouring U3As, there were all the adjuncts, in advice and in kind by way of publicity materials, of how to plan carefully, alerting press and radio, dealing with mailings and posters, and making contact with local agencies, among whom the public libraries still remained one of the safest bets. There was, by this time, a bank of counsel on many answers to many questions, on such subjects as arranging meeting rooms, subscriptions, insurance, interest-groups and many other items. The pattern was laid down of the public meeting; the formation of the steering committee; the planning of the programme; the election of an official committee, and, one hoped, the request for Third Age Trust membership. In many ways, this was all a sophistication, on the sound basis of the experience of this having happened over a hundred times, of Dianne Norton's simple outline of how to approach the task of forming a U3A, published in various forms, including in her chapter in *Mutual Aid Universities.*

Audrey Cloet thought very long and hard about her experience and her report, as well as recording the log of successful formations, she raised several pertinent questions about the nature of the U3A phenomenon, the relation of central and local bodies, the styling and direction of U3A groups, the peculiar problems of rural areas and conurbations, and a dozen other questions.

One particular aspect was that of definition. For a development officer, so Audrey Cloet stressed, the answer to the reasonable question, 'what is a U3A?' was difficult to answer, for 'the most striking feature of local U3As is their diversity'. She believed that it would have been 'unrealistic to expect the movement to stay on 'hold'' pending the working out of a 'prototype', that is, a complete model. Here she was thinking of the notion that the Cambridge U3A format, once formulated in 1982, might have been replicated across the nation. As we have already noted, variety had soon become the spice of U3A life, with the Cambridge formula, if anything, less typical than some others. That said, the chief motive for investing so much in one local U3A had been to demonstrate that, regardless of detailed style, it was possible for any sort of Third Age self-mobilised educational outfit to be established.

However, Audrey Cloet was undoubtedly correct to state that, of the hundred or so U3As extant in 1990, there was 'no two exactly alike.' This reflected the varied demands of members and the varied pattern of resources available in each locality, but it also sometimes reflected, according to Audrey Cloet, the fixed view of founder members. One example was the U3As where a prior determination had been made never to use members' homes, which was, of course, a major mode of provision in most U3As. It was also felt that there had been some abandonment of the self-help principle in the seeking of local sponsorship by several U3As, although some might have retorted that God self-helps those who self-help themselves. The object of the Third Age Trust itself spoke of 'the advancement of education, and, in particular, the education of middle aged and older people who are not in full-time gainful employment.' Thus spoke the voice of the charity lawyer, a being well-attuned to the business of daring to make the charitable objective as wide as is decently possible, thinking that, in one or two hundred years, it might just be convenient not to be too tightly bound.

Audrey Cloet's point about 'diversity' was well-made; it led her to adopt 'an open approach', simply because there was no such creature as a typical U3A. 'Localised and autonomous' was, as she underlined, an accurate briefing. One is back to one of the major themes of a study such as this; namely, the brave attempt to organise a national movement in which, against a desire to allow the maximum flexibility, 'diversity' does not become so flagrantly abused that little trace of a confederate creed may be found – or, alternatively, that, fearful of such discordance, the central authority tries to wield the big stick and knock everyone into a sterile, wooden shape.

Among the many benefits of Audrey Cloet's incumbency was that she understood much of this and somehow managed to balance the practical counsel with a continuing attentiveness to the overarching theory. It might be suggested that, during this three year phase and in some large part because of her endeavours, there was some growing sense of what a U3A was and could be. The colourful variety remained, to the enormous advantage of the movement, but, for the most part, there was something recognisable about the practice and habits of every U3A. Just as no two members of any species are ever quite alike, so was it with U3A groups – yet each one could be identified as a member of the distinctive species.

Audrey Cloet remained a figure of radical vigour in the annals of U3A development. For example, and as a kind of *coda* to the Rank fellowship phase, she organised a series of 'Up and Away' Days, with a useful subsidy from the Frizzell Trust. These she ran with Eric Midwinter in 1994. These were arranged regionally, in part to encourage the sense of cross-U3A support, at locations such as Cardiff, Norwich, Exeter, Salford and other provincial nubs. There were some ten of them in all. The morning was devoted to a highly practical workshop for those responsible for organising group leaders; these were variously called programme organisers or secretaries, group development officers and so on. The workshop addressed how to recruit, how to maintain and how to reward these seminal tillers of the U3A fields. The afternoon was turned over to something approaching a rumbustious rally for U3A members in the germane region, with speeches retelling the history of U3A and underlining the message of its crusading mission.

It had all amounted to three years and then more of successful campaigning. During this fruitful spell, new U3As were established at the rate of more than one every fortnight. Audrey Cloet's one-woman band had obviously played some stirring music.

ii. Local Development

Several of the local U3A stories received refer to the impact of Audrey Cloet. One is Lincoln, where, as Mary Elliott, its first Chairman, writes, it was Audrey Cloet who spoke at the inaugural meeting in 1992. Mary Elliott had heard something of the York U3A and, on phoning headquarters, her husband and she had been offered the usual advice: 'go ye and do likewise.' This they did, with 40 people attending that meeting and six groups being formed instantly. The Lincoln U3A grew rapidly and there were to be several others to follow in the area. A Lincoln member spoke at one of the early meetings of the Boston U3A, where John Richards and Ray Hurst were instrumental in launching a U3A there. John Knight, the experienced and ever-helpful Peterborough *impresario*, also made a number of useful visits. When there was a slough in the membership, the initiative of obtaining lottery funding for a recruitment drive more than doubled the numbers to 120. An interesting feature of Boston's schedule is the definition of the interest-groups into A. clearly defined and academic study; B. social study with clearly defined aim; C1. social recreational and C2. physical recreational – all designed to encourage a balanced programme not over-reliant on leisure pursuits.

Another such was Stamford, formed a year later, chiefly at the behest of a member of a U3A elsewhere who had moved into Stamford. He and his wife involved the local Volunteer Bureau and now there are some 400 members, with 50 or so study groups. Of later vintage is Sleaford, started in 1999, when a newcomer to the district, who had been a member of another U3A, placed an advertisement in the local adult education brochure. Mike Long, the current National Development Officer, and John Richards, Chairman of the Boston U3A, were among several who supported this venture, which has paid off to the tune of some 150 members.

However, the main thrust towards comprehensive coverage in Lincolnshire was to come from Sarah Hardman, of the Lincoln U3A, who was aware both of the sometimes isolated terrain of rural Lincolnshire and of the slight reluctance of some U3As to push their memberships too high against the problem of accommodation and other organisational posers. She hit upon the plan of creating a series of small but compact U3As across the county and, in concert with like-minded colleagues and with other support, she became something of the Audrey Cloet of Lincs. Lincolnshire now has seventeen U3As, nine of them 21st century origins, and with none earlier than Grimsby and Cleethorpes in 1991, many of them the consequence of this single-minded and hardy campaign. In essence, it means that practically all of Lincolnshire's Third Agers are residing within not insuperable distance from a U3A.

Wrekin U3A in Shropshire was another group that had backing from Audrey Cloet in 1990. It is also a first-class example of how well the national land-line worked. Pat Yarnell, keen to get involved, contacted the National Office and was given three names of possible Salopian connections. One had left the area; one, Valerie Atkinson, became the first Treasurer; one, Evelyn Nichol, became tutor of the French Conversation group; whilst Pat Yarnell became Chairman. After 'a very long phone call from Audrey Cloet', who offered 'a very full and detailed explanation' of U3A's aims, she attended a London meeting for would-be organisers, headed up by Audrey Cloet. 'The day I spent at this meeting was a fantastic experience. My decision was made – we were meant to have a U3A in our location. Very many thanks to the staff at the National Office for advice and 'opening the doors'.' Audrey Cloet attended the first public meeting in the January of 1991 and 25 people signed up: now there are 144, with sixteen special interest groups.

Shropshire has half a dozen U3As in all. These include Shrewsbury, where two women, Betty Green and Alwyn Kind 'who had met quite by chance, discovered a common interest in U3A'. Undaunted by a couple of abortive efforts in Shrewsbury, they touted the supermarket foyers and drop-in coffee mornings and gained enough support to risk a public meeting in September 1992. A month later the ubiquitous Audrey Cloet was in town to give 'an inspiring talk' to the original 33 members. Today there are 192 members, enjoying some 30 interest groups, including hand bell ringing, as one might have hoped and expected in the home of Brother Cadfael.

Ludlow is the biggest of the Shropshire U3As with 350 members and 35 groups, a remarkable exercise over a sure-fire five or six years span since 1997, when, as Chairman David Hughes reports, local individuals, with the help of the National Office and neighbouring U3As, set things moving so ably. Then there is Whitchurch and District U3A, parented in 1994 by an ex-grammar school teacher, Bill Cambridge, in concert with Joan Letchford, who had had U3A experience in the south of England. Dolly White, now the Secretary, explains how they were helped by other U3As and by Roy Wilson, by now the Development Co-ordinator nationally. It currently has 168 members and organises some 30 groups.

Staying close to these midland areas, Staffordshire, apart from the 1985 rise of Tamworth, has, like Lincolnshire, primarily been the scene of post 1990 evolution. An example is Lichfield, which now boasts a membership 225 strong, with more than a score of interest-groups at their disposal. Janice Moore tells how she met three other women in 1991 at a local history class, one of whom, the main inspiration, Phyl Armitage, had seen a notice about the Tamworth U3A and another, Jean Edlington, had been a member of the Sutton Coldfield U3A, before moving to Lichfield. Wheels were set in motion. Norman Richards, of the Swindon U3A and a man who was destined to play a major role in U3A development, met with this intrepid quartet and spoke at the inaugural meeting. They 'worked out the subscription on the back of a serviette and the figure we arrived at (£7.50) still stands' and the four adopted committee roles: Jean Malkin became Secretary; Janice Moore, Treasurer; Jean Edlington, Hostess; and Phyl Armitage 'our much-loved Chairman and Founder', who sadly and suddenly died in 2002. One likes the idea of a 'Hostess': every U3A should have one.

Leek U3A 'may be the only one', writes Jean Levitt, the Group Coordinator, 'which sprang out of a need to find an appropriate use for a building'. This arose when Jean Levitt was Chairman of the Staffordshire Moorlands Council for Voluntary Service, which came to the rescue of Norton House, a building dedicated to charitable purposes. Having raised the money to refurbish this Victorian edifice, the newly constituted Norton House Committee, taking its cue from the Newcastle under Lyme College of the Third Age, raised some £2000 and set out the U3A stall. 50 were expected at the inaugural meeting in 1995; 250 attended: 'it was if we had come with water tanks to a settlement in drought'. A hundred members were registered immediately, that number 'only limited by the size of the receipt book' and now there are 35 subject groups and a membership of over 600, an amazing result in a predominantly rural area. It is a rewarding tale and, as Joan Levitt concludes, 'we have a good cross section of our local population . . . the intermingling of different tastes and abilities is of great benefit as we sustain one another in our later years.'

Cheadle U3A, also in Staffordshire, was initiated in 1997 by two individuals. Vaughan Richardson tells us that one had been an educationalist and one the coordinator of an older persons' resource centre – 'some might say a perfect combination to start a U3A'. It was assuredly an effective combination. Cheadle has a strong membership of over 400 and over 30 groups, ranging from sugar craft to barber's shop singing.

A little further north in Derbyshire there are just five U3As, all of then well-established, with sturdy memberships, in total, about 1500. An early starter was Derby, in 1985, when Harry Muscutt was able to help a retired headmistress, Margaret Johnson, who was keen to start a group. As today's Secretary, John Smith, explains, she now lives in Germany, but is honoured with the Presidency in appreciation of her enterprise. Chesterfield was launched in 1994. Here Peter Johnson, the Manager of a local further education centre, as Jean Tindall, one of the current officers, recalls, included in his annual programme the date for a public meeting to ascertain whether there was a demand for a U3A in the district. There was. It now organises over 40 groups and, in paying due credit to Peter Johnson for this starter and for his other help, one must pause to reflect on how, in not too many years, education officers were actually taking up the gauntlet where some hitherto had felt imperilled by it.

Glossop and Buxton U3As came along in 1996. Again it was a continuing education venture. 'In January 1996, writes Olive Middleton, the Buxton Public Relations Officer, 'just 23 Third Agers made their tentative response to a quizzical advertisement in the local paper'. A friendly adult education officer had placed it and, inside a month, a steering group was formed and 86 people voiced their approval for the formal establishment of a U3A. Leek's Jean Levitt was 'our early mentor', while, in turn, Buxton U3A, which now arranges 40 interest groups for 400plus members in a town of 30,000 population, have helped Macclesfield and Bakewell U3As to get started. Bakewell U3A originated in 1998, the brainchild of prominent figures, John Evans, a former distinguished Derbyshire Chief Education Officer and Meg Laird, a former head teacher. George Hambleton, of the Bakewell U3A, reports that there are now some 30 interest-groups organised for a large membership of 356.

Shifting slightly southwards once more, one arrives in Nottinghamshire, where, truth to tell, the U3A harvest has not been as fruitful as in some other shires, despite its excellent start with the long-standing Nottingham U3A, launched as one of the first fifteen in 1983. The other four Nottinghamshire U3As are of later date. The Dukeries U3A originated with 25 members, as the Correspondence Secretary relates, in 1992, to serve the catchment area in and around Retford and Mansfield, but, in 1999, the Mansfield district members decided to form a splinter group. The Dukeries U3A runs a programme of sixteen study groups. There is a U3A group at Bingham, which began in 2001, while the Soar Valley U3A started in 1999. It did so on the initiative of M J Johnson, the Chairman, who had heard good things about the Leamington Spa U3A but knew that the two Loughborough U3As were finding it difficult to accommodate all those who wished to join. The Soar Valley outfit, whilst centred on Sutton Bonnington, nestles among the string of villages on the Nottinghamshire border with Leicestershire and endeavours to carry the word into those settlements. Such was the interest, that twelve interest-groups were started immediately and there are now almost double that amount. It is also unusual in that, by dint of some endeavour, half its membership is male.

That round up of U3As in Lincolnshire, Shropshire, Staffordshire, Derbyshire and Nottinghamshire needs little further exegis. It would be superfluous to underline too heavily the dependence of the U3A movement on the flair and ingenuity of individuals, often two or three individuals, frequently drawing solace and encouragement the one from the other. Again, as Audrey Cloet pointed out, there seemed to be, especially when the rough-and-tumble days of the 1980s had passed and some degree of respectability had been earned, a larger measure of enterprise on the part of adult education and other professional officers. These illustrations also demonstrate the incredible variety of the beginnings of U3As all over the country. By hook or by crook, U3As were swiftly being set up in every county of Great Britain.

iii. Office Politics and Economics

Meanwhile, back at the Ponderosa ranch of central oversight, there were signs of consolidation, not unlike those on the prairie after the first unsettled, pioneering years, with, for instance, the adoption of a U3A's first non-domestic office. In 1988 a room was sublet from the British Association of Settlements and Social Action Centres (BASSAC) in Stockwell, South London. It was very difficult for just one person, working from home, to handle all the administrative chores and this small office allowed Dianne Norton to pursue her duties, with the aid of a part-time administrative assistant and of volunteers from local U3As. One good result was that the busy telephone line could be staffed for much longer periods than was possible on a home basis, not least because Dianne Norton still divided her work-load between U3A and Age Concern England, where she still acted as Education and Leisure Officer.

The office and its setting had something of the *ambience* of 'Hernando's Hideaway' in the 1954 hit musical, *The Pajama Game*. Provincial visitors approached with caution and trepidation, but it was a step forward (or, more correctly, upward – as the office was perched at the top of several flights of stairs). Two years later, after much negotiation and administrative travail, the national office moved to new premises at Stockwell Green, not far distant from the first stop, but into more spacious accommodation in a building specifically refurbished for charitable usage with a grant from the Elmfield Charitable Trust. Here there was room to house staff, equipment and materials in decent order and it suited the U3A national purpose for six effective years.

In 1990 Graham Woodman, of the Brighton and Hove U3A, took over the national chairmanship from Eric Dyke. An ex-civil servant, he had risen to the heights of Assistant Secretary with the Department of Health and Social Security. Quietly spoken and careful in judgement, this slimly built, bespectacled, smiling figure proved to be an able leader at a time of modest expansion in several fields, apart from the salient one of extending the number of U3A groups. Graham Woodman, inheriting the temporary stable financial condition procured under Eric Dyke's prudent rule, led an enlarged Committee, as provided for in the new constitution. For the first time there was a recognised and formally appointed Vice-chairman, Secretary and Treasurer.

One of the first organisational changes was to establish four important sub-committees, as under: conference organisation; finance; research; services to local U3As, and travel, the last a portent of the strides already made nationally in this area. Such action indicated the growing activity of the movement both nationally and locally. A major step was the appointment of a part-time Chief Executive, leaving Dianne Norton, also on a part-time basis, to concentrate on publications and publicity. Another appointment was made from within U3A circles. Charles Braybrook, of the Brighton U3A, was invited, after interview, to take the post and this he readily did. A lively, affable man of distinct skills – like Graham Woodman, his background was in the senior levels of the Civil Service - he was poised to offer the movement a willing combine of shrewd command and friendly presence when, abruptly, sorrowfully, he died.

He had served barely eight weeks. It was a shattering blow both at an acutely personal level and also to the delicately erected fabric of the U3A as a national institution. The concept of a mainline manager, especially one with U3A as well as professional credence, standing at the focal point of the organisation, was a far-sighted one. It would have presented the agency in a more convincing style, for it could have meant that one or other of the senior administrators would have been on tap for callers more or less all the time. One yardstick of the national acceptability of an institution is its readiness and availability to make that kind of response, to, for instance, not only private inquiries but also public questions, from the press and media or from governmental and other authorities. It would be another six years before U3A nationally was able to reconstruct that degree of centrality of day-by-day management.

Dianne Norton gamely undertook the role of acting Chief Executive, with support from the Administrative Assistant, Barbara Adkins. Barbara Adkins gave selfless and unself-regarding service to the Third Age Trust, carrying out her manifold clerical and other duties with the minimum of fuss and the maximum of dispatch. She later became Office Manager and Company Secretary in 1991. At this point Dianne Norton reverted to her post of Publicity and Publications Officer, while Betty Carden, joined the staff as Administrative Assistant. Jinny Schofield acted as the Trust's very conscientious bookkeeper. Barbara Adkins held the senior post until her retirement, in grievous ill-health (but now, happily, much recovered) at the Christmas of 1995. By and large, the everyday running of the office proceeded with some smoothness, as, out and about, the U3A movement grew in size and visibility. To give some flavour of its jobs, 2500 postal inquiries were dealt with in the year 1993/94.

A further token of its developing power was the strengthening of its networking sinews. There began to be signs of togetherness, of joint educational action across the local groups. Possibly the first general example of this was the *Pickwick Papers* project of 1985. The rollicking early Dickensian novel was being televised in what used to be the 'family' spot at Sunday tea-time, when classic tales were for years presented by the BBC. Eric Midwinter was then serving terms on the BBC Advisory Committees for both Educational Broadcasting and for Broadcasting for Older People. He persuaded the BBC to surrender copies of the working script, something rarely released presumably because of the peril of TV's equivalent of industrial espionage – he recalls being asked to convey the scripts away from the BBC in two innocuous looking carrier bags. Brian Walsh, a sympathetic and knowledgeable expert in the fields of literature and education, agreed to prepare a guide for groups who wished to participate. This aligned the scripts to the text and raised various issues for discussion. The notion was that the groups would, on a weekly basis, read the apposite text and watch, either severally (perhaps using a video copy) or alone, the appropriate episode, before joining in a group discussion, with the option of written pieces or different members agreeing to lead the discourse.

Sixteen local U3As formed groups that took part; it went extremely well; and a report, based on group leader and group member responses, was completed and was quite widely circulated, the BBC itself making some active use of it. Several of these literary groups remained in business thereafter. The Harpenden subgroup, for example, became interested in the mini-art form of adaptation of books for the media. It composed its own mock-radio version of *A Christmas Carol* and presented it at one of the local U3A's general meetings.

It is worth dwelling on this pioneer effort – 'what are you going to do about the forthcoming production of *Bleak House*?' was one plaintive remark on the questionnaires – because it obviously was a little portent of the future potential for providing U3A groups locally with national sources. It also had a cultural resonance in terms of the late 20th century self-help agency. £500,000 had been expended on the production of the televised antics of Samuel Pickwick and his colleagues and a national expert had prepared the back-up material. Technically, then, the basic presentation was of a very high level, probably beyond the means and skills of most teachers in most schools. On the other side, groups of people gathered in someone's house for a chat about it. Admittedly, it was a structured and guided chat, but it had something of what, nostalgically, one might have believed happened in the past when interested and interesting people met in the coffee house or the barber's shop or the tavern or the reading room to discuss events or the latest story. The combine of television and localised discussion appeared, therefore, to bring together the best of the ancient and modern. It was another piece in the developing picture of an educational service that was setting high standards in the provision of adult learning, properly valued as bringing benefit to the self-realisation and self-esteem of individuals.

There were other cheery portents. Thanks to a grant from the Arthur Andersen Foundation, it became possible to make and distribute a U3A Reference File to all member groups; this was followed up in 1993 with an Information Supplement in *The Third Age*, which provided every member with basic data about the organisation and the way in which it was organised. There were other signs of national collaboration at a subject level. In 1987 there had been a once-off tour arranged to Paris for art-lovers from among the U3A groups and this had been very satisfactory. Now with a travel sub-committee in being, what was too fast becoming a significant dimension of U3A life was ready for a much more structured approach. The Travel Club was launched in 1990. It offered members, for an annual fee of £3.00, the chance to receive a travel network newsletter by post and thereby receive prior notice of U3A travel plans. The notion of the educational holiday, not unlike one of the original ideas considered during the early 1980s in the light of the Elderhostel programme, was to become a major, burgeoning element for those in U3A membership. By 1994 it had a thousand members and recent tours had embraced Mexico and Iceland among an itinerary of ten trips home and abroad.

A little earlier in 1989 another interactive approach had been launched. This was the highly productive concept of the Subject Network, a mechanism for encouraging and supporting the local incidence of a given theme or discipline. Jean Thompson, of the Reading U3A, had been one of those volunteers who had helped out in that first cramped Stockwell office. It was but the humble beginning to a career not only of national but also of international U3A fame, rather as the understudy in the chorus seizes the opportunity to demonstrate her talents and take the leading role to glittering acclaim. Energetically bright and sharply intelligent, she was elected to the National Executive Committee in 1989 and soon became the very first Subject Network Co-ordinator. It was one that was to be something of a model for others as well as a first-class contribution to the world of U3A.

It was the Languages Network. The link with the travel set-up is self-evident enough; together they pointed to a mainline U3A interest in the world outside the United Kingdom. Perhaps one of the most surprising and certainly one of the most gratifying aspects of U3A development has been this sense of eyes lifted to more distant horizons, this desire to journey the better to understand and to learn languages the better to comprehend the wider globe. Not for the U3A membership a battening down of the intellectual hatches and a retreat into the be-shuttered cabins of the known and familiar.

Jean Thompson chose, as she recalls, the day when the road and pavement outside were being excavated to hold on the ground floor of the makeshift Stockwell premises the first-ever Subject Network study day. The meeting gallantly continued regardless. Jean Thompson later began the Creative Writing Subject Network and soon others – art, music, sci-tech. – followed. 1989 also saw the first residential weekend workshop with a thematic base. This was for Oral History, another firm favourite among U3A ranks. This led to the establishment of another Subject Network and the launch of several local projects of this brand. In 1993 the Creative Writing Network held its first general meeting and an anthology of their collated thoughts, *What U3A Means To Me*, was published. U3As were looking backwards and sideways as well as outwards. Gwen Parrish, sprightly of mind and a consistently top-rate operator among the creative and literary ranks of U3A, would edit for U3A publication, latterly in conjunction with Tony Thornton, a number of anthologies of U3A writings, among them *Turn Back the Clock* (1998), *Travellers' Tales* (1999) and *Tinker, Tailor, Soldier, Sailor . . .* (2003).

The U3A's national existence revolved around the by now well-established annual conference. The pattern of shifting venues, with local U3As enjoying a moment in the sun by way of helping with the arrangements, and with a distinguished guest delivering the annual Third Age lecture, was now rationally in place. The 1990 Conference was at the Askham Bryan College, Sutton Bonnington, near Nottingham and this was the first to be organised by the new Conference sub-committee. To encourage recruitment, efforts were made to keep the costs below £100 for the weekend, for, obviously, some groups were finding it hard to justify the cost of travel and accommodation for delegates to these annual gatherings.

Sutton Bonnington in 1990 witnessed another first. Peter Shea is a man of many parts. We have already encountered him in his role as psychologist, adult tutor and supporter of both the London and Stevenage U3As. At Sutton Bonnington he was revealed, not, as he might have been, as noted chrysanthemum grower, expert wine fancier or collector of first edition Penguins, but as barn dance caller. Not only is he a reputed barn dance caller but he is also a trainer of barn dance callers and a choreographer of the barn dances they call. Here at Sutton Bonnington he was invited to organise a barn dance, which he did with his accustomed mellow humour – 'perhaps I had better just go over that again; there seems to be one person who's not quite got it right': this in response to a *mêlée* resembling a packed commuter train unloading at Victoria Station. He capped an enjoyable evening with the first ever performance of his specially designed dance, 'the U3Amble'. Gently sedate in tempo, it also had a demographic resonance: the sets were made up of trios of one man with a woman on either side of him, a closer analogue of U3A membership and of gender population divisions in older age than the more straightforward duo.

It is worth pausing over this charming if, on the shallow face of it, unimportant moment. It captured some of the essential ingredient of U3A-dom; that is, its friendliness and togetherness. Moreover, whatever accolades are showered on institutions, how many do you know that have their own dance?

York was the site of the 1991 conference. Attendance was high. There were over 200 U3A members, representing over 100 U3As, some probably attracted by the temptations of a 'social weekend'. This experiment of surrounding the business and professional elements with a wholesome mix of local visits and activities was successful enough to endure for a dozen years. Although, of course, it did not help by way of costings, many felt that, if they were to travel to, as in this instance, York, they might as well take the chance to enjoy the environs and find a little more about them. It was Julie Andrews who famously warbled that 'a spoonful of sugar helps the medicine go down.' The bitter tang in the medicine at York was the need to raise the affiliation fees from £1.00 to £1.25 a head.

Len Haynes of the Milton Keynes U3A was elected chairman at this highly successful conference. It was an excellent choice. Len Haynes was the recently retired inaugural Professor of Chemistry at the Open University, with whom U3A in the UK shared emotional and philosophic ties. He had also been, from its inception in 1969, responsible for the OU's degree programme. He was a most thoughtful and considerate man, quietly spoken, ready to listen and ready to give due weight to the opinions of others. The bout of bad luck that seemed over this brief span to haunt the organisation's senior officers struck once more. First there had been the death of Charles Braybrook; then Graham Woodman had suffered a heart attack and was insufficiently recuperated to pursue his major role for more than one year, hence the election of Len Haynes; next Len Haynes himself fell severely ill. His ill-health drastically curtailed his activities, although he was responsible for one sound practical benefit. Wearing his emeritus Open University hat, he arranged for the transfer of redundant OU materials for use by U3A local groups, a service arranged after his death by his widow, Mary Haynes.

Stan Llewellin, of the Chorley U3A and a steadfast NEC member, took control of this valuable *cache* of materials – he also, incidentally, was responsible for finding the money to purchase the NEC's first-ever photocopying machine and was otherwise engaged in fund raising measures. From his garage in Chorley, where these OU treasures were stored, he dispatched them throughout the nation, the beginnings of what soon became known as the Swap Shop, as these and other materials were redistributed to U3As. These were to be of great advantage to many U3A subject groups, for whom the purchase of necessary materials was an onerous one. In the year 1992/93, for instance, 200 OU courses in 85 parcels were distributed to 78 U3As. It serves as a sorrowful but proud memorial to the decency and dedication of Len Haynes, who died in the June of 1991. Valorously, Jean Thompson, who had already deputised for the chairman on many occasions, became acting Chairman, until, at the 1992 Conference at Exeter (where that lively, prominent and progressively-minded educationalist, Professor Ted Wragg, gave the Third Age Lecture) she was appointed to the chair in her own sovereign right, bringing to that role vivid gifts of *élan* and forward thinking.

The years 1991 and 1992 were times of substantial activity both in and around the U3A movement. At the office level the delivery of a desktop publishing unit, courtesy of British Telecom, was an enormous boon. It became possible to publish *The Third Age* newspaper more attractively, as well as producing all the other manifold pieces of national literature with more *panache*. A grant of £5000 from Barclays Bank enabled the central body to design and distribute a brand-new national leaflet and to undertake some further development work. There were also grants of £5000 each from the Esmée Fairbairn Foundation, not the last time that charity was to assist the national office, and from Telethon '92.

March 1992 was properly designated the tenth anniversary of the U3A in the UK. At this exact point the U3A movement in the UK boasted 161 groups and roughly 22,000 members. As emblems of this success, the first U3A badges, and later the first scarves and ties went on sale. The long-serving Treasurer, Harold Potts, was much involved with these ventures, anxious as he was to give some value for money to local groups in return for the capitation fee, and that marketing would later be extended. It was he who was to negotiate the inclusion of public liability insurance as a component of the group fee, a most judicious and practical adjunct, one that, by bringing some degree of relief to anxious organisers in a litigious age, was money well spent.

The Third Age published a special tenth anniversary supplement in 1992 and local U3As were encouraged to organise celebrations. Many did, some combining events to coincide with recognition of the first National Learners' Week. That mildly political focus was to the fore over the later months of 1991 and the earlier months of 1992, when several U3A members were actively engaged in what turned out to be a successful lobby for the conventional support for non-vocational adult education to be retained. This had been menaced by a government white paper that had voiced a heavy preference for strictly employment oriented training courses and proposed high fees for anything sniffing of enjoyment or relaxation. It will be remembered that these were 'Hard Times' for any expenditure not harshly measurable in utilitarian terms. In 1991 the National Executive Committee had made an appeal to the Department of Education for help with funding, but, in that atmosphere of Gradgrindery, in vain. As some cultural consolation, an Early Day Motion was tabled in the House of Commons in 1991, in the name of Simon Coombs MP and signed by 75 MPs of all parties, in support of the valuable work of the U3A movement. In 1992 the senior officers met with Tim Boswell MP, Under Secretary of State for Further and Higher Education, to discuss the U3A cause.

There was other evidence that the concept of the Third Age in general and the University of the Third Age in particular was gaining in identification in the land. A little earlier, in 1987, Peter Laslett had published another definitive text, *A Fresh Map of Life*, in which he had updated his findings about the worldwide Third Age phenomenon and in which the idea of the University of the Third Age received special commentary. There was another boost to the awakening of knowledge about the Third Age when, in 1992, after two years of investigation, the Carnegie Inquiry into the Third Age reported by way of nine specific studies into aspects of Third Age life and again in 1993 when a final report was published and widely discussed. Eric Midwinter was a member of the Advisory Committee to the Inquiry and he produced the special reports on 'Leisure' and 'Citizenship'. At its simplest it might be argued that, had the inquiry reported ten years earlier, many fewer people would have understood to what the title referred. It is a two-edged sword. If the growing awareness of the Third Age was a publicity fillip for U3A, then it must be urged that, as just about the only national organisation with the Third Age in its name, the U3A was doing much to impress upon public consciousness locally the precept of Third Agehood.

During 1992 the U3As were invited to plan ahead for the 1993 European Year of Older People and Solidarity between the Nations. Indeed, many U3As were involved in the events of that year and the U3A movement, as a whole, gained from the attached publicity. What attracted the bulk of the admiring comment was Jean Thompson's marvellous brainchild, emerging in some part from her Languages Network, of a U3A service of Translators and Interpreters for non-profit making bodies. This did extremely useful work and reached the heights of offering over a hundred linguists, recruited from U3As, and covering 26 languages. As may well be imagined, this was in chief demand during 1993, with its focus on cross-European liaison.

While mention is being made of Jean Thompson, this might be the point to intersperse a later item that she initiated. Stimulated by Peter Laslett and then published in his memory in 2002, this was *A Voice Not Heard Before*, the moving yet sharply perceptive views of U3A members over 80, compiled by Jean Thompson and a valued addition to the U3A canon.

What might be called the outreach actions – the parliamentary lobbying on behalf of non-vocational adult education; the brilliant *tour de force* of establishing a translation and interpretation service – appealed much to Peter Laslett and Michael Young. They appealed to the very postulates laid down by the Founders; they appealed to the very roots of their beliefs in civic engagement.

iv. More Local Development

After the authoritative reign of Frank Pedley, with his authentic northern roots, the succeeding national Chairmen were drawn from Oxfordshire, Sussex, Buckinghamshire and Berkshire. This possibly personified the fact that, with certain glowing exceptions, the incidence of U3A groups was more intense, in the opening decade of U3A history, in the home and southern counties. Although there were signs of stirring, it did appear that, on the U3A map, the further one travelled from London the more speckled became the pattern.

Len Haynes' Milton Keynes U3A, for instance, was established in 1987 at the instigation of the local Age Concern and the brother of one of its founding members was, we are told by Jackie Jones, now the Secretary of MKU3A, a fellow-student of Peter Laslett's at Cambridge. Its membership now touches on a thousand, with some 59 interest-groups scheduled. This is an astounding achievement, but perhaps the major accent to stress in respect of that amazing number plate, MKU3A, is demographic. Milton Keynes has the youngest age profile in the nation. Only 12 % of its population are of pensionable age, suggesting an estimated Third Age echelon of 22,000. Compared, for example, with the 35% of the Christchurch citizenry who are in the pensionable category, it appears quite tiny. What is striking is that 'only': 12% is not a small figure. In effect, there is no district in Britain where there is not a substantial coterie of Third Agers. There are now more old age pensioners in the UK than there are children on the school registers. That said, the attainment of MKU3A in persuading one in 22 of their *confrères* to enlist in the U3A colours is very creditable. Whenever someone argues that it is easier to start a U3A in a seaside resort where there is a large retired population, whisper the magic ciphers: MKU3A.

Two years later, in 1989, Eric Dorrance, a retired secondary headteacher, founded the Aylesbury Vale U3A in Buckinghamshire, attracting no less than 200 people to the initial meeting in the Aylesbury civic centre and, as today's Secretary, Shirley Stokes, records, immediately setting up a twelve-strong steering committee. Help chiefly came by way of free use of school premises, while a recent £4400 lottery grant for equipment has naturally been most welcome by this 350 strong U3A. Aylesbury Vale maintains a profitable liaison with the statutory authorities, exemplified by its registration as a Community Outreach Partner of the local grammar school under the government's Life Long Learning initiative. Such was the growth of Aylesbury Vale U3A that, some years on in 1997, another Aylesbury-oriented U3A launched under the aegis of the original one. One of its leaders, Ann Currie, tells how this second combine, the Mid-Bucks U3A, attracted over 60 interested parties to the inaugural meeting and now there are 30 activity groups and a membership of 220.

Haddenham and Princes Risborough U3As were both started in 2001. Peter Wenham, its Chairman, recalls that Haddenham was established on the initiative of a keen local person, with aid from the Third Age Trust; it has already topped the hundred mark and runs a dozen activity groups. James Scott-Smith, Secretary of Princes Risborough U3A, remembers how he penned personal letters to likely takers for a second exploratory meeting in the local community centre and how the local Community Association was very supportive: there are 186 members here and seventeen interest-groups are organised for and by them.

Jean Thompson's Reading group was affiliated to the Third Age Trust, like Len Haynes' Milton Keynes U3A, in 1987, it being one of Berkshire's five current U3As. Originally known as STAR (Students of the Third Age Reading), it was not until 1993 that, after heated debate and the resignation of a founder-member, the U3A logo was adopted. Janet Johnson, the present Secretary, explains how, yet again, it was the librarian, this time at the local college of education, who gave initial support. Reading U3A has 365 members and organises nearly 50 interest-groups. Jean Thompson persuaded a Reading U3A colleague, Joan Butler, to consider a U3A in nearby Wokingham. Joan Butler hosted a coffee morning, with Audrey Cloet in support, in 1990, and, although progress was initially slow, Colin Mitchell, the current Secretary, records the present existence of 41 interest-groups and, with 467 members, this bustling and efficiently managed outfit is the largest in the county.

Newbury, Bracknell Forest and Maidenhead comprise the remainder of the Berkshire quintet. We hear from Michael Tucker, in charge of Maidenhead's information services, how the local Rotary branch, anxious to extend its charitable interest with the launching of a U3A, had approached a colleague and himself. A working party was formed; 125 attended the opening meeting; there are now over 300 members, enjoying 30plus activities, and, with the help of external grants, a healthy financial position. Bracknell Forest U3A is of newer dating. 50 people attended a public meeting called by the Director of the Bracknell Council for Voluntary Service in November 2000, and, not least with the friendly backing of Wokingham and Maidenhead U3As, membership already approaches 200 and there are fifteen interest-groups.

Across in Bedfordshire there are six U3As. Among them are Bedford, Leighton-Linslade and Dunstable. Bob Wane, the Vice-chairman of Bedford, tells the tale of someone at the local Community College whose mother told him about the one she attended. Showing commendable respect for this maternal counsel, he persuaded the College to back the notion of a Bedford U3A, and, although educational politics and economics have made that linkage redundant, the U3A thrives, with its 351 members and 33 groups. When the large Luton U3A seemed to have out-grown itself, its officers lent support to a resident who wished to start a new U3A in close-by Dunstable. That now numbers well over 500 members and organises over 50 activities, a rapid and splendid growth in but three or four years. Janet Mardle, now its Chairman, reports on the backing that was also received from the local council and, ineluctably, the local library.

Brian Hayes, Founder-Chairman of Leighton-Linslade U3A, recollects that his project was another with the Audrey Cloet stamp upon it. She had been invited to speak in 1992 at a Library Club meeting for the over 50s – another 'library' involvement - and Brian Hayes was invited to take the lead among a gathering band of enthusiasts. Len Haynes spoke at the first public meeting and soon there were over 80 members. There are over 600 members currently in this flourishing U3A, with its programme of 63 interest-groups.

As Brian Hayes succinctly comments, 'the U3A is a simple idea, but very powerful'.

v. International Vistas

The University of the Third Age throws a lengthy perspective. It is by deliberate choice that one sets beside the animated reality of the interest-groups of, say, Milton Keynes or Reading, some account of the U3A worldwide and of the UK's stance thereof.

Jean Thompson, organiser of the Language Network and the Translation/ Interpretation Service, was the key internationalist. It was she who was primarily responsible for taking Britain into the global reckoning in respect of U3A. In 1991 Len Haynes had been invited, as the Third Age Trust Chairman, to address an Association International d'Université du Troisième Age (AIUTA) conference in the Netherlands and, because of his illness, Jean Thompson deputised for him and made an impressive appeal to this international union of U3As about the integrity and thrust of the British model. Marian Bieber, of the London U3A, had previously attended an AIUTA Congress in Hull, Canada in 1990, where there had been such financial difficulties and clashes of opinion that she had wisely advised that the time was not yet ripe for too close an alliance. However, it was concerns among some AIUTA leaders that its scale was too restrictive that led to this specially convened meeting at which the British U3A movement was asked to say its piece.

There were those present from backgrounds of institutional and governmental resourced programmes, who thought that self-mobilisation was a mirage, but they could not explain away the obvious arithmetic of the British U3As' successes, nor were they blind to the *imprimatur* that Peter Laslett's international reputation stamped on the project, nor, indeed, unsusceptible to Jean Thompson's strongly stated case.

In 1992 the General Secretary of AIUTA visited the Third Age Trust, bringing a personal invitation to Jean Thompson, now Chairman in her own right, to join the AIUTA governing board as the British representative, along with Professor Zahn of Germany, where another special case presented itself.

The AIUTA statutes had to be altered to allow for this, for its membership tended to be based on individual U3As conventionally linked with an old-style university; a national confederation of self-help cells of differing shapes and styles was alien to this constitution. To summarise the point in a nutshell, where scores of member U3As were paying individual fees, the British U3A could only be expected to pay one, and this to a financially embarrassed agency. Matters were righted at an extraordinary general meeting of AIUTA with an amendment that gave its board power 'to adapt membership requirements, bearing in mind the legislations and usages in different countries'. In 1993, with the ratification of the National Executive Committee, Jean Thompson joined the AIUTA board as a non-voting member.

Since then Jean Thompson remained the British delegate, and, along with fellow U3A members, has taken an active part in the last six biennial AIUTA Congresses. She has spoken in ten AIUTA countries, extolling the virtues of the British model in the appropriate language. In 1994 Jean Thompson started the practice of inviting two overseas visitors, at their own expense, to the U3A National Conference. She has, to a large degree single-handedly, put the British U3A on the global map and, crucially, there is now widespread recognition that U3As come in two boxes.

The international debate continues. The posers are often raised at U3A gatherings. It is the local/central discussion writ large. There is an annual fee of £1000, plus travel and accommodation costs for board meetings and Congresses. Some reasonably ponder on the value of this outlay and wonder, too, whether the gulf between the French and British models is not so wide as to make collaboration negligible in pragmatic terms.

The internationalist response to this by no means irrational questioning is that the U3A in the UK did take its inspiration from this worldwide movement and should not be insular; that we profit from learning how other countries deal with Third Agers – and here the miracles of e-mail and WWW have been a technical boon – and that, for all its limitations, AIUTA does offer an opportunity for U3A members to meet and swap ideas. At the 2002 Conference a motion to disaffiliate from AIUTA was discussed but there were reassurances that the international body was determined on reform. Roger Cloet, of the Bath U3A, who has also contributed much to the much-appreciated development of computer studies nationally in U3A circles, is now the British representative on its governing board and he told the 2003 Conference at York that AIUTA had 'subjected itself to a period of intense soul-searching' and would now be much more accepting of the British model, a reformation, he argued, that would be in evidence at the next Congress, in Shanghai in 2004. In the light of these changes of heart, it has been decided that U3A in the UK will retain its membership for the time being, while AIUTA's proposed reforms are kept under review.

It might be worthwhile, at this juncture, to glance briefly at the global U3A picture, as of the mid 1990s. By the time the British U3A was launched, AIUTA had 170 institutional members, drawn principally from France, but also from Belgium, Poland, Switzerland, Spain, Italy, Canada and the United States. Such numbers have obviously grown over the last twenty or so years. To take one dramatic example, China has 400 U3As with 470,000 students, although the host older age population is 100m. These are organised on traditional lines, as part of some 5300 educational organisms made available to the older population.

The conventional 'French' regime of alliance with a neighbouring university continues to be the norm. There are 21 such U3As in Switzerland, 25 in the Netherlands, 16 in Poland, 152 in Italy, some 34 in South America, and many others dotted about the globe. The British model, however, is gaining some ground. Australia is the most spectacular illustration of this.

Soon after the launch of the British U3As, the percipient Australian academic, Jack McDonell visited Europe on a study tour and appraised the various facilities offered older people. He was impressed by the British U3A format and carried it back with him to the Antipodes. In 1984 the Melbourne U3A was established. There developed over the next decade 'a wide variety of intellectually demanding courses, crafts workshops and social activities for 18,000 older learners in more than 108 independent campuses operating in all states and territories of Australia'. This is a striking rate of epic proportion, a tribute to the far-sighted Jack McDonell and his colleagues.

New Zealand also adopted the British/Australian formula with some success, as from 1989 beginning with the Auckland group, with the great majority of interest-groups meeting in private homes while there are intriguing reports of British-styled U3As in several other nations, among them the Czech Republic, where there were, in the 1990s, some 45 U3As, and with odd examples in Bolivia, Ecuador, Brazil, Paraguay and Argentine.

This was intended as a glimpse at the international U3A scene, without any pretence of being an exhaustive log of either the

French or the British models, to say nothing of the several other hybrid versions that are also to be discovered. This sketch was included to hymn the progress made across the world in terms of educational provision of this kind particularly aimed at the Third Ager. It is at one and the same time a recognition of the compelling power of the Third Age concept as such, and some token of the recognition that Third Agers require, like everyone else, educational amenities of whatever kind.

To the British U3A member, settling down for his play reading group or her computer course one Thursday morning, it must be of some curiosity and comfort to recall that, in the Czech Republic, in Australia and in Ecuador, there are other Third Agers embroiled in similar activities under similar regulos. In all of this, to repeat the plaudit, Jean Thompson has been the key internationalist.

By the end of 1994 the number of U3As in the United Kingdom was hovering around the 250 mark, halfway towards the magical figure of 500plus of the present day dispensation. Allowing for the comings and the goings, one is able to log the name of Melbourn and District as the 250th on the roster – a budding U3A, as we previously observed, and, not without a certain satisfaction to close watchers of the U3A scene, firmly located in Cambridgeshire.

Eight: DEVELOPMENT, DEVELOPMENT, DEVELOPMENT

Development was the keynote of the mid-1990s. There was a general feeling that it was important to cover the ground, to guarantee that, as far as was humanly possible, anyone who wished to might have reasonably prompt access to a U3A. Thus the thrust was about forming U3A groups and, this was, rightly at that time, felt to be a higher priority than overall membership. After all, one could not have members unless one had groups. That truism is inserted because, eventually and by the end of the century, it was possible to suggest that the number of groups proportionately outstripped the total membership. Then it would be necessary to address the other side of the group/membership equation.

Equally important was the condition of the national machinery that already had to deal with well over 200 affiliates and was driving onwards to register many more. It had not advanced much in terms of administrative modernity. The finances remained precarious, with an admixture of capitation fees and occasional grants only just about meeting the needs of this still small-scale organism. In January 1994 Bill Hawes, of the Kennet U3A, completed a highly useful survey of the central office for the National Executive Committee. There he found four half-time staff, with Isobel Markham of the Bexley U3A, the committee member with direct responsibility for their work, lodged in three rooms at Stockwell Green. He reported that everything was 'neat and efficient'. Isobel

Markham was to offer dedicated and quietly unsung service to the national office for some time. One insight into the internal workings of the office was his analysis of 500 letters received in the months prior to 22 November 1993. Of this correspondence, 200 were enquiries from existing U3As, 200 were from educational institutions and such like organisations and 100 were from the general public, usually asking for information about U3A matters. Bill Hawes also included comments on the thorny issue of regional development, leading to his proposal that there should be nine such regions, each with its own chairman and/or 'group leader'. He also added that during the year of 1993 no less than 50 U3As had been added to the reckoning, a continuing and welcome growth, but one that automatically placed pressure on so tiny and under-resourced an administrative team, despite its tidy and effective dealing with these matters.

There was a contextual aspect. As the years of the 20th century drew to a close, there was an ever-increasing sense of exciting technological change, with its menu of 'microchips with everything'. In a world of vivid imagery and colourful appeal, there was a rising expectation about the presentation of corporate affairs. The sober-sided scrubbed look of the voluntary movement of mid 20th century, all make-do-and-mend and cyclostyled sheets, was forced to cede ground to newer yardsticks of public presence. The staid black and whites of the 1970s and early 1980s had yielded to the rainbow affects of the late 1980s and 1990s. Bodies like the Third Age Trust, known in the political trade as 'vol orgs', were faced with something of a quandary. If they presented themselves as earnestly impoverished and reach-me-down, they ran the risk of being regarded as old hat. If they adopted modernistic mechanics of communication, they ran the risk of being viewed as flashy and spendthrift.

However, in respect of image, it was imperative that the U3A in the UK, upholder of the notion of a positive older age, should not be overshadowed or seem publicly to be threadbare and woebegone and, in any event, the determining factor of optimum efficiency was paramount. What was necessary was to unfold some golden mean between the ostentatiously extravagant and the dismally poverty-stricken. Over these years, then, efforts were made to overhaul the central machinery and to find ways of resourcing it more substantially.

i. National Development – the Alan Willey Approach

Whether it was the guiding hand of a benign providence or the astute political sagacity of its membership and committee, the national U3A movement contrived to find leaders suitable to the hour and its needs. Frank Pedley had been invaluable as the U3A nationally struggled with constitutional and related questions; Jean Thompson had been ideally suited to securing for Britain a place on the international U3A plane and, indeed, for ensuring that U3A was much better known on the national stage. She had also encouraged the blessings of subject networks and other forms of cross-group collaboration.

Now it was the turn of Alan Willey. A leading member of the Tynedale (Hexham) U3A and the first return to northern pastures in search of a Chairman since the critical days of Frank Pedley, Alan Willey was also the first in that post to hail from a primarily industrial background, whereas his distinguished predecessors had usually enjoyed sterling careers in educational settings. He was elected to the National Executive Committee at the Exeter AGM of 1992, where he famously and accurately forecast that U3A membership would quadruple to over 100,000 by the end of the century –with the essential concomitant that the national framework must be tough enough to tolerate that degree of growth. His first committee posting was that of Subject Networks Coordinator, in which role he successfully organised the first pre-conference study weekend. This temporarily replaced the 'social weekend' that had been run in conjunction with the business matters of the AGM and was, in effect, an opportunity for the Subject Network personnel to meet and discuss their particular interests.

A mellow-humoured figure, imbued with a quiet confidence, his engaging personality and shrewd organisational judgements were to be of great value to the Third Age Trust. He was elected Chairman at Lancaster in 1994 and brought a business-like approach to all the U3A procedures. Not the least of his assets was a clarity about what he felt was more and less important; he seldom departed from this critical arbitration of priorities. He made no secret of the fact that he did not warm to pettifogging issues consuming valuable time at AGMs; as with most voluntary bodies, one still found the 'Paper Clip Syndrome' in evidence, that tendency, already referred to in the explanation of U3A constitutional affairs, of rather constipated debate, at well above room temperature, on smallish posers. He was not keen on governmental financial support, believing that one risked losing control of one's actions in such circumstances. Then again, and on his own admission, he was not very interested in the international U3A movement, suspecting that the chasm between the 'French' and 'Anglo-Saxon' concepts was well nigh unbridgeable. In any event – and here one sees those complementary qualities of different Chairmen in play – Jean Thompson had, in the event, and with the help of other *confrères*, resolved that issue and was able to continue to lead for the British U3A as the equivalent of a Secretary of State for Foreign Affairs.

What Alan Willey was passionate about was managing the 'business' – and he did not demur from usage of that word – 'professionally' – and he did not baulk at that adverb either.

Speaking to his Lancaster audience, he vowed to bring dynamic leadership to the cause - and then proceeded to supply it. With well over 200 member groups, he avidly seized the nettle of communications. He inaugurated the Chairman's regular letter to U3As groups, 14 of them in all over his period in office; he urged NEC members to present affiliation certificates personally to the ever-extending list of new groups and otherwise to make countrywide visits; he promoted the concept of regional structures and subject networks, seeing such devices as necessary for the gluing together of these rapidly expanding numbers. At board level, he insisted on all committee members participating even-handedly not only in decision making but also in the sharing of senior responsibilities. He also recruited a Chairman's Advisory

Panel of U3A members with specialist managerial skills to counsel the board.

He promised the Lancaster delegates a business plan and, next year, he announced it to the Swansea delegates, where he diplomatically began his address with a few sentences in Welsh. The business plan was greeted with the acclaim of, to Alan Willey's slight embarrassment, a standing ovation. This plan, *Facing the Future*, was updated, under the title *Investing in the Future*, in 1996, when the conference was held in Edinburgh. Detailed yet lucid, sharpened with clear objectives, it touched on development, the regions, central administration, publications and public relations, links with other organisations, subject networks, research, fundraising and finance.

There had been precursors. Norman Richards, when Vice-chairman, had led a review of U3A organisation over the years 1993/94. This, after widespread local and national discussion, had proposed plans to improve the NEC's development programme and returned once more to the idea of a full-time chief officer. Then, in 1994, Morris Brodie had presented a well-informed and concise report.

Morris Brodie had been a senior consultant with the United Nations and had undertaken assignments for the UN in no less than sixteen countries. His review came as the consequence of a recommendation by an NEC policy review working party, chaired by Idris Davey of the Swansea U3A. *The Brodie Report*, sparsely written and sparklingly crystal-clear, touched on many matters to do with day-by-day administration, particularly the duty of NEC members to evade the temptation to become busy officials instead of concentrating on strategic planning and leadership. The fundamental question was put in a nutshell: was the U3A 'a pretentious leisure club' or, as Morris Brodie hoped and believed, 'an adult education movement imbued with intellectual and social purpose'?

It also dealt with pressing issues *vis-à-vis* local groups. To ensure the central organisation could fulfil its responsibilities adequately, it advocated a capitation fee of £3.00, instead of the then current £1.35, grudgingly paid by some. That suggested augmentation seemed swingeing to many, but the report spelled out succinctly for what purposes the funds were required. One of them was the truth, well-understood by charity managers, that, unless an agency was on a solid footing to begin with, funders were less, not more, willing to come across with the required monies, fearing that they might be throwing them into a deep sump.

Some national bodies adopt the Stalinist approach of collecting all the individual subscriptions centrally and then deciding how to allocate them for regional and district activities. True to its belief in the primacy of the local unit, the national U3A had never for a moment considered that overmighty route. Nonetheless, it led Morris Brodie to make an observation that should be inscribed on the portals of all U3A groups. '. . . it is one thing', he coolly wrote, 'to be locally autonomous. It is another if autonomy is claimed in order to imply (local U3As) can feel free of any obligation to the larger movement . . . The self-help philosophy is to be applauded, but it can be read as self-serving.' Amen to that prayer.

These surveys and reviews, culminating in that important document, *Investing in the Future*, transformed the mood as well as the mechanics of the U3A nationally. There was a sober but gratifying recognition that not only had the embryonic U3A emerged from the chrysalis stage into maturity, but that it also faced a future of unprecedented growth and influence.

ii. National Development – The Saga Saga

A major step forward toward a more secure financial base was taken with the agreement to accept the sponsorship of the Saga company, one of perhaps the two most significant financial settlements negotiated by the U3A nationally.

An approach was made by Saga in 1993. It arose from a deputation of U3A officers who had waited on the Saga chiefs with a request for a grant of £20,000 for the hiring of a chief executive. Saga were interested but preferred something a little more substantial and two-way in value. The proposal was for Saga to undertake the publication of *Third Age News* for two years (this period was subsequently extended to three years), which, in turn, would provide an outlet for its own product in a field where U3A members were already very involved. This would immediately have the effect of releasing funds, for enlivening the development plans and sustaining the national structure. It was a tempting offer, but there was, at all levels, fiery and even acrimonious debate, with, in certain areas, dread murmurs of disaffiliation in the sombre air.

To deploy equine imagery, the protagonists thought it would be looking a gift-horse in the mouth to refuse such help, given that the *quid pro quo* was some discreet advertising by Saga of their product in a *niche* market where there was already substantial interest. The antagonists were mindful of Virgil's warning, 'do not trust the horse, Trojans', with its sobering implications about the Greeks when bearing gifts. There were fears that independence would be menaced by so close an association, while, as the responses to the questionnaire distributed to local U3As by the then Chairman, Jean Thompson, indicated, there were suspicions that the address database of the Third Age Trust might be vulnerable to possible Saga depredations and that the Saga image was a bit too ancient for up-and-thrusting U3A-ers.

A small majority at the 1994 Lancaster AGM agreed the proposal. Roger de Haan, the entrepreneurial Saga boss, had dispelled some of the overt suspicion with disarming charm and sensible comment: in reply to the suggestion that SAGA wished to take over U3A, he replied 'who would want to take over you lot?' It was an amiable but astute answer, for, to all but the most self-important minds, it had the ring of wounding truth.

Gerry Hitchen, who began a busy and productive spell in 1993 as Secretary and then Vice-chairman, became much involved in these negotiations. With a career in adult education and a formative phase among the North Devon U3As behind him, he was to be a crucial figure in several noteworthy events over the next few years. A friendly countenance and an alert mind were part of his stock-in-trade, together with a fine devotion to detail, that express trait of the good administrator. He recalls how, at the subsequent negotiations about how exactly the newspaper would be edited and produced, the 'sticking-point was their wish for only an advisory editorial committee', which would have left the Saga-appointed journalist in sole command. Gerry Hitchen insisted that the formal contract should allow the Third Age Trust to have a final say in editorial matters, a clause that, as Gerry Hitchen reminds, was to be of pertinent use over the next years when there were disagreements over what might be included.

The first Saga-backed newspaper appeared, the 35th in the series, with 24 pages in A4 format, and with colour following the next year. From the economic viewpoint, and apart from the glories of improved production, the telling fact was that this was all accomplished without resort to U3A funds. Saga was to publish the magazine for three years from the summer of 1996 to the summer of 1999.

There was a very useful corollary to the Saga connection. Gerry Hitchen has recounted how Roger de Haan was also persuaded, more or less free of charge to U3A, to request the Saga solicitors to obtain copyright on the U3A logo and the trade marking of the title. This was accomplished in 1996. Alan Willey rightly described the U3A title and logo as 'our most precious asset'. The Founders had, so to speak, foundered in this regard. It had been briefly discussed but then shelved, the belief being that friendly persuasion was the preferred option to legal enforcement, especially in the early stages of development, when there were so many sensitivities about the central/local relationship. In a tough world, however, with non-affiliated bodies determined to deploy the title, it was the correct decision to seek the sanctuary of the law and protect the integrity of the U3A in the UK. That said, it does appear that there are a few mavericks still acting under the U3A heading up and down the land: it is not easy to compel them to stay their hand.

Gerry Hitchen duly made legal dispositions at a solicitors' office in Bideford and the deed was done. Despite the continuing problem of some malcontents, it is Gerry Hitchen's judgement that it has stopped some illegitimate U3As from passing themselves off as nationally 'official' and persuaded others to come into the licit fold. It was obviously a proper step to take. It is well worthwhile emphasising in this, the formally commissioned history of the U3A, that any agency still utilising the U3A title and logo could well be infringing the civil law.

Soon afterwards there was another and allied legal nicety to which to attend. It was to prove to be one of the quaintest curios of U3A's chequered legislative history.

Gerry Hitchen, relaxing in blissful innocence at his wife's house in Great Holland, Essex, was disturbed by a peremptory knock at the front door. It was two officers of the Essex county trading standards department. They had arrived, without warning, on the advice of their Bridgend counterparts, where a complaint had been made that the Third Age Trust was deploying the term 'University' against the express instruction of the Privy Council.

As a follow-up to the patenting of the U3A title and logo, the NEC, on the promptings of John Lloyd, of the Wearside U3A, and an active committee man –he was Chairman of the Development Sub- committee – who brought much vigour and sensibility to the NEC's proceedings at this stage, had resolved to change the umbrella label. It was deemed more meaningful to use the overall title of 'University of the Third Age', particularly now that the name had such legal validity. Interestingly, one of the reasons Michael Young, ever an observer of the far horizons, had plumped for 'Third Age Trust' was in case the charity might have spotted an opportunity to start another arm. This might have been another strategy for bringing educational succour to those in the Third Age and it could thus have been inaugurated without the bother of registering another charity.

However, that likelihood had not appeared and 'Third Age Trust' did not of itself resonate of U3A.

As Secretary, Gerry Hitchen had approached the Charity Commission and Companies House with a view to changing the name of the charity. The Charity Commission agreed without comment but U3A's old friends at Companies House passed on the letter to the Privy Council office. Naturally, the Privy Council rejection only applied to the national body, in consequence of the Companies House relationship, and had no general application to local U3As, all properly registered as charities.

Gerry Hitchen explained to these suspicious officials that the problem arose because two arms of government – the Patent Office and the Charity Commission – were happy with the notion of a national University of the Third Age, whilst a third – the Privy Council – were unhappy. Further, he pointed out that it would hardly be possible, certainly without creating confusion bordering on anarchy, to issue an edict against the general use of the term 'University', especially in this case where there were already hundreds of legally established and autonomous voluntary bodies using the word in their titles. He described the French origins of the mechanism and its worldwide usage.

He never heard from them again. He has since learned that the Australian U3As had some similar difficulties and that there has been a British case of a college being disallowed from using the term 'University'. The combine of Companies House and the trading standards agencies offers the probable explanation for this visitation, for it touches on the possible commercial ramifications. It is highly likely that the official worry was that they had uncovered a meretricious gang of confidence tricksters flogging gimcrack degrees at extravagant prices to a gullible public. Once perceived as a genuine charitable and non-profit making venture, all was apparently well, although 'Third Age Trust' remains the charity's name, so that if there were a desire to launch a separate digital TV channel (one of Peter Laslett's dreams) or a correspondence college (one of Michael Young's visions), there would be less of a legal barrier.

Gerry Hitchen has described how his comprehensive counter-argument, when so abruptly caught on the doorstep by the visiting bureaucrats, was a plea quickly fashioned by a mind concentrated by the thought that they might 'come to cart me off to the Tower'. No one would have wished to see Gerry Hitchen languishing in the Tower, brooding over the prospect, like Colonel Fairfax in *The Yeomen of the Guard* ('Is life a boon? If so, it must befall/That Death, whene'er he call,/Must call too soon') of facing the axe for his treasonable offence. Nevertheless, there is just a lurking regret that the matter had not been taken a step further. It might have been worth it for the chance of watching and listening to Peter Laslett fiercely addressing the Right Honourable Members of the Privy Council on the meaning of 'University'.

iii. National Development - the Lottery-backed Resource Centre

There could be no greater contrast than that between the medieval vestiges of Privy Council potency and the ultra-modern materialist allure of the National Lottery, but Gerry Hitchen bestrode the past flummery of the one and the up-to-the-minute glamour of the other without quailing. Naturally, the long-serving Treasurer, John Moyes, also played a major part, especially when it came to the various calculations required, as well as later when this huge hoist in U3A finances had to be managed.

Those who have not been confronted with the Byzantine intricacies of a national Lottery application may not wholly appreciate the zeal and persistence shown by the U3A Secretary as he tackled this task. Gerry Hitchen had a month to prepare the material, including a lengthy business plan, in order to meet the Lottery Board deadline. Lottery grants officers also interviewed him. Although the principal need was a permanent office base and support for *Third Age News*, he was well aware that core funding is always the more difficult case to urge. Thus the argument was for a Resource Centre and for a linked publication in support of development and the spread of ideas.

One minor reward for Gerry Hitchen was a Lottery Board accolade. He was told that his application was a model of its kind. It pressed the need for U3A to move beyond its chiefly administrative duties in a condition where low income had precluded all but a minimal engagement with educational development *per se*. Remarking that a recent MORI/NIACE survey in 1995 revealed 'the scandalous fact' that 60% of older people had never participated in formal educational activities since leaving school, and pressing as a leading text, 'Help U3A groups develop their learning opportunities', the bid was made for two main elements:

'A Resource Centre of learning material, electronically stored and delivered

A Periodical to disseminate good learning practice'

It was pointed out that 1000 sq ft of space was available at the Third Age Trust headquarters for the Resource Centre. Attention was drawn to the 56,594 members in their 333 groups as 'a living testimony to the importance and value of providing learning opportunities for the older age group . . . Narrowly vocational education and training receives massive support from the government, but there is no help and even less understanding of the value to older people and to the community at large of providing a U3A-type service.'

It was a powerful and fluently crafted appeal. It did not fall on deaf ears. A grant of nearly £300,000 was received from the Lottery Board, to the joy of most and the consternation of some. By U3A yardsticks, it was a colossal sum and, of course, would require watchful management to secure the best dividends from such a bonanza. Apart from the organisational concern, there had been some worried noises at the outset about whether Lottery funding flouted the U3A precept of self-help.

The question of the boundaries of self-help has already been considered and needs must be considered still further, for it was and remains a basic predicament within the U3A movement. Like the

American Constitution, it is open to 'loose' and 'tight' interpretations. At the ascetic extreme, self-help was all but a synonym for self-sufficiency or self-sustenance, in the sense of the members being the sole providers of revenue or other forms of help and any turning to an outside source contravened the ethic. This presumably included the equivalent of bazaars or sales of work and there are many U3As who make a tidy sum from, in illustration, the retail of the plants nurtured by the gardening group. At an absurd level, one might debate, like an item of medieval theology, the pros and cons of a non-member buying a raffle ticket in aid of a U3A . . . and so could one pursue these instances into trivial logic-splitting.

For those at the other end of the spectrum, self-help has the connotation of raising funds in any way imaginable, so long as the steadfast character and unrestricted control of the organisation is not impugned. In this interpretation, self-help is about devilling for whatever resources one can uncover, without the expectation that one should expect aid, financial or otherwise, to be heaped on U3As as if they were social casualties in distress. There are two important rules. First, that self-help is not passive; it is about the active pursuit of one's objects, in a society where older people have for too long been viewed as the object of varied forms of institutional alms-giving, about which they have had neither say nor influence. Second, as a complement of this, self-help implies that one has maximum authority over the use of the monies or materials acquired. It is other people, offices and officers, making the decision about how the funds should be utilised that is the sticking point and which fundamentally offends the self-help *credo*.

Self-help is, essentially and above all, a statement about citizenship. It is about the citizen being, in the argot of the leisure industry, the 'origin' rather than the 'pawn', the Svengali not the Trilby in the social relationship, or, a more homely example, the Peter Brough and not the Archie Andrews.

It is an appropriate point to muse over the self-help conundrum, for U3A in the UK was confronted with its most overwhelming windfall ever, one that challenged the leadership to recognise that U3A was a big player on the educational playing field. In 1997, the year the national conference met in Liverpool, the Resource Centre was established and in 1998, looking a little ahead, the first edition of the educational bulletin *Sources* was published.

The Resource Centre soon became the focus for a much more elaborate supply of materials than anyone had envisioned. Its highly qualified Manager, Elizabeth Gibson, a Chartered Librarian, has kindly provided an up-to-date description of its present standing. It is, at base, a growing collection of non-book materials, freely available to U3A members, and it consists of slides, video-cassettes, audio-cassettes, Cd-roms, DVDs and multimedia packs and, in addition, materials of that ilk produced by local U3As and, after use, donated for other members to use. As of late 2003, there were over 1800 individuals on an ever increasing database, held, as is the stock catalogue, on the computerised library management system, Limes Millennia. The service operates a standard form of postal delivery, irrespective of distance, with no charge made for outward postage, although the recipient must find the charge for the return of the loan.

Requests pour in by letter, e-mail, fax and telephone, with items booked for immediate use or reserved for future use; the Resource Centre is usually holding reservations for up to nine months in advance. Some groups block book materials for every meeting of a session, giving all the dates well in advance, a tribute to the careful planning of the group leaders. Many of the items have been bought on the recommendation or request of members, making it, as befits a self-mobilising organisation, very much the creation of the membership. Free subject lists are available, detailing useful information, like the number of slides in a pack or the running times of video and audio cassettes. The major U3A subjects are covered, with some particular emphasis on art, science, music and history.

The general aim has been to build an unusual collection, that is, one that does not duplicate the normal public library provision. The results have been excellent. There are now many U3A interest-groups that are heavily dependent on what the Resource Centre is able to provide to run existing courses and develop new areas of study.

Sources has proved to be of great value to the movement. It is distributed three times annually to the homes of subscribers on an entirely free basis and, theme by theme, it has offered takers a wealth of admirable content. Over 20 issues have been posted to its eager readers since its inception in 1998, with each issue concentrating on one or other of the subjects or activities with which U3A members are involved. To take one edition at random, the June 2003 issue majors on music and proceeds by highlighting some of the musical wonders to be found across the nation's U3As. These range from the eight groups, from opera to jazz, of the huge London U3A to the four groups of 'modest village-based' Wonersh in Surrey, with G & S in Chichester ('The very model of a modern U3A', we are informed); 'Singing for Pleasure' in Peterborough – 'and not forgetting the tea-break'; the 'sweet harmonies' of 'Barbershopping' in Cheadle, Staffordshire, and Pembrokeshire's own jazz band, all designed to make the ears do whatever the equivalent of mouth-watering may be. The founder editor was the brilliantly inspirational David Ensor of Salisbury U3A, who gave *Sources* a splendid start and masterminded its progress for over three years. Now edited by the enthusiastic, lucid and well-organised Mike Williams of the Hastings & Rother U3A, *Sources* catches the tenor of self-help learning with verve and dispatch.

There were other national contributions to U3A development during these middle years. In 1993 Peter Laslett had brought Roger Coleman into the U3A fold. He was instrumental in forming and directing the 'Design for Age' project for U3A art and design fans, based on the Royal College of Art. Members acted as informants on specified items, such as tetra milk cartons, with the hope of evaluating and improving the design of products used by older people. In 1995 there was the Cochrane Foundation collaboration, whereby, again at Peter Laslett's behest, Mark Lodge was introduced to U3As with his plan for engaging its members in very practical research. He trained U3A members to search medical documents, with a view to building up data about hip replacements and other medical procedures and problems. Peter Laslett was always keen to further the cause of volunteer research by older people.

In 1996 the first week-long 'Summer University' was mounted. It was at the University of Surrey in Guildford, home both of one of the country's most supportive universities and one of its leading U3As. Organised by Jean Thompson and Professor Peter Jarvis, it explored 'The Makings of a Modern European Consciousness' and there was a contingent of visitors from German U3As to add true verisimilitude to that up-to-the-mark and animated discussion. The second of the series, in 1997, was also at Guildford. It considered 'Understanding of a Changing Society' and was extended to two weeks duration to allow for a related week of English language tuition run by U3A convenors.

iv. National Development – New Technology

The advent of new technology has been of some significance for a growing self-mobilised body such as U3A. Luckily for the British U3A, the expert figure of Roger Cloet – already encountered as the U3A's international representative - was on helpful hand and he has provided notes about this development that have been indispensable in the preparation of the following account.

In 1988 he was asked by his wife, Audrey Cloet (for here is another of those Sidney and Beatrice Webb-type marriages that have stood the U3A movement in such good stead) to advise the Bath U3A on applying the computer to its membership lists. He obliged, demonstrating to a wondering committee how a database could be constructed and how multiple letters could be fabricated. 'It intrigued me', writes Roger Cloet, 'to discover that otherwise well qualified people often had little conception of what data processing involved, nor of the economy of effort that could be achieved'. This set him on designing a course for 'literate adults', over against his usual clientele of 'recalcitrant juveniles with limited attention spans.' He was able to try out the course on the little group of Bath activists.

In 1994, accompanying Audrey Cloet to the Exeter Conference, he complained to the then Chairman, Alan Willey, about the dearth of U3A group activities in the sciences.

This was tantamount to the callow soldier who asks aloud about the lack of music in the canteen and is ordered to move the piano. Roger Cloet of a sudden found himself launching an appeal on this theme, leading the resultant Sci/Tech Subject Network and editing its newsletter. In 1995 he was encouraged by the next Chairman, Len Street, to seek grant-aid for IT activity for older people. He applied to the Nuffield Foundation Phoenix Fund, on which Committee it so happened Eric Midwinter was a member, and landed a sum of £11,227, made available in the summer of 1996. In the autumn of that year, with the necessary equipment purchased, the first presentation was made to the Lewes U3A.

In the course of the next two and a half years 23 U3As were visited, ranging from Dumfries to St Ives, averaging about a couple a month, often with members of neighbouring U3As attending. Local good will and assistance enabled the number of visits to exceed those possible merely within the given budget. The first priority of these presentations was to enable local U3As to deploy such technology for their own administration. A final small grant from the Phoenix Fund underwrote a meeting of the Sci/Tech Network at Bath at which the next IT development was explored and thereafter the NEC continued to sponsor such one-day events. In the meanwhile, many U3As were seeking local help from schools and colleges for support in this regard, with, of course, the Internet becoming a growing attraction.

The experience gained through the Phoenix Fund project was made the subject of a paper, entitled *IT Learning in Peer Groups*, presented by Roger Cloet to the AIUTA Conference at Quebec in 2000. This resulted in an improved appreciation of the UK U3A's self-help approach among fellow-members in other nations, some of which are reconsidering the value of the Anglo-Saxon U3A attitudes. Roger Cloet concludes that, 'by concentrating on teaching the simplest practical software, people have been encouraged to engage in using computers both for personal and management purposes. It has been stressed that older learners wish to be both users, and interpreters, of collected data, not merely substitutes for the traditional typing pool as slavish assistants to a management structure. This is another aspect of self-help, since the U3A committees are often also the 'workers' or 'the staff''

George Canning once spoke of calling the new world into existence to redress the balance of the old. It is in this exemplary fashion that new technology has been called into action on behalf of old age. The U3A website was set up in 1998, with Paul Baron as webmaster; in 2001 'Signposts', the monthly electronic magazine was started, and in 2003 Jean Thompson and Tom Holloway established a new domain, 'World U3A', to promote the U3A internationally. By 2004 online courses included four tutored courses, involving a five hours weekly commitment by participants, in short story writing; 'English; the language of the world'; 'Visiting Artists in Rome' and 'Artists of Spain'. There are eight untutored courses, chiefly in the arts and creative writing, plus a couple of free 'course frameworks' in genetics and lighthouses; links to other free course material in wartime reminiscence, medieval timber-framed houses and Victorian art. Finally, places have been booked on Australian U3A online courses in 'the Night Sky', 'Religions of the World' and 'Autobiography and Journalling.'

Before leaving the centre for another tour of the radii and the circumference of U3A action, there was another vital ingredient in the fare prepared by an industrious NEC for the affiliated groups. This concerned insurance, not the most exotic of questions, but one that was of the utmost significance for U3A groups, especially when one remembers how ageist tends to be the insurance business in respect of older people. As an aside, it might be suggested that, with regard to social responsibility, the insurance matrix is completely the inverse of what common sense might dictate. It is the 35 year old, with, in Tommy Handley's famous descriptor, 'three widows, 16 orphans and a football team to support' who may be taking inordinate risks with some death-defying pursuit. It is the 85 year old, keen to go hang gliding, with all his social duties discharged, who threatens little or no dent in the social fabric.

Harold Potts, the Treasurer, had persuaded the NEC to include public liability insurance as part of the affiliation fee and later, with the help of advice from Saga's insurance experts, this was sophisticated during Gerry Hitchen's secretaryship. Although this has become more expensive of late, this offers cover for some of the more risky outdoor activities of U3A personnel, negligence claims against organisers of activities and the possibility of U3A members accidentally hurting one another. One shudders at the thought that they might envision such an objective purposefully. As Harold Potts and Gerry Hitchen shrewdly judge, this simple but highly pragmatic device is much valued by local U3A groups, who would otherwise find the insurance costs prohibitive and, in mundane practice, it has been a benefit that has proffered a gratifying answer to that oft-cited question 'what are we getting for our affiliation fee?' Both of these officers are adamant that insurance cover has proved invaluable in tempting several reluctant U3As to join the flock.

Gradually, then, the central office was developing a balanced recipe of fine comestibles for the member U3As. The toothsome delicacies of learning aids, such as *Sources* and IT provision, were no less appetising to U3A groups than the wholesome diet of insurance cover.

v. Local Development – the South West

One critic of Charles Dickens' picaresque novel, *Nicholas Nickleby*, said of it that 'while Nicholas Nickleby took to the road, Ralph Nickleby stayed at home and looked after the plot.' Having examined something of the mid 1990s Ralph Nickleby role in terms of the national plot-line, it is time again to take to the road and see what was happening in these years by way of burgeoning U3A groups.

At this stage, Norman Richards, founder of the momentously bustling Swindon U3A, grasped the adventurous part of Nicholas Nickleby wholeheartedly. Although admittedly nearer in age to

Uncle Ralph than nephew Nicholas, this doughty, dryly cheery figure brought the same intrepid sense of enterprising vigour that characterised the mettlesome hero to the development fray. Like several U3A *aficionados*, he had enjoyed a successful career in adult education – and, aptly, he had been a mature student himself at Ruskin College, Oxford and at Bristol University - before turning his steady gaze on to the needs of the older adult. Soon after election to the NEC, he became Chairman of the Development Sub-committee, which was charged, in the aftermath of the Audrey Cloet Fellowship and on something of a shoestring, to sustain the developmental package. Audrey Cloet remained very much a part of this venture, while Eric Midwinter also served as a consultant advisor. Norman Richards was also Vice-chairman of the national committee.

With a combine of personal visits to individual sites and joint meetings of new and recently formed U3As, a broad vision of enlarging the scope of U3A provision was evolved. It was open-minded and open-handed and there was even some attempt to risk the icy draughts of 'cold starts'. It was a rugged consolidation of and building upon Audrey Cloet's work. Of Norman Richards, it may fairly be said that, throughout the history of the U3A movement, few enthusiasts have so clearly grasped the concept of U3A, as prefigured by its founders, nor been so perspicacious in transforming concept into practice. During these years the number of U3A groups rose dramatically once more.

It is the moment to embark on another of our regional visitations, all aimed at capturing some of the flavour of local action and practice, and it is decidedly relevant to begin in the south-west, with Wiltshire, Dorset and the Norman Richards' show. It is all the more apposite, for the Swindon foundation owed something to the support of those two old faithfuls, Dianne Norton and Audrey Cloet. Norman Richards, a reader, like all the best adult educators of his generation, of *New Society*, had learned of U3A in the columns of that once influential magazine just after his retirement. Gathering about him a number of likely activists, he carefully planned a launch meeting attended by a hundred potential customers and addressed by Dianne Norton, Audrey Cloet and Dorothy Sutton of the Taunton U3A. This was followed by the election of a committee and, enterprisingly, Norman Richards sought funding, not only from local charities, such as Age Concern, but from the commercial sector, to the immediate tune of £500 from Allied Dunbar, the Swindon based insurance company. The strategy of local commercial sponsorship was, for many in the voluntary movement, especially at a parochial level, something of an innovation.

Registered in 1988, the Swindon U3A grew rapidly, before settling down to its current membership of well over 800, with scores of activities in play. Features include its week-long arts festivals and its music group that transmuted into a rhapsodic dance orchestra *à la* Geraldo or Henry Hall, with its U3A-logoed music stands and its increasing list of requests to play at dinner dances and the like. Norman Richards, like several other local founders in their respective bailiwicks, was elected Life President of the Swindon group.

In 1998 Norman Richards moved to the temperate coastal delights of Christchurch, Dorset, vowing never to allow himself to be drawn again into U3A affairs. In 1996 the Christchurch U3A had registered with the Third Age Trust and, soon after his arrival there, Norman Richards bumped into the Christchurch U3A Secretary. It now has a membership of 450 and over 50 activities – and Norman Richards is the Chairman. One recalls how fire horses, put out to pasture, stir and prick back their ears at the sound of the fire bell. In both these enterprises, Norman Richards has had as his spirited adjutant, his wife, Pauline Richards, a perfect example of another strand not uncommon in the U3A story, the dedicated husband and wife duo.

Christchurch U3A
UNIVERSITY OF THE THIRD AGE
LEARNING OPPORTUNITIES FOR THE OVER 50'S
U3A
2003/2004 PROGRAMME

Still in Dorset, Bournemouth U3A had little or no organisational aid in establishing itself, in fact, it is one of those places where there was some opposition in local educational quarters. It was chiefly the brainchild of Aubrey Weinberg, its Organising Chairman for seven years and a man who brought great devotion and intellectual strengths to this, the first U3A in Dorset. It was in the spring of 1988 that Robin Segal, another active figure in the Bournemouth tale, had moved from London, where he had been a member of the London U3A. He rightly envisaged that Bournemouth was ripe for the U3A treatment. Bournemouth U3A, amazingly, started with no less than 200 members and reached a high of over 900 members, with close on a hundred weekly activities, in the mid 1990s. It has now settled back to some 600 members.

It has been a very ambitious and successful venture. Aubrey Weinberg worked solidly and well, the culmination of his endeavours coming in 1994, when, in concert with the Help and Care charity and with the assistance of a Lottery grant of £150,000, the Pokesdown Centre was purchased and refurbished as a focus for U3A activity. Bournemouth has had only three Chairmen in its busy history, and Aubrey Weinberg was, until his recent death, its Life President. That part-ownership of the Pokesdown Centre did lead to some uneasy moments in the story, but, as Aubrey Weinberg reports, 'a strong and devoted committee is strengthening its structure and range of activities'.

Aubrey Weinberg was also helpful in the formation of other Dorset U3As, among them Dorchester and Poole. Miriam Kays, Chairman of Poole U3A, reports on how her group began in 1993 and has sprung to be one of the nation's largest bodies, with just on a thousand members, a most impressive development. A glittering array of some 70 activities tempt the Poole members, among them sugar craft and industrial and military archaeology, whilst the newsletter tells of all sorts of events from pub strolls to that exotic trip to Istanbul and North Cyprus; names are named of those gentlemen who were obviously excited by the belly dancer.

Lucas Korwin tells how he started the Shaftesbury and Gillingham U3A. He had not long been a member of the Poole group when Dennis Cooper, the Poole Chairman and a man interested in spreading the word throughout the region, asked him to take on this task. This he did with an inaugural meeting, attended by 70 people, in 1999: a walking sub-group formed within days and now there are 246 members and 25 interest groups – and, very properly, Lucas Korwin is President. In total, there are eleven U3As serving the beautiful county of Dorset.

Back in Wiltshire, Swindon was by no means the only contender. Wiltshire proved to be fertile territory: there are nine exceedingly well-established U3As there, with a joint membership topping 3000. Among them are West Wilts, based on Trowbridge, which began in 1989, and, as its Groups Co-ordinator, Kit Desoutter, explains, it originated in local initiatives, with national office help, and now has over 300 members with some 30-odd activities. Then there is North Wilts, based on Chippenham, which started in 1993 and has over 200 members, as Ann Hurcomb, the Chairman, reports. The ballroom dancing group sounds enticing. Its leader, Malcolm Hodges, writes about it in the newsletter. A reluctant scribe, he had yielded to the 'nagging' of the editor and explains that 'well, we dance – and then we dance some more – and then for a change we dance again': 'it was worth nagging' is the editor's laconic postscript. Shades of Victor Silvester.

Bill Hawes, whom we encountered earlier in this chapter as an office surveyor for U3A and a man much concerned with regional developments, forwarded a succinct account of the doings of Kennet U3A. This covers Marlborough and the surrounding villages and was something of a child of the Swindon U3A, that thriving town being only ten miles distant. It affiliated in 1993; it has 300 or so members and runs 32 groups. Warminster is a later growth. It was registered with the Third Age Trust in 2001 but already has 239 members and an attractive list of 31 group activities.

Phyll Babb has written a fine account of the interesting U3A life of Salisbury and its surrounding area. Salisbury and District U3A was founded in 1988 and flourished profusely, reaching the 500 membership mark by 1994. Phyll Babb was then the U3A Course Co-ordinator, and, together with the Secretary, Peter Tee, she called a meeting of some 50 people who were demanding access to the fold. They collectively decided to start another group and Sarum U3A was born. This also blossomed: quickly it had 280 members and now has 40 plus interest groups (including two 'Latin without tears' ventures). Thus in 1998 the Spire U3A was established, with, to retain the family connection, the Sarum Chairman's wife becoming the Spire Chairman. Spire U3A also burgeoned fruitfully and now has well over 200 members, so that the Salisbury district has approaching a thousand of its inhabitants in U3A membership.

It is an intriguing solution to the problem of growth against the wish, oft expressed in U3A circles, to retain the much appreciated friendliness of relative smallness. In each case group leaders offered to do extra courses to ensure a good start, while there is excellent co-operation among the threesome, with the Chairmen attending, a tribute to their devotion, all three committee meetings. Vacancies on activities are advertised across the three groups and outings and other events are open to all. There is a shared web site. It is an ingenious solution and it is also worth noting that most of the Sarum groups 'have no 'tutor' but are run by members taking turns to present material or follow some form of shared learning'. It sounds like a model of the ideal.

John Gooch, its Chairman, writes informatively about the Ferndown U3A, which affiliated in 1997. A younger woman working in a youth centre told her mother, who just happened to have been a past officer of the Bournemouth U3A, that the building was mostly empty during the day and was crying out for her to start a U3A. The gallant mother stood outside Tesco with posters and other materials, until she had gathered around her a nucleus of thirty or so members. In a few years that has leaped to 469, with over 70 activities on offer, a splendid achievement. John Gooch's wife, in a fine instance of U3A motivation, became so enthralled by and with the Egyptology group that she subsequently set up the Wessex Ancient Egyptian Society and became research assistant to an Egyptologist.

In nearby Gloucestershire there are ten U3As. Four examples may be noted. Cirencester U3A originated in 1992, on the initiative of local enthusiasts, such as Pam McGrath, the first Chairman, and Jane Brewin, and with the help of Audrey Cloet and others. It has nearly 250 members and organises nearly 30 groups and it published a delicious little booklet to commemorate its tenth anniversary in 2002. One of the fascinations of researching U3A materials is the curious items that turn up in newsletters: we learn from Eric Roberts, the Cirencester Chairman and courtesy of its history group, how most of Europe had £sd currency, rather than anything like Euros, in Carolingian times and beyond.

But back to the grindstone of U3A historical records . . . with the cheery notice from Group Co-ordinator Joy Davey on the origins of Thornbury U3A in South Gloucestershire in 1998. Three people responded to a letter in the local paper about forming a U3A and the resultant quartet organised a meeting. They were helped by Kate Wedd, the national Chairman, 'who is still helping' and by Roy Wilson. 'We were afraid no one would turn up to the meeting, but over 80 came and the queue to get to the room went down the stairs of the building and out of the door. We never looked back and now we have around 700 members,' There are nearly 40 activities arranged, from world religions to cycling – including 40 mile spins – while one interesting variation on the monthly meeting is Thornbury's thematic approach, such as 'The River', a series of monthly talks on the Severn.

Thirdly, there is Gloucester & District. Its Chairman, Gordon Brown, concisely describes how local individuals, the neighbouring U3A of Cheltenham and the national office, including a heartening visit from Eric Dyke, the national Chairman, was the impetus. This was in 1988. Now there are over 600 members and about 40 activities, including the 'Open Minds Forum', 'What the Papers Say' and 'Write Your Own Life Story'.

Finally, another big Gloucestershire U3A is Tewkesbury or TUTA, founded in 1991. It had been a slow burn. Its founder, the lively and assiduous Brenda Perkins, had heard Dianne Norton and Eric Midwinter talking about U3A at Toynbee Hall, London in the early 1980s. When she retired to Tewkesbury in 1991, she recalled the concept when told there was little for active retirees in the area. Audrey Cloet was once more recruited for the fray, along with Rona Dow of the Gloucester U3A, itself established in 1988 and now having over 600 members. By the end of the year, as the present Chairman, Nora White retails, there were 170 members and 19 groups; nowadays there are 842 members, a remarkable turn-out for a market town district, and 44 activities. The euphonically sounding TUTA adds lustre to the very animated experience of U3A in the south west of England.

vi. Local Development – the North East

Travelling on a diagonal across the kingdom to the north east, one finds now a score of U3As within the ancient shire bounds of Northumberland and Durham. Although the 300-strong Tynedale U3A had been started in 1984 and the 200-strong Stockton U3A in 1986, most of these were foundations of the 1990s, when stalwart U3A warriors like Alan Willey and John Lloyd emerged as national leaders. Indeed, it was this intrepid pair who were responsible for the inauguration of the Newcastle U3A in 1998, as Mary Dodds recalls. Both men were eager to develop the regional spread of U3A. This U3A has 220 members; 27 interest-groups; a monthly coffee morning at the Centurion, Newcastle Central Station, and its own office that doubles as a venue for group activities.

John Lloyd's Wearside group was also the progenitor, along with keen local interested parties, of the Washington U3A, founded, as Pat Gauntlett, the Secretary, reports, in 2000 and now arranging a pleasing little programme of fourteen groups for its nearly a hundred members. Peeking into yet another attractive newsletter, one discovers news of the marriage of Peter Wigley and Minda Nichol at the Minster Church, Sunderland, with cakes and drinks after the Washington U3A AGM, provided by Peter Wigley, by way of celebration. Alnwick U3A followed from an article in the local paper inviting those interested to come forward and, in 2000, it was in business, with a developing band of 74 members and sixteen interest-groups, an admirably high proportion for that membership. Our correspondent, Maureen Stephenson, was, at the time of writing, about to submit her PhD thesis, for which Alnwick members provided some action research on the use by older people of computers and the Internet.

John Lloyd was also involved, along with Brian Stephenson of Morpeth U3A and others, in the foundation of the North Northumberland U3A, based on Wooler, in 1996. Among the locals involved, special credit redounds on Joyce and Geoff Moore. Joyce Moore, recollects Barbara Ratcliff, the Secretary, 'had read something about U3A in an Age Concern leaflet.' The membership is now over a hundred , with a dozen or so activities arranged, while, emulating the Norman and Pauline Richards Swindon/ Christchurch exploits, Joyce and Geoff Moore moved to Thirsk and started a U3A there a year later. The missionary spirit endures.

The Darlington U3A story is a highly personal one. Audrey Williams, its Secretary writes: 'Darlington U3A started on the initiative of one person . . . myself. I had seen articles over the years and thought that I might do something about it. After a brief second marriage, my husband died and I found myself in a strange town, knowing virtually no one and wondering what to do with a life that had fallen apart. After a few years of feeling sorry for myself I made an effort to start living again. I wrote to the national office to inquire about nearby groups. They said, 'why don't you start one?' That wasn't what I had in mind but I knew that I had to do something worthwhile, so I did start one. The office sent me thirteen names it had received from people in my area during the previous four years. That gave me a few names and eventually four new people sat around my dining table to talk about the idea. We divided our town into sections and went around with posters . . . ' So for some months the hard toil continued, with press and institutional support tapped. Audrey Cloet made one of her magical appearances, while the Northallerton and Stockton U3As also proved extremely helpful. This was 1992. Now Darlington has 234 members and sixteen groups.

That is indeed a highly personal tale, but it is not untypical of the many individual autobiographies that comprise the full account of the U3A epic in the UK. Moreover, as Darlington U3A grew, steps were taken to start another Darlington-oriented group, to be known as South Durham, in part to attract new members from the rural outskirts of the town. Mrs Sandy Hood undertook much of the burden and, with the help of Mike Long, now the U3A Development Officer, called a meeting. Judith Hall writes, 'I went along to the meeting . . . and, after a very informative discussion, we decided to proceed', with Judith Hall being among those who formed a steering committee. Beginning with just sixteen members, there are now over a hundred, and about twenty activities are organised for them.

Another new kid on the block is the Wear-Tees U3A, formed in the Crook area in 2001. The Secretary, Norma Robinson, forwarded a short history of her U3A in the first edition of *U3Alink*, which begins with the heart-gladdening words – for the historian – 'the origins of organisations tend to be lost in the mist of the past; before that happens to Wear-Tees U3A I would like to put on record my recollections.' Thus Norma Robinson is able to describe how Allen Dobson, of the Durham U3A, had obtained £1000 Lottery grant to establish U3As both in the Easington and Wear-Tees areas; how twenty people met 'all waiting for someone to volunteer to be an officer'; how 'to her everlasting credit and our gratitude', Sylvia Beadle took the plunge and the chairmanship; how 'in a moment of aberration, not realising what the future might hold, I offered to act as Secretary'; how a committee of just three strove mightily; and how now there are over a hundred customers for the well managed programme of Wear-Tees U3A.

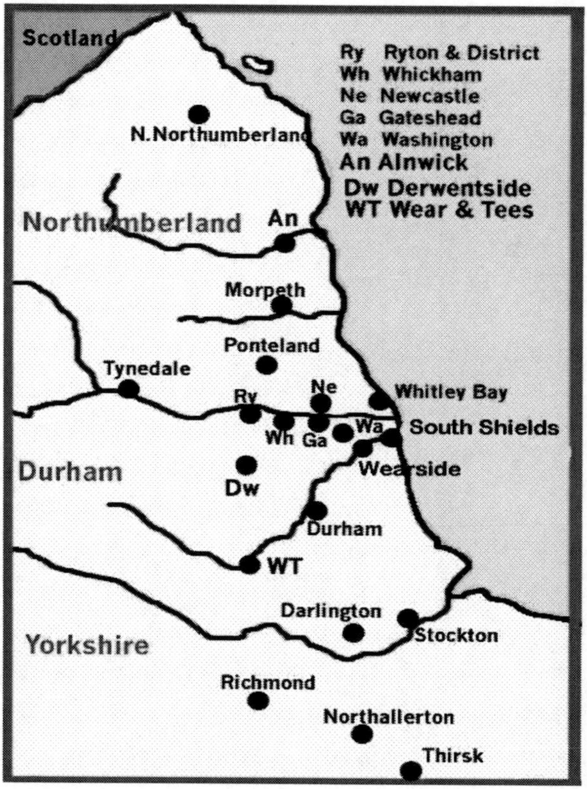

The reign of Alan Willey also included significant changes of premises and personnel at the centre and significant shifts in the momentum of U3A development in Wales, Scotland and Northern Ireland. Attention will next be turned in those directions, but not before an apt mention of what Alan Willey's chairmanship may, overall, be best remembered for, and what he himself hopes will be the case. This was his insistence that the essence of U3A-dom was fun. Unless there was enjoyment, there was nothing, a truth largely forgotten, if ever recognised, by a multitude of educational theorists and administrators. His counsel to U3A conferences – 'enjoy yourselves and be nice to each other' – is relevant not only to U3A experience but to the educational process at large.

Nine: EXCELSIOR!

Onward, ever onward, was the U3A cry, as more and more groups flocked to join the legions. Longfellow's youth, climbing steadfastly upwards, with his 'strange device' and 'clarion voice' of 'Excelsior!' could not have been more adamant than was the British U3A in its resolve to conquer. It is true that, metaphorically speaking and by definition, 'the shades of night were falling fast' in relative terms on the UK's Third Agers but still they contrived to create the huge spectacle of a country-wide organisation and, unlike Longfellow's unlucky youth, were able to look toward the Millennium with alert confidence.

i. 'Uppards'

Before his honourable retirement, Alan Willey presided over two other major moves, one of fabric and one of personnel, that were to consolidate the Third Age Trust's by now strong institutional position. In April 1996, aided by the generosity of British Telecom, the national office was moved from Stockwell to much more imposing quarters at 26 Harrison Street in the more central Gray's Inn Road area of the capital. One person much involved in this advantageous shift was Albert Hill, himself an ex-BT officer. Another was the highly effective John Lloyd, who was also competently on hand when the move to Bromley was organised. Apart from the improved WC1 geographic situation, there was much more room for administrative work and meetings. The whole social climate was much more benign in regard of everyday office life for the staff there. Had it not been for the 1000 sq ft space available, it would have been pointless to seek funds for a Resource Centre. It could now be boldly affirmed that the Third Age Trust had lost an office and gained a headquarters. It was to remain the buzzing focus of national U3A action for seven eventful years.

In the same year, 1996 and just before this move, the significant step was taken of appointing a full-time Company Secretary. With brilliance of foresight, the NEC appointed Lin Jonas, who, for eight years, has brought sane, cheery and composed control to the charity's affairs.

Lin Jonas, a daughter of Chester, was, in the doubtlessly entrancing years of her youth, a frequent visitor to Manchester United's Old Trafford in the glory days of Bobby Charlton, George Best and Dennis Law. Did some of the zest and *panache* of those immortals rub off on to the admiring young fan? Did some of their honourable sense of ambition and undaunted striving for achievement inspire her when, thrust into professional oversight of a developing enterprise, she brought such devoted resource to the post?

Whatever the motivation, and after taking a history degree at Queen Mary College, London and working as a personnel and office manager in various businesses, including footwear, wholesale foodstuffs, publishing, theatre design and law, Lin Jonas found herself at something of a loose end in the mid 1990s. She spotted what she calls 'a funny little advert' in the London *Evening Standard*. It invited applications for an national office administrator for a small educational charity. After a preliminary interview and some further reading, she became hooked on the simplicity and value of the U3A ideal. Suddenly it was a post she quite badly wanted and, once appointed, it is one she continues to cherish. It started off being 'a bit special' and then Lin Jonas realised 'how special'.

'I find', she writes, 'the U3A organisation inspirational and its members inspiring. I get an enormous amount of pleasure in being able to help and support groups and individual members and it is unusual to be eight years down the road in a job and to feel more committed than at the beginning . . . and I do'. She has presided, in her executive role as Company Secretary and National Administrator, over a movement that has grown to 539 groups and she has contrived to sophisticate and adapt an office system to cope with that level of expansion.

Obtaining more salubrious premises and engaging a full-time chief officer plainly marked the ascendancy of the charity into a condition of maturity. Having run the adolescent gauntlet of barely adequate rooms, staffing and resources, it was now an adult among 'vol orgs', well able to take care of itself and to be perceived as a power in the educational arena. Such maturity had come gradually, the desired outcome of the trials and travails of many strong-minded committee members and officers.

Alan Willey was replaced as Chairman by Noel Martin of the Newcastle-under-Lyme U3A. He had joined the national committee in 1994 and, from his background of management in the brewery and victualling trades, he brought a basic and pragmatic approach to the business of running both local U3As and the national U3A that was very refreshing. His practical briskness made quite an impact, for instance, at meetings with nascent groups. Unfortunately, he encountered harsh personal problems, outside the remit of his U3A involvement, and was obliged to resign. Alan Willey generously returned to take up the crown for an extra six months, until it was time for another election in the autumn of 1997. There were one or two other changes at the top. Harold Potts, the long-serving and, given the state of the finances for most of his rule, long-suffering, Treasurer gave way, first, to Roger Strachan of the Hessle U3A (where, he was, incidentally, the convenor of a magicianship interest-group), and then, for what was to prove a long and profitable spell, John Moyse of the Swansea U3A. He was to give over six years of service in that capacity, an era replete with all sorts of financial matters, not least the Lottery funding, for and in which he played a main part, the later major grant from the Esmée Fairbairn Foundation and from government, as well as dealing with the financial implications of two office moves.

Treasurerships are often thankless jobs; John Moyse earned heartfelt thanks for his labours from his appreciative colleagues.

The Saga deal effectively marked the end of Dianne Norton's illustrious thirteen years career in several roles on behalf of the national U3A. By 1995 her key job had become editing the *Third Age News*, something she had done since its inception, even unto, as Frank Pedley, recollects, writing every single word of one early edition. As the fourth member of that originating quartet, the three national Founders had leaned very heavily upon her for administrative back-up, but it should not be forgotten that, as well as providing clerical and allied support, she had frequently been the public face, mouth and pen of the movement. Dianne Norton's intelligent comprehension of and fluent ability to elaborate the theory and practice of U3A had been a gainful advantage to the evolving organisation. The movement deservedly rewarded her with Honorary Associate Life Membership of the national U3A. In the words of the 1995 Annual Report: 'Dianne Norton, without whose efforts since the early days of 1982 there would be no U3A today . . . '

In the meantime, Norman Richards' Development Sub-committee had, among many other things, attracted a grant of £10,000 from the Calouste Gulbenkian Foundation for its work. This was split into two parts. One purpose was to undertake a review of the growth of U3A nationally, to identify its strengths and weaknesses, especially in respect of incidence, and to make recommendations accordingly. Eric Midwinter was invited to take on this task, which, under the title of *Thriving People*, was published in 1995 and distributed to all U3As. In 2002 he updated his findings in a much briefer format, entitled *Thriving People Revisited*, which was also forwarded to all U3As. Be still the anxious fluttering of the thwarted reader: the content of these two documents will be employed in a later chapter, when some attempt will be made to analyse the character and status of the U3A in the UK at the present time.

At this point the number of U3As was 266. By the end of 1996 that total had jumped again to well over 300. Fans of Stanley

Holloway's monologues (mostly written, for U3A addicts with a thirst for knowledge, by Marriott Edgar, also formulator of most of Will Hay's screen-plays) may remember that his parody on the poem *Excelsior!*, was 'Uppards'. Roughly speaking, U3A in the UK was heading in that same direction.

ii. 'Missionary Work in the Celtic Backwoods?'

Stay the irate complaint of political correctness: the sub-head is borrowed from Swansea U3A. That was their wry take on the decision to deploy a major portion of the Gulbenkian grant in development work in Wales, Scotland and Northern Ireland. In fact, it was largely a decision made by the Gulbenkian Foundation itself. As happens with funding trusts, specific themes are sometimes chosen for specific periods of funding and the three other 'kingdoms' of the UK had been selected for particular treatment at this time.

Nonetheless, outside of South Wales, U3A penetration had not been too pronounced in these areas. In 1995 there were fifteen U3As, total membership about 1800, chiefly in the south, in Wales; seven U3As, total membership about 500, in Scotland; and one U3A, with a membership of some 300, in Northern Ireland.

U3A was not yet a truly going concern in these parts. This possibly reflected a mix of factors. In the first place, the element of 'contagion', already considered, meant that, at this stage, there was a severe imbalance between regions that were saturated with U3As and those where development had been lethargic. There were still several counties and conurbations in England where this rule of thumb applied, so, from this standpoint, there was no need to wrack one's brains for added cultural grounds for a reluctance to bring U3As to Wales, Scotland and Northern Ireland. The seeming difficulty of spreading the U3A word both in large cities and in remote agricultural districts, as opposed to the relatively more fertile soil of suburban and market townships may also have had some bearing on this.

In the second place, there was some evidence, again of a comparative rather than exclusive kind, that the U3A evangelical impetus, like many another British organisational process, was, in chief, rooted in the home counties. However strenuous the attempts to safeguard the decentralised rights of localities, distance does not always lend enchantment to the ear. The first counties to be more or less fully U3A-ified were Surrey, Oxfordshire, Hertfordshire and others in the south east, closer, that is, to the national centre point and perhaps feeling more comfortable with that relationship. The anxieties of Cornwall; the prevarications of Lancashire; the vicissitudes of the West Midlands and Greater Manchester; the uncertain responses of the large industrial cities; the withdrawals of some Yorkshire U3As: these have all been rehearsed. Against the weight of the splendid advances in all those areas, those difficulties may now appear minor and, in truth, it would be misleading to over-emphasise them. Nevertheless, in so far as, with any programme asking for a central/local harmony, distance from the hub may become a disbenefit, this may also have affected the outcomes in the outlying 'kingdoms'. Once more, the reasons were probably more geographical than cultural or social.

It is true that, again as elsewhere, there was some suspicious resentment of the U3A presence in certain parts of these vicinities, although, as we shall observe, several professional educators were to demonstrate crucial enthusiasm. For example, in 1982, soon after the launch of U3A nationally, Eric Midwinter was invited by Robin Webster, then Director of Age Concern Scotland and later to be widely responsible for the sowing of the U3A seed in the Irish Republic, to address a large and predominantly professional audience in Glasgow. It was to prove the most difficult occasion for Eric Midwinter, weary survivor of a long line of difficult occasions. Ken Dodd's nickname for the Glasgow Empire – 'the House of Terror' – sprang to mind. Apart from the usual worries about tutorial employment being undermined by the tactics of U3A, there was an additional accusation. It was averred that allowing 'ordinary', that is, unqualified, people to organise educational classes was 'dangerous'. One had never heard the antidemocratic and exclusively professional case put so strongly or, to be fair, so honestly, for one began to wonder whether, behind the conventional plea constantly heard about U3A imperilling jobs in adult education, lingered this manifest distrust of lay people, this clinging to, as George Bernard Shaw opined, the idea of the profession as 'a conspiracy against the laity.'

Be that as it may, and whatever the reasons for some slight tardiness in Welsh, Scottish and Irish development, there was now a chance to advance proactively.

- Wales

Swansea U3A stands out in Wales as an early riser that is healthy and wise and certainly wealthy in educational riches. It registered with the Third Age Trust in 1988 and now has 400 or more members and a schedule of 30 or more activities. Betty Lowe, of its Editorial Sub-committee, forwarded a copy of *The Story of Swansea U3A*, published in 2002, and a really fascinating read. Harry Muscutt addressed a meeting in the YMCA in 1986 and Edwin Lewis was adopted as Chairman. In spite of some early fluctuations of membership and disappointments with premises, the Swansea U3A made great progress, much of it to the credit of the 'dynamism' and 'determined efforts' of Edwin Lewis. He tells the anecdote of approaching *The Herald of Wales* newspaper, where he overheard the editor, who owed him a favour, instruct, 'get rid of him at any price and make it snappy,' The result was a very favourable account, while the interview ended with the reporter saying, 'Great; can't wait to enrol my mother.'

They were fortunate, too, in persuading the well-humoured and sapient character of Professor Maurice Broady as President. He had had connections with French UTAs and was surprised one evening by the arrival at his front door of 'what I took to be a small cortege of Jehovah's Witnesses.' Before he could administer his 'standard one-sentence rebuff', 'this tall, thin and obviously vigorous chap', whom it transpired was Edwin Lewis, had successfully broached him on the subject of the presidency. Swansea, under this kind of positive leadership, has managed two aspects that have escaped several U3As. First, they have built up a big membership in a traditional industrial base and, second, they have, very unusually, sustained a weekly series of meetings. These are regularly attended by about two-thirds of the membership, alongside a wide-ranging series of activities. Other U3As that have stuck to the weekly general meeting as the core activity have sometimes found difficulty in building a large membership and programme of interest-groups. Among its many attributes, the Swansea U3A publishes, as well as the usual newsletter, the twice-yearly *Swansea Chronicle*, an in-house publication of stories, poems and articles, while highly advantageous relations are maintained with the very helpful University of Swansea.

It makes for an inspiring tale and Swansea was also to the fore in pushing the cause in South Wales. In the Audrey Cloet days, the Swansea officers assisted, *inter alia*, with the launching of Llanelli U3A in 1992; its Secretary, Pamela Lewis, reports that it now runs 18 groups and has 113 members. In turn, Rosemary Lloyd, its founder, and Sheila Ablett, its current Secretary have explained how, with Llanelli's support, the Cefn Sidan (Burry Port) U3A, now with ten groups and some 50 members and having survived some internal ups and downs, was started in 1994. It was while working with groups of people with learning difficulties, that the caretaker of the hall where Rosemary Lloyd was based told her about the Llanelli U3A's meetings there: it was another of those chance encounters that crop up so frequently in the U3A history. 'He planted the seed': she contacted Les Tabbs, then its Secretary, and 'he was wonderful and very enthusiastic.' Swansea U3A and Norman Richards were also involved in this launch.

With the help of the Gulbenkian monies, Swansea was instrumental in setting up further U3As, among them Porthcawl and Carmarthen. Doug Jones, Vice-Chairman of the Porthcawl U3A, has unstintingly provided valuable testimony to the work and character of his U3A. He recalls how the first programmed meeting was in 1996, 'when our guest speaker rather inauspiciously chose as his title 'the Sinking of the *Titanic*'. Nevertheless, we sailed on with relatively little trouble since.' The good ship 'Porthcawl U3A' voyages on with over 400 crew, making it one of the biggest of the Welsh U3As and with about a quarter of the members travelling from outside the town to enjoy the amenities. Doug Jones, in response to the call to revisit the U3A founding principles on the occasion of its 21st birthday in 2003, contributed an interesting article on the precursors of self-organised learning in Britain, from the 'penny universities' of the coffee houses via the Mechanics' Institutes to the Mutual Improvement Societies.

Carmarthen held its inaugural meeting in 1994, the speakers being Margaret Hammond of the Swansea U3A and Idris Davey, also of the Swansea U3A and a cheerful, hard-working NEC member with a willing heart in regard of development. Hazel Drew, the Carmarthen Chairman, tells how Llanelli members were also there in support; now there are some fifteen activities and a membership approaching a hundred.

It was the solidly supported Chepstow U3A that, in 1988, invited six Monmouth residents to one of their meetings and, as the Secretary, Paul Bearne, records, 'they were immediately inspired to form a U3A.' Beginning with nineteen enthusiasts, there are now 273 members, enjoying a range of 32 activities. Caldicot U3A was another started during the Gulbenkian period. Here it was, as Peter Shreeve, the Chairman, describes, the Chepstow U3A, growing ever larger, that again initiated the move in 1995. There are over 200 members and there are a dozen or so groups. Of particular note may be the aspect of social responsibility, a feature of the activity of many U3As. For example, the walking group takes part in a county path care scheme and helps repair country walking tracks, whilst the handicraft group makes up children's comfort quilts for the ambulance service.

Trixie Stevens, the present-day Secretary, sends details of the inauguration of Newport U3A in 1993. Pam Ambrosen writes in the tenth anniversary newsletter, 'I am very proud of my membership number – one – which is partly because my name begins with A, but also because I was there from the beginning.' Pat Singleton and Jo New from the local college were great helpmeets, but, faced with an inaugural crowd of 120, they 'were amazed and frantically looked around for extra chairs.' That running thread of organisers frantically looking around for extra chairs is a pictorial image signifying much about the unmet needs U3A has revealed. Newport is now 328 strong, with 26 groups, focused on the use of rooms at the Shaftesbury Methodist Church – and with Joblot, the musical troupe, playing at village country dances, and the U3A old time music hall, catching the eye.

All in all, there are now 26 U3As in the South Wales and Severnside areas, a remarkable attainment and one that gives rational U3A coverage on a par with most regions in the United Kingdom. Away from the more heavily populated south, there are fewer U3As in the remainder of Wales, but these half a dozen are still sufficient to make their presence felt. They include Dywfor and Merionnnydd U3A, based on the beautiful town of Porthmadog. It was today's Secretary, Beryl Davies, who was yesterday's inaugurator. In its simple phrases, her account echoes scores of other such experiences all over the country. Beryl Davies, having heard of U3A from a friend who belonged to a U3A elsewhere, contacted the national office, received a start-up grant of £75, invited her acquaintances to her home for a meeting, formed a steering committee, took receipt of leaflets and posters, held a public meeting, received regional and local U3A support, launched a programme, affiliated in 2002, and already has over a hundred members and more than a score of interest-groups. Superficially, it sounds preposterously easy: in deep reality, it entails, of course, substantial dedication.

On the north coast is the Abergele and District U3A, about which John Morris, its Chairman, is the informant. It registered in 1991 and has 191 members and eighteen activities. It was started by local individuals and, given the terrain, the bird watching, botany and gardening programmes sound extremely tempting. George Adams, the Secretary, writes in about the Flintshire U3A, recently started in 2002 on Deeside, with 40 members and eight interest-groups. The Flintshire Library and Education Service promoted an open day at Flint library to give the U3A its initial boost. George Adams, made redundant by BSC Shotton years ago, heeded the call of Community Education and became imbued with its philosophy, an important strand, of course, in the U3A ideal. Finally, at Bangor, the U3A was established, according to Chris Cave, the Chairman, on the joint initiative of several members of the Anglesey U3A, based on Holyhead, and other local inhabitants. A key figure was Pamela Fox-Russell, the North Wales Regional Representative. Meetings began in 2000 and now 160 members enjoy eleven activities, as well as an interesting programme of weekly meetings and visits.

In brief, the U3A movement in Wales has more than doubled its groups since 1995 and more than trebled its membership, to well over 5000 in sum.

- Scotland

Edinburgh U3A is one of the largest in Scotland and it is yet another in which Audrey Cloet was involved. It began in 1989 with Edinburgh Third Agers seeking help and materials from the national office. Marjorie Langdon is our Edinburgh correspondent and she reports on how well went the first meeting, in March 1990, and how Helen Cairns, who was to become one of the U3A powers in Scotland, was appointed Chairman. That original 50 has grown more than tenfold; membership is now 556, and there are upward of 65 interest-groups, including no less than five book groups. *The Clarion* is the excellent Edinburgh newsletter, which heralds the doings of this exceptionally fine development.

In the three other instances to hand, it was local education bodies that led the way. The Secretary of East Lothian U3A, Julie Murphy, relates how Edinburgh U3A was helpful to the East Lothian effort, but it was Frances McLennan, from the local Lifelong Learning Centre, who was the catalyst. She called a meeting, ensured a steering committee was formed and provided some free accommodation and now the group has blossomed, with 226 members, drawn from over a fairly rural county, and more than a score of activities. Dundee U3A also had the bonus of aid from the local community education service, plus help from Audrey Cloet and the national office, while the first Chairman had been a U3A member in Australia. As its Secretary, Irene Dowie, explains, it was originally the Craigie U3A, when it was formed in 1992; now, under the Dundee label, it has 170 members and some fourteen interest-groups. A final Scottish example is Arbroath, described for us by its Chairperson, Jocelyn Slater. Here the A ngus community education service was to the fore, advertising in the local press and holding a meeting in Arbroath library, preparatory to affiliation in 1996. There are now 64 members and ten groups.

The general situation in Scotland is that there are currently 15 U3As, with Edinburgh U3A by far the biggest, and a total membership approaching 2000, double the number of groups since 1995 and quadruple the membership.

- Northern Ireland

For some time the powerful Foyle U3A in Londonderry, which began business in 1990 and became registered with the Third Age Trust in 1990, was the sole Northern Irish entry on that roster. It is an amazing story of fruitful endeavour, inspired by the vision and work of the charismatic Pascal McDonald, after whom the Foyle U3A headquarters are meritoriously named. It is an intensely busy history of building contacts with educational and sponsoring bodies. The winter 2001 newsletter describes how Pascal McDonald House, Gransha Park, was bought, refurbished and extended, with the help of a massive outlay of £322,490 from the Community Fund in 1999. Foyle now has 536 members and runs 77 groups and activities

We are indebted to Ann Hayes, Convenor of the U3As in Northern Ireland and a member of the NEC, for providing these facts for a pen-picture of U3A life in Ulster. Apart from the large Foyle operation, there are a further eight U3As, with Causeway U3A in Coleraine and Down U3A having biggish memberships, and with the others – Newry U3A, Strabane U3A, North Down & Down U3A in Bangor, Enniskillen, Belfast U3A and Sperin U3A in Magherafelt – being somewhat smaller. There is a total membership of about 2000. All these U3A groups meet monthly in a variety of venues ranging from colleges and church halls to council premises and even a theatre, while interest groups follow the usual pattern as in the rest of the UK, gathering in people's homes and other places, including the occasional golf club. Area meetings are held every six months, hosted by different U3As each time and the geographic compactness of the region allows for a reasonably high level of inter-group contact. Growth is 'slow but steady' and there are plans to extend the already existing contacts with U3As in the rest of the island of Ireland.

Especially at the time of the Gulbenkian subvention, Foyle U3A was instrumental in encouraging other U3As to establish themselves in Northern Ireland. The Causeway U3A, also in Londonderry, was certainly assisted by Foyle (formerly known as the U3A in Derry), as its Chairman, Gwen Appleby, recounts. The initiating individual was Ray Morrison, who became the first Chairman. It began with 47 members in 1995 and now has about 300, with fifteen activities, and its general monthly meetings are held in the resplendent comfort of the Portstewart Golf Club. Gerald Bourn reminds us that development continues. He was a member of the Newry U3A and this led him to transform a social group at nearby Crossmaglen into a brother/sister U3A. It only began in 2003, with 23 members and five activities: it was good to hear from one of the babies of the movement and we wish it well.

Where in 1995 there was just the noble Foyle U3A, now there are nine U3As in Ulster, with a joint membership of approaching 1700, nearly six times the 1995 total, a highly creditable shift in U3A activity.

A word in season about the Irish Republic, which, although strictly outside the legal limits of this study, perhaps deserves a neighbourly paragraph or two. Soon after the launch of the U3A in the UK, exploratory contacts were made in the Republic. Robin Webster, already encountered in his role as Director of Age Concern Scotland, was carving out for himself an illustrious career, first as Director of Aontas, the Irish adult education centre, and later as founder and Director of Age Action Ireland, the mainstream Irish charity concerned with older age. A radiantly effective organiser and generous adherent to the U3A cause, he has regularly used Eric Midwinter as a consultant and, in the early 1980s, two Harpenden U3A stalwarts, Reg Davis and Wilf Plimley, crossed the Irish Sea with the message. The Gulbenkian Foundation grant of 1994 and, in 1999, a three-year grant from the Irish Department of Education and Science, further helped the work.

As a result of this and other initiatives, there are now fourteen Irish U3As, beginning with the Finglas U3A, Dublin, in 1995, and there are a number of welcome cross-border connections. Several of these were formed latterly, a credit to the new and pro-actively energising National Education Development Officer, Mary Colclough. The story of development and a guide to self-help learning for older people may be enjoyed in the beautifully produced

I'm Not Finished Yet, edited by Pamela Whitaker, then the National Education Development Officer for Age Action Ireland and published in 2001. On the cover Doirin Creamer, of the successful Blackrock U3A, Dublin, is appropriately cited: 'the University of the Third Age sends the message – you are not alone. It's the strength that we give each other that is important'.

iii. Street's Ahead

Once more either some politically inclined god touched the shoulder of the Third Age Trust or its members demonstrated inexorable wisdom. Once more the U3A movement was rewarded with the Chairman it required at that point in its evolution. In 1997, at the Liverpool Conference, Len Street, of the Lea Valley U3A, was elected by an overwhelming majority from four candidates and acceded to the national chairmanship in place of Alan Willey.

Len Street brought an air of kindly authority to the role. His expertise lay in the educational field, but his competence embraced many other qualities. He could manage and he could lead. A gently imposing figure of a man, his presence on a platform or at the head of a committee table won and commanded decent respect. His chairmanship was to oversee expansion in several directions, much of it without undue hassle. Len Street had served on the NEC throughout Alan Willey's three year reign, serving on both the Development and Finance Sub-committees and having some responsibility for fund-raising.

It was just after his appointment as Chairman that the munificent lottery funding was awarded. He immediately showed his gift for prudence. £282,000 would be received over a three year term, but this involved the engagement of part-time staff and Len Street realised there was no 'exit strategy', namely, a method of dealing with the material and staffing implications of the Resource Centre beyond the lottery-oriented phase. He adroitly delayed the acceptance of the money until there had been some renegotiation and a modified spending plan agreed. That done, all went ahead swimmingly and Len Street acknowledges what a tremendous difference the grant made. As well as opening the Resource Centre and publishing *Sources*, the refined financial strategy enabled the NEC to survive the withdrawal of the Saga sponsorship of *Third Age News*. This was now relaunched as *U3A News* under fresh, freelance editorship. In 1997 Marie Hardie of the Salisbury U3A joined the NEC as its first member to assume responsibility for public relations and media contacts; she did a superb job. At the same time, it proved feasible to keep the capitation fee, always something of a bone of contention, at a comparatively low level. This all made for a solid and productive beginning to the Len Street era.

The NEC agreed on three critical tasks: support for existing U3As; help for new U3As, and raising the level of awareness about U3As. Of the first, there was emphasis on organisational backing from the centre for the actual learning activities of member U3As. Of the second, the crucial work was masterminded by Roy Wilson, the National Development Co-ordinator, whose vital contribution will be reviewed in later chapters. Of the third, there were to be, under Len Street's aegis, plenty of meetings with government ministers, attempts to form links with other educational agencies and the procurement of governmental funding for specific projects. The NEC also grew much more alert about the possibilities of making submissions to studies and enquiries of a relevant kind.

Since that point governmental contacts have been sustained. Among the files are to be found correspondence that, for example, includes letters from Kim Howells, Parliamentary Under-Secretary of State for Education, on the issue of Lifelong Learning (1998); from John Denham, Minister of State for Social Security and the Prime Minister's Office about a strategy for older people (1998); from Jeff Rooker, Minister of State for Social Security in regard of the Inter-Ministerial Group for Older People (2001); and from Margaret Hodge, Parliamentary Under-Secretary of State, then Minister of State, for Education and Employment on a number of topics (1998-2001). Various submissions – for instance, on 'the Learning Age' and on the Welfare Reform Green Paper, both in 1998; on 'Learning and Working

Together' in 1999 – were made to the appropriate departments in response for calls for consultation. There was also communication with senior ministers, among then Alistair Darling, when he was Secretary of State for Social Security, and Estelle Morris, during her tenure as Secretary of State for Education and Employment, both in 2001.

This third component was important. Naturally enough, for many of the early years the U3A nationally was chiefly concerned with ensuring its own salvation and consolidating its internal position, although – its engagement with AIUTA is a fine example – there had been some concerted efforts to reach out to similarly inclined partners. The move to raise public awareness, not just as a means of prompting direct support or canvassing for new members and extra funds, was sound in principle and practice. On the one hand, a generally raised consciousness of the U3A approach was, pragmatically speaking, a utilitarian way of creating a mood in which the more direct appeals for support would be the easier to make. On the other hand, this was a straightforward acknowledgement of the founding principles that the U3As, nationally and locally, had some duty to broadcast the existence of the Third Age as a recognisable social phenomenon and to assert the rights and expectations of those in the Third Age.

The liaison with AIUTA was sustained, although there was always a modicum of criticism within the movement about linkages with the continental style U3As. Roger Cloet, from Bath U3A and already revealed as an IT specialist, took over from Jean Thompson as the Trust's representative. Len Street provided accommodation for one of the AIUTA Council meetings in London, which gave a chance for NEC members to meet AIUTA delegates. This led to Roger Cloet becoming a voting representative as opposed to a mere observer and he was the better forearmed for the task of persuading his colleagues of the value of self-help learning.

Len Street's aim was to create an *ambience* for the U3A in the UK in which innovative ideas might flourish, as flourish they did. A wholesome range of activities were either begun or reinforced during these three years. There were Summer Schools, Study Days, group leader support schemes and an expansion of the Subject Networks; there were *Sources*, videos, online learning, the beginnings of the Royal Institution lectures, the first of them in 2000, and with as many as 400 members attending the 2003 series *U3A Explores Science*, and many other similar ventures.

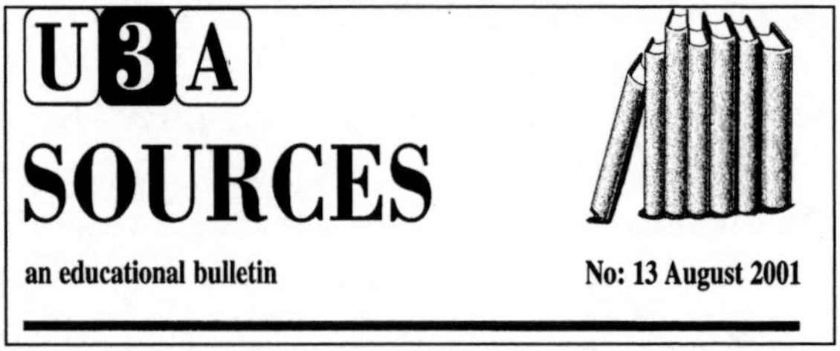

These instances all illustrate what Len Street regarded as his priority and what, in effect, was the telling characteristic that made his accession to the chairmanship so opportune. He recognised that this organisation, which had gradually and successfully struggled through the pressing challenges of building constitutional, financial and structural stability, could now afford the time to consider its basic essence as an educational agency. He also believed that the U3A movement should take up this opportunity seriously. Fundamentally, he felt that, for an educational association, there was not enough educational talking.

Thus in 1996 he persuaded the NEC to establish a Standing Committee for Education (SCE) on a three year trial basis, with Bill Fletcher of the Cirencester U3A and himself as the trail blazers. Its remit was to make recommendations to the NEC about the implementation of educational policy and to succour local U3As in their educational duties. It was under the aegis of this committee that many of the more purely educative aspects of U3A were promoted. At the Edinburgh Conference in 1996 this agenda was agreed in some detail. It was accepted that the SCE should work to encourage individual U3A members to realise their best educational selves; to provide training days for group co-ordinators; to publish relevant materials; to support and increase Subject Networks, with workshops and other forms of training, and to establish links with other appropriate educational suppliers.

The SCE operated to strengthen existing, and start new, initiatives and make them a coherent whole. The first year, 1996/97, showed how possible this was. As a base for the planned Resource Centre, some 5000 slides were acquired; more 'Subject Start Up' leaflets were published; the first one day seminar for group leaders was planned; active links were forged with organisations like the BBC Pilot Learning Zone, with which ten U3As became involved, and the first of a number of submissions was made to the DfEE, the Department of Education, as was. In 1998 the SCE established a sub-group for Group Leader Support.

The advent of lottery financing obviously buoyed these endeavours marvellously well, with the Resource Centre and *Sources* the keystones. The SCE was able to organise more seminars in aid of group leaders and Subject Network convenors. Summer Schools followed – the first at York in 1999; the second at Chester in 2000; the third at Exeter in 2001. Now there were an absolute plethora of meetings and seminars for the critical players in U3A educational action, while the number of Subject Networks had leapt, by 2000, to no less than 27. During that year 25 study days and similar occasions were organised or backed by the SCE.

2001 marked the end of the lottery funding but the work continued unabated, helped by grants, among them one from the Nuffield Foundation's Phoenix Fund to develop on-line courses, the first two of which were delivered in that year. In 2002 a U3A Learning Support Group was formed. It had been a whirlwind of activity, with the educational standards of the local U3As its vortex. The success of the SCE effort was celebrated sedately in 2000, when its construct was incorporated within the Third Age Trust constitution and it adopted some proper legal identity.

It is a breathless tale of intense and eminently sensible enterprise. In a study such as this one may only sketch the outline of this six or seven years of astounding progress on the more purely educational front. Building – as Len Street and the members of the SCE would be the first to admit – on ten and 15 years of remarkable achievement by their predecessors, a highly sophisticated national service was developed for the member U3As. At the lowest and most pragmatic level, it was becoming more and more difficult for local U3As rationally to bemoan the payment of a (rather small) affiliation fee, when this elaborate supports system was at their disposal. At the highest and most philosophic level, the gradual creation of a well-ordered national hub – it had been astutely constituted; it had been shrewdly made business-like; it had learned to maintain financial steadiness; now it was humming on all its educational cylinders – was the culmination of one of the Founders' chief desires. This was the fervent hope that the centre and the points on the circumference – the national office and the local groups – would forge ahead steadfastly, the one reinforcing the other in harmonious and profitable partnership.

In 2003 Len Street went to Buckingham Palace to meet the Queen, who asked him if U3A was a new idea. One might suppose that, compared with the monarchy, it still has a certain novelty factor. He had been appointed to the Order of the British Empire for services to the U3A movement. As many will be aware, and as Len Street OBE was eager to point out, the state authorities use the honours system in part to recognise worthy organisations and institutions by acknowledging the contribution of one of their leaders. Both Len Street and U3A had earned that reward by diligence and endeavour, sprinkled with the magical dust of imagination. It was the rich icing on the 21st birthday cake.

iv. Wedd Site

U3A's Midas Touch in respect of Chairmen was not about to desert it. The Millennium greeted Kate Wedd, of the Bristol U3A, to the chair, although that sedentary sounding piece of furniture hardly does justice to this woman of vigorous energy and infinite capacity. A former head teacher in the south east of England and a U3A member since 1988, for three years she bestrode the realm, visiting over a hundred U3As and sustaining an acute commentary in *U3A News* under the delicious label of 'Wedd Site'.

In the last of these, in the autumn of 2003, she reviewed her three years of whirlwind action and incisive leadership. She listed the achievements of that phase, among them a more democratic selection method for trustees; the growth of technological aids, including more outline courses; direct mailing of *U3A News* to members (a device that gradually began to mend the somewhat sporadic dispatch of the newspaper via the local group route; some 80 U3As and 30,000 members take advantage of this offer), and 'hard-won major grants' that supported the central administration and avoided expensive hikes in the capitation fee, which had only risen 50p under Kate Wedd's sway.

Among those 'hard-won major grants' was one that possibly gave her especial pleasure. This was a large award of £63,000 from the Esmée Fairbairn Foundation for the continuance and development of the Resource Centre. This certainly deserves particular note, for it ensured that the mid-term future of the Resource Centre was more or less secured. The donors made an unusual and far-sighted condition of acceptance of such a big grant. It was proposed that the Third Age Trust should retain a professional fund-raiser, for it was felt that, for such a large membership organisation, a few tricks were being missed and the national U3A was under-achieving financially. In consequence, Christine Buccella has been recruited on an consultancy basis. One result has been the 'Friends of U3A' scheme, which has steadily built up to a roster of more than 400 such adherents to the cause.

Kate Wedd was keen to stress how she had kept to the 'simple rules and few', firm in her belief in the founding principles. She counselled on the wholesome value, for Chairman and member alike, of renewing that belief in the enunciated creed and she marvelled at how little it had been necessary to amend the original tenets in the light of experience. She quoted the concise definition of the British U3A: 'a self-help, low-cost learning organisation for older people no longer in full-time paid employment'. She emphasised that 'it was a startling idea for the UK that older people could direct their own learning, keep their brains lively and still make a valuable contribution to society at large.'

Kate Wedd had invited U3As, on the occasion of the national 21st birthday, to re-examine the founding *credo* and, at the York Conference, there were a set of group discussions on specific clauses.

The findings were summarised by Ivor Manley, Vice-chairman and a former senior civil servant, and Stanley Miller, an NEC member and former education advisor and inspector. These were described as 'often heated discussions', but the general view seemed to be that fine tuning rather than wholesale change was required. 'No one wants to throw out the baby with the bath water', reported *U3A News*. Ivor Manley of the Farnborough U3A and Stan Miller of the Hall Green U3A had proved to be wily, wise old owls in their direction of this telling piece of retrospection.

One major conclusion was that 'in spite of difficulties, group sizes and group leadership, the U3A approach to learning was working', but that it was essential to 'promote the notion of shared responsibility for learning' and to insist that 'the greatest resource available to U3A learning is its membership'. 'Experience as a resource' was an arch stone of the U3A building. Although there were genuine concerns about some of the severity of the language of the founding principles and their uncompromising, even austere, tones in respect of funding, research, voluntary endeavour and campaigning, there was an equally strong determination that, in any updating and amendment, there should be no deviation from the central precept of lifelong learning in the self-help mode.

In the late 1980s there had been those who had wondered whether or not U3A might lose its 'pioneer spirit' and become a trifle comatose, even complacent. The radical and deep thought implicit in that kind of debate signifies otherwise; rather that the message of the originating philosophy is gradually taking profound root. Some of that is down to Kate Wedd, with her fervent conviction in those guiding principles, no less her sharp-witted grasp of exactly what they entail. It is said that in 1823 William Webb Ellis, at Rugby School became the accidental creator of rugby football, when he picked up the ball and ran with it. Vivacious Kate Wedd, rather more purposefully, picked up the U3A ball and ran with it, enthusing others were her faith in, hope for and charity about the U3A idea. It was no coincidence that this period marked a point where the public image of the U3A and, by that token, a positive stance on older age, showed up more brightly on the societal radar screen.

It had been an evangelical *tour de force*. Once more the British U3A had been served by the Chairman that, humbly, it needed and, less modestly, deserved. As *U3A News* affectionately reported, 'a much-loved figure at conference, she led the U3A through a successful period in its history, and left the platform to a standing ovation' after a personal and poetic tribute from Lin Jonas, beginning:

So you'll go no more a-roving;
So late into the night;
Never knowing if you're coming
To an accolade or fight.

One of Kate Wedd's last acts was, at the York conference, the bestowal of the title of 'Founder Member Emeritus' on Brian Groombridge, on whose gifts these pages dilated in the opening chapters. His contribution to the enormous and very critical success of the movement in the London region; his unquenchable thirst for proselytising about U3A wherever he finds himself; his highly intelligent understanding of the place of U3A in the context of the history and current condition of adult learning; above all, his largeness of heart meeting with his vastness of mind – these were grounds for his most meritorious award. In receipt of it, he enthralled his audience with a mapping of the five 'milestones' on the road toward making education more democratic, a journey beginning in 1903 with the founding of the Workers Educational Association and continuing with the 1922 establishment of the BBC, the provision of universal secondary education by dint of the 1944 Education Act, the creation of the Open University in 1969 and then, the terminus, perhaps the temporary terminus on the tour, the opening of U3A in 1982.

It was apt that this award was made as part of the 21st birthday celebration of the national U3A, held at the York conference and focused on an exhibition of U3A's history, efficaciously organised by the current Secretary, Glenys Tuersley, and contributed to by Brian Groombridge.

v. Back Home

After such a giddy ride to the exhilarating heights of national U3A philosophy in thought and practice, it is right to return, once more, to the front line of U3A, to the localities, where, every day, small groups of older people gather to demonstrate that philosophy.

Our latest little tour takes us north again to Cheshire. Roy Wilson, who became National Development Co-ordinator in 1995, hailed from the Chester area. He had not long been a 'native' U3A product, although his progressive credentials in adult education circles were well bespoken, and, as the equivalent of a national organiser, he renewed an old acquaintance with Eric Midwinter from the latter's days in Liverpool. Slimly built, tall and extremely competent, this acute-minded, ever-friendly officer brought something of a new look to development, as the forthcoming chapter on regional development will underline. Once more, the U3A nationally was to benefit from the strengths and not suffer from the weaknesses of a senior officer's stance. Where the likes of Harry Muscutt and Audrey Cloet had built on the advantage of their intense U3A upbringing, without allowing themselves to be too much the introverted U3A counterpart of 'little Englanders', Roy Wilson brought a freshness of outlook to the task, seeing the U3A with admiring but new eyes. At the same time, he was soon imbued with the spirit of the organisation, chiefly because it matched the open-mindedness he had always brought to his educational work. His untimely death was a bitter blow and a much-mourned loss to the movement.

It followed that some of the mainsprings of his efforts were close to home, where, in Cheshire, a series of thirteen U3A groups were assembling, in a relatively late but crowded piece of development, beginning with Chester in 1993, through to Neston and Cheadle Hulme in 2002. Indeed, Roy Wilson was the progenitor of the Chester U3A. It was he who, as Carol Ferris, the Chester Business Secretary, explains, contacted the National Office, and met in Chester Cathedral with the other six, all women, on the national address list for the area. Would anyone else be interested? The beautifully presented *The Chester U3A Millennium Document* picks up the tale: 'then we heard the first footfalls on the stairs and soon the room was filled to overflowing . . . 87 enrolled there and then.' Now there are nearly 500 members and 45 interest-groups. The *Millennium Document* calls 'this ongoing success' the 'greatest tribute we can pay to Roy, our first Chairman, remembering his paraphrasing of President Kennedy, 'ask not what U3A can do for you, but what you can do for U3A.'

Congleton was one of Roy Wilson's 'foundlings'. He 'gave lots of invaluable advice and encouragement', when, in 1997, and as something of a complement to the formation of the nearby Alsager group, Congleton, aided with a small grants from the Mayor's charity and materials provided by Lin Jonas, established itself. At the first public meeting in 1998 over a hundred people enrolled and, within five years, there are over 400, with more than 30 activities from which to choose. As for Frodsham, affiliated in 1996 and now with 76 members, this was the child of Millie Wilson, who had previously been the leader of the Kirkham Lifelong Learning group, one of Jim Soulsby's set-up, described in an early chapter. Moving to Frodsham, she once again seized the initiative and organised newspaper advertising, a small committee and a public meeting, as well as getting help from the local council and the U3A regional network.

Roy Wilson was also instrumental in giving good advice to and, with Helen Smith of the Sale U3A, speaking at the first meeting of the Macclesfield Rural U3A. This was in 1997. Lucinda Hodges, of the Langley Teachers' Centre, and Audrey O'Neill had run the U3A hare and they were backed by other local U3As and the national office, as they proceeded to begin with 70 members and seven group leaders – today the figures are 286 and 25 interest-groups, all well advertised in Macclesfield's excellent newsletter. Crewe and Nantwich is the largest of the Cheshire U3As with a remarkable register of 777 and they organise 47 courses. Millie Carter, now the President, was one of those who responded to a letter in the *Chester Chronicle*, and a small group went ahead in 1995, enrolling 52 initially. 'I wonder', writes Sheila Healey, the present Secretary, 'if Millie Carter and her friends realised what an unqualified success story was to follow.' A 'minor panic' in 1996 over accommodation apart, it has been a comparatively smooth ascent to such glory.

Roy Wilson was also busy over on neighbouring Merseyside. There are now eleven U3As in that region, apart from Wirral, all of them post 1993 in affiliation date. Wirral Hundred, for instance, originated as a splinter group from the Wirral U3A who, along with the national office, leant support at this time. Wirral Hundred affiliated with the Third Age Trust in 1997 and now, according to its Secretary, Val Leah, has a hundred plus members and runs fifteen activities.

Diana Selmer writes in about the Bebington U3A, started in 1993 and registered nationally a year later. Pressure of numbers on the existing Wirral U3A, meeting in Birkenhead, was the cause and Eric Barnes, later to join the NEC, was first Chairman. Of its 106 members, 96 belong to at least one study group, a very high proportion indeed, and 'one busy man belongs to nine.' The gardening group have, with 'meticulous planning' organised holidays for the last eight years. 'What', asks Diana rhetorically, 'characterises Bebington U3A?' Unlike jesting Pilate, she stays for an answer: 'the willingness by the majority to get involved', in research, in charity work and the 'fair trade' of catering, groceries and handicrafts. In a climate where some U3As are not alone among voluntary organisations in bemoaning the lack of enthusiasm of ordinary members that is a heart-warming little yarn.

Bromborough, also on the Wirral, was established with the backing of and part funding by Bebbington U3A, when the latter's membership grew precipitately. Ian Norris, its Publicity Secretary, tells how the Bromborough group began with just 38 members in 1998 and now has 192, with more than a score of activities on offer and an attractive 'welcome pack' for new members. Ian Norris argues that there is room for twelve U3As on the Wirral Peninsula, although he very sanely points out some of the pitfalls of organising U3As in the area. There are in fact, five U3As on the Wirral. In turn, Bromborough was responsible for the launch of the Neston U3A, affiliated in 2002. It has a hundred members, but, such are the infelicities of local authority divisions, it appears to fall into Cheshire.

In the old Lancashire area of Merseyside lies the Huyton U3A, which began, as Alison Williams relates, in 1997 and has built up slowly to 64 members with six or seven groups. Elsewhere north of the Mersey are groups such as Formby U3A, with close on 700 members, and Liverpool itself with 375 members, two of the seven U3As on that side of the famous river.

The U3A journey now zooms from north-west to south-east, to Kent, a well-harvested field for U3A, where there are twelve U3A groups, all of them more than a hundred strong and three of them around or above the 600 mark. Orpington U3A, with its 660 members and over 50 study groups, is one of that enterprising trio. Its Secretary, Ron Holmes, records how it was founded in 1988, another feather in the Bromley U3A cap, for its officers gave 'considerable help' in the formation of what has proved an encouragingly rapid and productive growth.

Magda Sweetland is our correspondent from another of Kent's big hitters, the Sevenoaks U3A, where she is President. She heard of U3A on holiday in Italy, when a fellow holiday-maker told of her membership of East Grinstead and how 'a local farmer had given a disused barn to the town's U3A and several groups, working together, had managed to turn it into a community theatre.' Magda Sweetland continues, 'that was a *Eureka*! moment for me. I realised this was a doing organisation and one where the expertise of retired people, co-operating positively, could be harnessed and utilised for the benefit of the whole community.' With an enthusiastic friend, a newspaper advertisement, financial help from the town council and the national office and local U3A support, she recruited a steering committee and a set of study group leaders, 'and I have never looked back.' 200 attended the launch meeting, a hundred joined immediately, 'which was an act of faith on their part' but 'the winning element was that so many had heard of the magnetic appeal of U3A from friends in other parts of the country.' Sevenoaks, with 86 interest-groups, touches on a membership now of 600.

Thanet U3A was only formed in 2002 but it already has 130 members and, says Secretary Gwenyth Kay, 'we have become an exciting and thriving group'. She says this against the background of a struggle to win through, after it had been decided that Thanet should operate separately from the Canterbury & District U3A, of 1986 vintage. The Thanet experience, both the battle and the winning of the battle, is not unlike that of many other U3As, a tacit reminder that all does not go swimmingly all of the time.

As a coda, it is worth mentioning that, although there are two or three famous drop-outs from the U3A homestead, there are several others that, for various reasons, have left the fold or folded up. Apart from the nine disaffiliates before and at the time of the great constitutional crisis of 1989, there have been another 23, making 32 all told, since then, including three in the year 2003. It is perhaps rather more than, off-hand, one might have guessed. Some of them just faded away; some of them are Lancashire-based Life Long Learning groups; some were involved with the reconstruction of the West Midlands U3As; some just did not want to belong to the greater community of U3As. In all cases, it is a salutary reminder that vigilance is the only safeguard and that no group may be sustained without constant refreshment of members and officers and thoughtful planning ahead.

That is the last of these *tours d'horizon*, although we might have paid a visit to the sunny strands of Spain, where there are three U3As affiliated to the British U3A. The itinerary of local U3As has touched almost every region of the British Isles, all in the knowledge that, without those local cameos of parochial initiative and energy, there would be no U3A, all in the hope that the distinctly domestic flavours will, for the reader, offer an additional taste to the rich savours of the national dish. One running thread has been, as the Cheshire and Kent visitations illustrate, the manner in which local U3As, for a mix of reasons, have worked hard to create more and more U3As. If one were to choose a biblical text as a memorial for U3A local history, it might well be one of those verses from the fourth chapter of Genesis, such as 'and Seth lived a hundred and five years and begat Enos.'

U3As are good at begetting.

Ten: The Regional Question

The bipartite construction of the British U3A movement, matching national oversight with bustling localism, has given this study a two-dimensional form, with the honest attempt made to balance the two elements as judiciously as possible. Adding a third component to the literary edifice would have been a precarious risk. It was judged better to pause at this stage and devote a chapter to that component, namely, the question of regional organisation.

i. The Argument

At the risk of some simplification, the long-running controversy – and that is not too fiery a word in the circumstances – about whether or not there was a regional role in the U3A structure boiled down to a contest between decentralisation and devolution. This pair of political science concepts are easily confused. The former is more about the determination of decision-making at a community level, close to what used to be known as a 'know everyone' system. The latter is more about the granting of special powers to a larger segment of whatever the central territory is. For example, there is a difference between the inhabitants of Rhyl running their own affairs in decentralised mode and being governed, in part, from Cardiff rather than London. This is not judgemental, for the *nuances* of advantage and disadvantage in these varied layers of governance is complex and changing.

Transferring that organisational dichotomy to U3A matters, there has been throughout its history, some debate as to whether regionalism should be left to the decentralised U3A groups to develop informally, as, when and how they felt, or whether, in a more devolutionary style, regionalism should be more formally imposed from the national headquarters, in the sane interest of retaining a coherent formation. It was, at base, a 'bottom up' *versus* 'top down' argument.

One has to recall that the rapid growth of U3As surprised the early managers in the same way that the spread of the motor car caught Edwardian England, complacent in its belief in the perfectabilty of the railway train, off guard. At the beginning, one was only too grateful that a national regime had been put in place – and those early crises about its financial support and constitutional propriety that led to the mourned loss of some U3As should remind that it was quite arduous to establish a national, let alone a regional tier. Moreover, at the onset, there were scarcely enough U3As to justify a national conference, never mind a regional structure. Robb Wilton, that lugubrious home guardsman, asked by his sceptical wife, Rita, whether he was the only one defending British shores from Nazi invasion, replied, 'No, of course not, there's Charlie Evans and one or two others.' In the first couple of years the U3A mustered something like that kind of martial complement. Often a U3A was its region's sole representative.

Even by 1995, when there were 266 U3A groups, only a hundred or so were engaged in the 17 loosely formed regional networks that had perforce emerged. In many regions the incidence of U3As was still too patchy to make administrative sense. At the same time, the counter-argument lay in that very factor. Were there a more formal regional structure, it was urged, then quicker progress might be made in poorly serviced areas. Conversely, with nascent U3As struggling to reach stability, there was often a feeling that there was neither time nor energy for their leaders to be adding regional duties. Nor resources . . . there was always the fear that subscriptions would be levied to aid regional action. Many felt that, in a relatively compact nation-state, there was no formal necessity for a third bureaucratic tier for what was still a relatively small national institution.

Yet, for all those dreads, there was considerable regional activity. If the foregoing records of local development have proved anything, it is that U3As have been remarkably keen to assist other new U3As locally. Of the 187 surveyed U3As, no less than 83 specifically refer to receiving often indispensable help from neighbouring U3As, a wonderful tribute to the co-operative mood and principle. Sometimes the motives had a colouration of self-interest, where, for example, a U3A, believing itself to be in danger of overcrowding, hit upon the solution of starting another U3A. However, that is, of course, a thousand times better than shutting the doors and doing nothing.

As we have observed on our armchair travels up and around the country, the U3A group as engine for more U3A groups has been a premier factor in the prevalence of many U3As in some neighbourhoods and, in converse, their insufficiency in others – an argument, in turn, for some form of regional arm to accomplish the missionary work in just such districts.

It followed that where U3As were in close contact and were, in fact, related by parenthood, there would be togetherness. Networks naturally began to flourish. This was commented on in earlier chapters, with Devon, Cornwall, Lancashire, the West Midlands, Oxfordshire and one or two other areas having their own varying take on this subject. There were one-day joint seminars or conferences and exchanges of information and other signs of mutual help. In 1986, for example, there was, as previously noticed, both the first Northern Conference and the first Preston get-together of the Lancashire groups, while, more formally, the Sussex Region association, first of the now characteristic 'networks', began in the same year. Soon there were others, although it is correct to point out that one or two were formed and then collapsed.

So the history of regional activity is not much shorter than the saga as a whole. Hilary Greenwood, a Chairman of the NEC Development Sub-committee and Chairman of the Hillingdon

U3A, is a sapient and articulate correspondent on this issue. 'It is curious', she writes, 'that this development, which goes back many years . . . has never been formally recognised as is the case with many other major charities.' The working party on U3A structure reported positively to the Warwick conference in 1998 on this as on other subjects and proposals to initiate a regional construct, with appropriate tiers of management and a much enlarged NEC, were agreed in principle by a large majority, but never transmuted into day-by-day practice.

The excellent Swansea U3A *Story*, published in 2002 and already cited in descriptions of the Welsh U3As, captured the mood of the regional row in a passage sub-headed 'Regionalisation – or Not?' ' . . . during the last four or five years, up to the turn of the century, much time was increasingly taken up by the politics of reorganisation of U3A nationally. A minority of U3As were pressing for a more formal multi-tiered organisation, at a time when public and private industry recognised that such pyramid structures were out of date and were changing to flatter and leaner organisations . . . Apart from increased cost and longer lines of communication, it was felt that U3A would lose its character of informality, helpfulness and friendliness and the structure would be cumbersome and unmanageable . . . Gradually, it became clear that many of the local U3As were prepared to drop out of the national organisation if the proposals were agreed . . . a large majority of local groups wanted to retain the flatter informal structure . . .'

The York conference of 2003 also discussed the regional question. The same old ground was ploughed over in what *U3A News* described as 'one of the fiercest debates' of the meeting. Although there are 'Areas', for the purpose of electing members to the NEC and thereby ensuring some fair degree of cross-representation, the Third Age Trust lends support to regional activity at an operational level, believing them to serve a useful purpose in promoting co-operation among U3As. It had been at the London conference in 1999 that this compromise area/regional structure had been accepted and it is worth a pause to clarify the distinction.

Initially nine – it is now thirteen - 'Areas' were designated, based on traditional national and county boundaries. U3As within each Area are asked to nominate someone for election to the NEC, in order to ensure that representation thereon has a broad geographic foundation. Such NEC members are expected to form a linkage between the 'Regions' within their 'Area' and generally act as a constitutional conduit for the Area in question. It is impressed upon these representatives that they are 'from' rather than 'for' an Area and the elections take place at the AGM. Thus some strengthening of the democratic base is assured without the undue strain of introducing another bureaucratic tier. In a nutshell, the 'Regions' are about decentralisation and the 'Areas' are about devolution. These areas comprise Scotland, Wales and Northern Ireland, North West, North East, Mercia, East Midlands, Eastern Area, Thames Valley, London, South West, Wessex and South East.

That said, it is still difficult to halt the ongoing and well-matched argument, as rehearsed at York in 2003. 'Regions have a culture and areas don't', argued Doris Dobson of Durham U3A, while opponents of the motion to formalise the regional structure and link it politically with the NEC claimed it was impracticable and that the current arrangements worked well enough. The motion was narrowly lost.

One suspects that the argument will return to the rostrum of future conferences. It is certainly true that the catalyst for regional growth has been educational rather than political, in so far as it has been about starting new and refreshing old U3As, rather than looking at the constitutional and administrative implications. When Roy Wilson was responsible for development in the 1990s, he very swiftly spotted the regional element as the grand key and acted accordingly. Under Norman Richards' aegis, a couple of workshops had been held for leaders of rising regional networks, chiefly in terms of establishing contacts and encouraging the start of new U3As. Then Roy Wilson pioneered the idea of forming small support teams in the regions to tap into groupings and help form and sustain U3As.

He recognised that, by this stage, the task had outgrown the compass of a national officer and required something like the equivalent of an Audrey Cloet or a Roy Wilson in almost every area. The regional network was the self-mobilising analogue of this. Since his much-mourned death in February 1999, another dedicated National Development Officer, Mike Long, also with solid experience of the adult education service, has devotedly taken up the cudgels. Five annual meeting were convened of regional representatives, two in London and three in different parts of the country.

In cursory summary, therefore, the 'bottom up', decentralising proclivity has been highly fruitful, whereas the 'top down' devolutionary trend has been postponed, apart from the constitutional deployment of the 'area' precept. It is a Regional system that has the advantages of the one – all groupings are, more or less, borne forward on the groundswell of underlying popular support, without the advantages of the other – the coherence of a fully structured overlay for operational purposes. Of the 522 U3As affiliated in mid-2003, 438 or 84% U3As were in one of the regional groupings, a triumph for popularism, whereas, self-evidently, 84 or 16% were not, to the despair of centralism.

ii. The Regional Mesh

The easiest way of purveying the all-round nature of this regional evolution is by listing the groupings, as of July 2003, together with the number of U3As in particular membership; thus:

Central Southern with 14; Cotswold Link with 10; Cumbria with 10; Dorset with 9; East Midlands Area Association of U3As with 33; East Hampshire with 7; Essex with 12; Hertfordshire with 14; Kent with 8; Lancashire Central with 9; the Greater London Forum with 22; Greater Manchester with 10; Merseyside & West Cheshire 15; Norfolk with 7; North Bucks, Bedfordshire and Northants with 8; Northumbria with 21; Ridings Region with 20; Shropshire with 7; Somerset, Bath, Bristol & Mid-Wiltshire with 24, but sub-divided into three sets; South Staffordshire Link with

4; South West Peninsula with 25; Suffolk with 10; Surrey Central with 12; Surrey Link with 6; Sussex with 23; Thames Valley with 24; West Midlands Liaison Link with 18; West Surrey with 5; North Wales with 4; South Wales and Severnside Network (West) with 7; South Wales and Severnside Network (East) with 16; plus Development Contacts with Scotland with 13, and Northern Ireland with 7.

There are, then 33 groupings, double the number in 1995, and bidding fair to cover the entire nation. Predictably enough, given that spontaneity has been the watchword, they vary wildly in number of groups and size and type of area represented. Perhaps more significantly, they vary in character, from the very active and well-formulated complex to the arrangement that is only occasionally and peripherally in motion. Again, the argument is evenly contested. As with the development of U3A groups initially, until a number had experimented and survived, one did not know what formulae would be successful. Indeed, philosophically, one might press the point that the non-formal regional evolution was U3A group self-help writ larger. Doubters could, on the other hand, claim, with some conviction, that, now that the secrets of wholesome regional life are revealed, it seems perverse not to spread such good practices to all regions and all U3As. It is fair to state that, although 84% of U3As are in some form of regional link-up, some of this is limited and threadbare in character.

iii. The Networks in Practice

As with the local U3A groups, activists have been generous in the provision of information about the work of the regional groupings. Most of the Regional Groups have appointed a 'Regional Contact' and the NEC's Development Committee has regular meetings with these contacts, further helping with inter-regional and other matters. It is proposed to offer some examples of the workings of these regional activities.

The Greater London Regional Forum (GLRF), as Hilary Greenwood reports, was established in 1994. Possibly the smaller London U3As had hitherto regarded their prosperous neighbour with some awe, but, in any

event, there had been few connections among the metropolitan U3As. The London U3A called a meeting of the other London based groups, chaired by Marjorie Ogilvy-Webb. The subject of shared activities was discussed but, admittedly, another topic was anxiety about the relationship with the national body. London U3A had been one of those soured by the decision to hand over to Saga the production of the U3A newspaper and, in general, felt that national consultation was disappointing. London U3A, whose unifying stance in the face of the reversals of 1986 had been so supportive, was disconcerted, even to the point of wondering whether, given its size and professional management, it should leave the national association.

Hilary Greenwood was active, as both co-optee on the NEC Development Sub-committee and member of the U3AL committee, acting as go-between, persuading the London membership they had much to offer the U3A union and persuading the national committee that regional contacts, as well as being vital to joint action in the districts, might be helpful in terms of improved communication. In 1995, for example, U3AL hosted a meeting, organised by Roy Wilson and John Lloyd, then Chairman of the NEC Development Committee, and chaired by Chairman Alan Willey, to promote the idea of regional contacts and thereby assist Roy Wilson's ambitious plans for growth. Hilary Greenwood is of the view that the move of the national office to central London, the appointment of a National Administrator, Lin Jonas, and the supply of materials available, particularly through the Resource Centre, considerably improved local, regional and national liaison and mutual respect, a fine tribute to the value of highly practical engagement.

Peter Sinclair, mastermind of the Harrow U3A, became Chairman of the GLRF, and sought help from the constitution of the New Zealand U3A regional bodies and, later, Hilary Greenwood was able to circulate a model constitution to all regional networks, just as, for many years, it had been the practice to send all new U3A groups a constitutional template. The GLRF has its own website; it holds three or four meetings a year and elects its own officers. Its activities, apart from the basic sharing of ideas, have included concerts and workshops, organised by Marion Bieber, including, by way of attractive sample, a study day on Beethoven Sonatas at the British Museum, while, in 2003, the first one day conference was held at Brunel University, with the help, among others, of Heinz Wolff.

Special commendatory note must be made of the expansion schemes attempted by GLRF in districts of multi-ethnic constituency, such as Haringey, Hillingdon and Wandsworth, together with an experimental project of similar kind in Hayes, one of two funded nationally by the DfES to engage in cross-cultural studies and promote social cohesion.

Further west, in the Thames Valley, there are now 28 U3As associated, from Banbury to Bracknell, north to south, and Swindon to Rickmansworth, west to east. Don Rankin, its Learning Support Group Network representative and a member of the High Wycombe and District U3A explains that the Thames Valley Region annual conference 'will remain an informal friendly gathering for U3A members to exchange information and experiences'. Apart from an important Chairman's meeting prior to the national AGM, to deal with matters concerned with national U3A affairs, this is the nuclear event. Interestingly, there is a 'troika' arrangement. The onus for planning rests on each U3A in turn, but the present U3A is supported by the immediate past and immediate future U3A in the interests of continuity. For instance the High Wycombe conference fielded an impressive team of speakers and presenters, among them Ivor Manley, Keith Richards, Jean Thompson, Elizabeth Gibson, Tom Holloway and other luminaries.

Up in the north east the Northumbria Region network offers another slant on such associationism, as Margaret Minns, the Northumbria Regional Contact and a member of Whickham and District U3A describes. It all began in 1994 when Alan Willey and John Lloyd, those famed notables from the U3A national arena, held a meeting in Durham and six U3As bound themselves together in the interests of common encouragement and support. Four more joined in 1995 and now the numbers have sprung to 24, comprising all the U3As in the region. There is now a simple constitution, a £12 levy on each group in membership and a newsletter.

Regional meetings are 'a swap shop of ideas, information, successes and failures', while joint activities include a bird watching group, 'Quiz Challenge!', joint outings, a constantly revised regional speakers' list, a regional travel group and the upkeep of a regional website, for which Sunderland University laid on a design course for regional members. There have already been seven one day and one two day learning events, generously made available to all UK members, as well as a couple of well-attended group leaders' workshops. The Northumbria Region actively helps to develop new U3As, assisted by a local fund specifically set up for the education of older people. By these means, new U3As are allowed free membership for a year and are given a start-up grant of £50 in addition to any Third Age Trust award.

John Craddock has forwarded details of the Association of East Midlands U3As (EMU3As). On a suggestion of John Knight of the Peterborough U3A, Ray Hirst of Boston U3A organised a meeting of East Midlands Chairmen, with a view to setting up an association that has met initially three times and latterly four times a year. In 2000 a constitution was adopted, with elected officers, and funding has been placed on a stable basis. The first thoughts were to 'form 'twinning' between towns and develop visits, friendships, outings for members and a general intermingling in an effort to boost membership and encourage the opening of new U3As throughout the region'. Inter-U3A meetings, boosting confidence and exchanging experiences, and one day summer schools were followed by three day residential summer schools, for example at Lincoln in 2002 and Stamford in 2003.

As awareness and assurance grew, there was some involvement in business matters, especially in terms of smaller U3As, some of whom, for instance, found it difficult to fund a representative to attend the national conference. In 2001 it was decided to adopt a pro-active approach to the formation of new U3As. This was (as was described in an earlier chapter) especially telling in Lincolnshire, resulting in six new U3As, together with one in Nottinghamshire. Since 1994 group membership has risen from twelve to 38.

The regional agenda is all-embracing. It comprehends the formation of new U3As and the encouragement of co-operation among U3As, along with the organisation of regional events and the discussion of national policy matters. EMU3As is one of the largest of the regional networks and it certainly generates plenty of action.

Forgive the *cliché*, but, as with the national row over regional devolution, the debate continues.

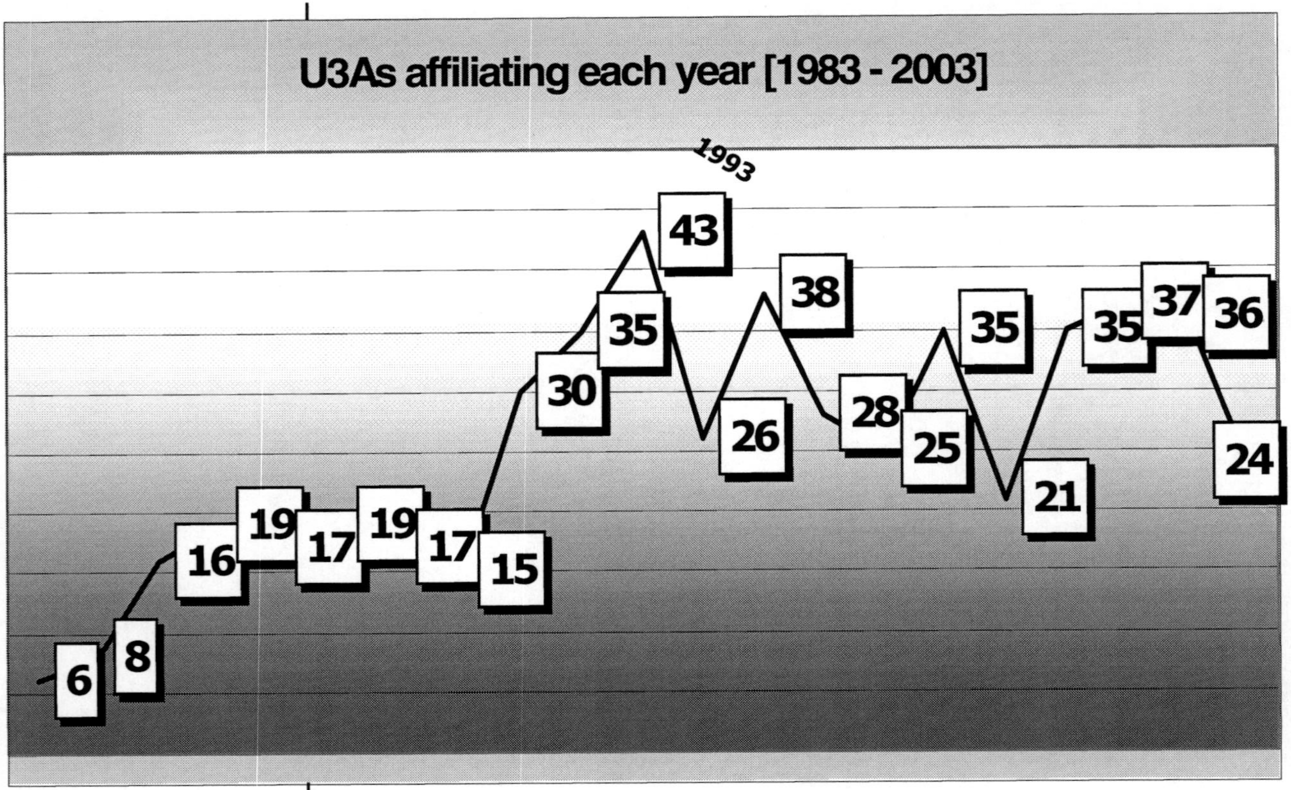
U3As affiliating each year [1983 - 2003]
1993
6
8
16
19
17
19
17
15
30
35
43
26
38
28
25
35
21
35
37
36
24

Eleven: Today

June 2004. There are 539 U3As in the UK and there are, in total, 141,301 members, and still counting. In 2002 Four Border Abbeys U3A, (Kelso) was recognised as the 500th. Cowton and Countryside U3A, near Northallerton, was the 539th U3A to sign on the dotted affiliation line. The groups stretch from Land's End U3A (Penzance), in the far south west to Inverness and Black Isle U3A miles away in the north east, with Limassol, Cyprus U3A slightly further south and east. The current rate of progress is three or four new U3As a month. The national office deals with about 50 inquiries a day, post, mail, fax and e-mail, while, should there be a major piece of national publicity, inquiries might rise to 500 over three days. This is now an effective and prospering enterprise. The Third Age Trust has an annual turnover of £500,000.

i. Grand National '04

The U3A in the UK retains its simple but heroic criteria for affiliation. U3As must proffer a broadly educational programme for those in the Third Age and have a democratic structure, with a model constitution and a format for charitable status available from the national headquarters. Let us not pass lightly over the momentous nature of that twofold rule. Engaging older people both in educational and democratic activity takes a swipe at several taboos: education is supposed to be exclusively for younger people; older people are not self-reliant; and education cannot be run on the base of popular democracy.

It is a good moment to run the rule over the key people and the decisive instruments of this successful organisation.

- the Chairman

Keith Richards, of the North London U3A, is now at the helm as U3A National Chairman. U3A could not ask for a wiser pilot. Once again U3A's feel-good fairy has waved her magic wand and contrived yet another 'right time; right place' spell. Bearded, prepossessing and with a self-deprecating line in diffident good humour, Keith Richards is an experienced educationalist. It is a lengthy experience, beginning with his national service in the Royal Army Education Corps, followed by teaching in north London schools, before lecturing posts at the Sidney Webb College of Education and the Polytechnic of Central London, later the University of Westminster, where he was Head of Continuing Education.

There are teachers and teachers. It has been said that teachers may be divided into 'distenders' and 'extenders', those that close students down and those that open them up. Keith Richards is one of the 'extenders'. He met Peter Laslett in 1994 and inhaled the giddy fumes of lifelong learning for older people. He was completely captivated by the U3A notion and has been on the NEC since 1998, becoming Vice-chairman in 2001. His key concern is the nature of the U3A learning process: 'we are', he exultantly claims', 'the real standard-bearers of lifelong learning . . . we're not about passive learning . . . in the U3A the learner is also the teacher. Every member has the potential to share learning with others. We get people leading groups who say: I never thought I'd be a teacher, but I'm doing it and I'm loving it'.

That knowledgeable grasp of and sympathetic acceptance of the special educational thrust of the British U3A has rarely been so articulated as it is by Keith Richards. It is timely. There has been resourceful development on the geographical, social, constitutional, financial, professional and business fronts. The U3A is both thriving and stable. The moment for educational development is at purposeful hand. Here again there is much upon which to build and one would expect, over the next years, to see some intensification of the discussion of the individual U3A member as the learner-teacher.

By heartening coincidence, or possibly prescient planning, the 2003 Third Age lecture at the York conference was given by David James, that long-term friend and expert adviser of U3A, on the germane subject of learning in later life. Ian Searle, a very active member of the LSG, supplied the précis from which these phrases are chosen. David James compared learning with eating, defining it as what happens 'when our experience changes our behaviour in some way' and arguing that 'if we stop learning we die'. He stressed the need for balance in life and how a derangement of the 'life strands' may cause distress, citing the extraordinary examples of Retirement and Bereavement Death Syndrome as being comparable to cot death. Learning in later life, David James claimed, was one way of redressing such imbalance.

Turning to the actual conduct of such learning, he spoke of how a range of motives, in terms of the fulfilment of various needs, might be met in group learning. 'Reinforcement learning' might, for example, bring some sense of security and esteem, while its complementary partner, 'extension learning' might satisfy one's curiosity and help realise unknown potentialities. In this respect, later life learning might have the value of being self-directed, as opposed (like much learning in early life) 'externally controlled', and it is the task of the U3A learning circle to offer, regulate, support and monitor that opportunity.

David James' counsel was timely, in that it gives an updated and upbeat espousal of and reassurance about the psychological rationale of the U3A movement and experience.

- the Development

A major element in the current business of developing the U3A concept and practice has been provided by an important DfES project, costed in varied parts at a total of over £50,000, and already mentioned briefly in passing. It began in 1999 and is now complete.

One of the chief components was the development of new U3As on 'greenfield' sites, what old stagers will recognise as 'cold starts', and as 'satellites' of a 'parent' U3A, with an extra experiment, already noted, in terms of multicultural development. The initial results were extremely impressive, far surpassing the original targets, with fourteen 'greenfield' and no less than 53 'satellite' U3As formed between May 1999 and March 2001, the activities of some of which have been reported in these pages.

Another element has been the provision of training for study group leaders and, in the same period, an amazing series of 25 'support' days were organised around the country. Some of these were subject-oriented but others were for new group leaders, groups co-ordinators and so on. All of this was immensely gratifying, in respect of quantity of activity and quality of practice. A detailed mapping survey of the membership was the third aspect of this invigorating project, and some of the results have been included below in the examination of the current U3A membership. Happily, a further project – on 'U3A learning methodologies' – has now been funded by the DfEE.

It is difficult to overestimate the value of these pieces of action research. It will be of incalculable value to the future organisation of the U3A in the UK and it again serves to underpin the prestige of U3A, as a body properly fitted to undertake such a close self-examination.

- the National Office

This educational success is only made possible by organisational success at the top.

A strong team of a score or more form the NEC, with ten offshoots, like the Standing Committee for Education, the Development Sub-committee, the Learning Support Group and the Finance Sub-committee, to help guide the now colossal business and professional work of the organisation. Bruce Cannon acts as the press, media and public relations officer and he has produced a simple but interesting Media Pack, including useful information about the U3A movement and often intriguing details about the background of its leaders. Chief among them now, as of 2004 and apart from Keith Richards in the chair, are the two Vice-chairmen, Ivor Manley and Rosemary McCulloch of the Deepings U3A, together with the Secretary, Glenys Tuersley of Harrow U3A and the Treasurer, Jean Goodeve of the Pembrokeshire U3A.

Of the professional staff, we have already encountered Lin Jonas and Elizabeth Gibson. There are six others, pride of place going to Lin Jonas' assistant, Sharon Ahtuam, who, being in the twelfth year of her diligent and unstinting service, is to be congratulated for such long devotion to the charity. Phillipa Bassett, interestingly, was a volunteer helper in the Stockwell days; she was and is an art group leader with the Croydon U3A and is now an invaluable member of the National Office team. Tim Harris, also ex-Stockwell, is the book-keeper, while Sue Redford, Grace Letley and Georgette Brown make up the complement that, in the main office and the Resource Centre, ensure that things go swimmingly.

This dedicated band are housed in a reasonably comfortable accommodation in the Old Municipal Buildings, Bromley, above an estate agents and with a branch of Sainsbury's within striking distance. With the Resource Centre also safely housed there, it forms an appropriate hub of efficient organisation for the U3A movement.

Lin Jonas sums up their task in a couple of words: 'starting' and 'supporting', that is, helping new U3As to take on active life and then ensuring the support mechanisms are in evidence thereafter. Despite towering costs, the Third Age Trust has managed to keep in place the comprehensive liability insurance cover that is such a boon to all U3As and, generally, the national office exists to advise and assist, its telephonic helpline always busy and its raft of leaflets and other materials forever ready to be forwarded across the nation. All the time the standing of the organisation continues to rise, its image burnished by the improved and more professional approaches and equipment that is available. The national U3A is very much now a player in the serious game of national education.

Communication is the archstone of the Lin Jonas managerial edifice. Hers is a service industry and her ambition is to guarantee that every U3A knows full well what this entails. Lin Jonas is eager to be on personal terms with as many U3As as possible, hence her determination, whilst running a hectic office, to try to make some two or three trips a month to local U3A groups. Only one aspect seems to disturb the even tenor of her moderate temperament and that is local U3A committees that do not pass on to their members the relevant information contained in the regular mailings from the National Office because they decide the members will not be interested. 'If individual U3A members are not' she explained, 'inclined to take advantage of the services provided and events organised by the Third Age Trust, that's fine and it's totally up to them but I am resolved to do all I can to ensure it is their choice'. Her visits to local U3As usually take the form of outlining the services that are available and she does frequently find there are misunderstandings about what the national office does. A much-repeated comment, so she finds, is 'how do you do all that on £2.50 a member?', a somewhat more realistic question than the one that echoes down the U3A ages and may still, regretfully, be overheard today, that is, 'what do we get for our £2.50?'

- the Subject Networks

The national strands that now weave across the nation create a veritable warp and weft effect. The Subject Networks are a highly practical example of this. The National Co-ordinator is Christine Dickson, who also manages the Genealogy Network, although in the autumn of 2004 she will be replaced by Daphne Sirett. Amazingly, there were by now 39 Networks, 39 steps, so to say, to stalwart group support on a nationwide basis.

Some of these cover popular subjects offered by most U3As of moderate size, such as art, bridge, creative writing, drama, environmental studies, European studies, history, oral history, languages, literature, music, photography, IT awareness, philosophy, sci-tech, sport, textile crafts, travel, walking and world religions. But they also include themes such as antiques/collectables, archaeology, architecture, bird watching, calligraphy, cinema, English folk dance, finance, genealogy, geology, health/well-being, Internetwork, jazz appreciation, law and government, psychology. To complete a mouth-watering list, there are inland waterways and story telling.

- the Development Officer

Mike Long has been Development Officer since 1999. Like several of his predecessors, his joint experience was as teacher in further education – for over 20 years, with a preference for mature students seizing a 'second chance' – and, having taken early retirement, as a U3A *alumnus*. Looking for shared learning in a relaxed setting, he joined the Tamworth U3A and quickly became its Secretary. In 1999 he was appointed to his national post, to which this optimistic and intelligently committed officer has brought his strong belief in lifelong learning and his innate capacity for organisation.

Just after his appointment, Lin Jonas had what Mike Long describes as 'the inspired idea' of packing him off to York for U3A's first-ever Summer School. He joined the literature group and met fellow U3A members enjoying shared study in convivial environs. Like his colleagues, he met and felt comfortable with U3A's leading lights and admired the presentational styles of Keith Richards, Shirley Thew of the Basildon and Billiericay U3A and others. 'I knew immediately and almost instinctively', he writes, 'that I belonged, that I found myself in harmony with my appointed role, so that the work has been a pleasure to me, more like an extended hobby than a job'.

A telling lesson for Mike Long on that occasion was the classic relationship of 'development' and 'education' and he has since practised the art of attempting both to organise new U3As or regional networks and raise the actual learning processes of U3As. And it was at Sleaford where he opened his innings, speaking for the first time in aid of the launch of a new U3A. 'Thank you, Sleaford, for giving me a good start', is his grateful blessing.

Working, then, with the Development Sub-committee and with the Standing Committee for Education in close attention, Mike Long has followed in the footsteps of his admired predecessor, Roy Wilson, in pressing for wider and deeper regional engagement with development. Over the last months, other groupings, among them East Cheshire and North Staffordshire, have been added to the list, while existing groupings have intensified their activities. Since his appointment, Mike Long has visited each region at least once. With the support of some DfES funding, specific areas where U3A's showing was sparse have been targeted. Particularly gratifying has been the successful establishment of U3As where previous efforts had failed – Lymington, Weymouth, for instance – or where it was said to be impossible because of the town's rival attractions – for example, Evesham, where a hundred people turned out for the exploratory meeting.

- the Editor

The longest-lived artefact in U3A lore is the newspaper, as old, in slightly differing forms, as the U3A in the UK itself. It now has the good fortune to be edited by Francis Beckett, a progressive educational journalist of national distinction. He is certainly right to believe that he has made the *U3A News* look more like a magazine, one that anyone might leaf through because of its general interest, and less like a newsletter, something that perhaps 'you'd only pick up if you were your local U3A secretary and you wanted to find out if the editor had used that picture of your bridge group you sent him two months ago.'

Like all those involved in the management of one or another elements of the increasingly full and complex world of U3A, Francis Beckett is ambitious. He recognises that there is a legitimate function of reporting on U3A events and debates, but is hopeful of persuading those in authority that these do not have to be pursued so exhaustively and, indeed, enjoy more impact if presented more snappily. He pins other hopes on improved advertising revenue, offering the possible chance of more pages or, the better option, more frequency. For Francis Beckett perceives that *U3A News* may have a mightier future role, as 'the magazine of Third Age learning', containing, 'news and features of interest to the sort of people who are, or may be, interested in Third Age learning', covering issues concerning relevant educational, political and social themes.

Heraclitus said that 'man steps but once in the same river'. The history of the U3A is replete with the actions of men and women who understood that nothing stays the same or, worse, if it does, it tends to stagnate. However, the Father of History must, at the last in this section, yield to the Queen of Communication, Lin Jonas. She amused a recent conference with her versified burlesque of the reluctant recipient of her evermore desperate attempts to make sure everyone knows what is going on:

DOT MATRIX HAS HER SAY

'ad 'em?
'ave I 'ad 'em?
every day in every way
since I joined the U3A,
reams of paper come my way.
excuse me, madam,
of course I've 'ad 'em!
Communications?
Abominations!
I get loads,
I get lots
at a flamin' rate of knots
I've even sealed my letter box,
to no avail,
your Third Age mail
keeps on coming through my door,
from some National Office bore,
who wants a bonus -
name of Jonas:
circulations,
abbreviations,
DSC and NEC
TAT and SCE
what do they mean?
are they obscene?
I've tried to type them in
on my Enigma machine
to crack their code –
it did no good.

I'm still confused,
I'm not amused;
in fact, I'm getting more than vexed
about your endless stream of text.
I don't need it;
I never read it;
I just throws it away,
so I'm glad you rang today;
I can finally have my say
- be sure you heed it,
I won't repeat it –
stuff your leaflets and your letters
to your olders and your betters;
stuff your facts and stuff your fiction;
stuff your Postman Pat addiction;
stuff your hand-outs and your flyers;
stuff your words that cross my wires;
stuff your information tech;
stuff the National Exec . . .
Get off the phone!
LEAVE ME ALONE!

ii. Down at the Local – the U3A Groups

We rapidly shift from that scene of poesy, of which Robert Browning might have been proud, to the healing calm of a final and wholesale look at the member U3A groups. The local picture provided here is a *pastiche* of the 187 local groups who corresponded with the author with details of their activities. For a number of logistical reasons, 181 of these are included in the statistical analysis. This represents some 35%, roughly a third of the U3As nationwide, an extremely large sample in terms of social policy analysis. Moreover, those 181 groups represent 63,000 members, 49%, just on a half of the national membership, an even more potent sample. The gross figures are those of June 2003, that is 522 groups and 130,500.

In terms of the timeline, they cover the entire gamut of U3A history, from Yeovil, starting in 1982 to Monks Brook, beginning in 2003. The fractions by date of affiliation are: 1982/89; 48 (47% of all those registered in that phase); 1989/94; 63 (42%); 1994/98; 45 (36%) and 1998/2003; 25 (17%). The slight imbalance, 'old' to 'young', from the norm of 35% has an obvious explanation. The older U3As have more of an history to relate, while the younger breed are still getting going and making their history.

The range in size, from Sheffield's teeming 2000 to Crossmaglen's newly-born 20 is not too different from the national range. Of the 181 in the survey, 22 or 12% have less than 100 members (compared with 25% of the national U3As as a whole); 57 or 32% have 100 to 250 (45.5%); 71 or 39% have 250-500 (24%); 17 or 9% have 500-750 (7%) and 14 or 8% have 750 and over (3.5%).

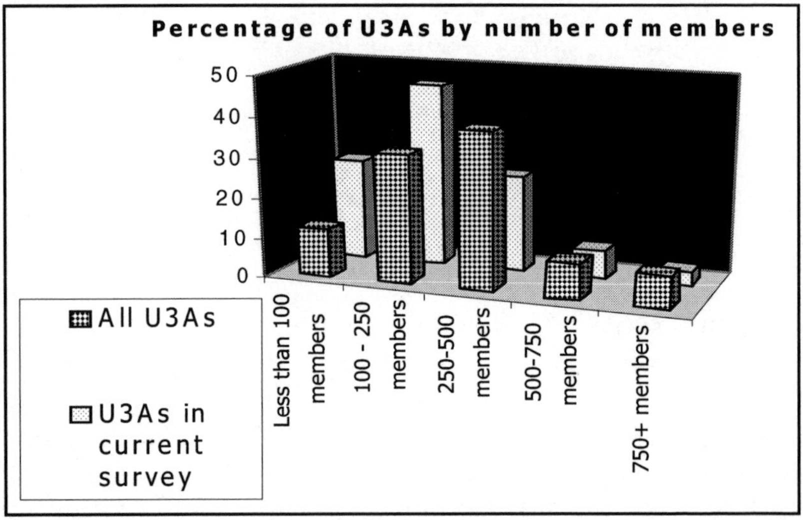

In overall terms, the average size of the British local U3A is about 250. However, the largest eighteen U3As, with 20,500 members among them, do raise that mean radically. If one withdraws that total from the calculation, then the average is nearer 218. The total membership of the U3As surveyed is some 63,000, an average of approximately 350 a group. This is higher than the national average, but, once more, the explanation is fairly self-evident, in that many newer groups, who were less likely, understandably, to have responded, are only just beginning to recruit members.

One of the interesting figures relates to the interest-groups and other activities mounted by the U3As. It has been possible to compute the number of these in the 181 U3As, indeed, that was one of the indices for inclusion in the mathematical part of the scrutiny. It is not the easiest of figures to calculate, as there is no exactly consistent definition (nor should there be) of what constitutes a U3A activity. Using a conservative guide, it may, however, be safely said that the 181 U3As arrange 5800 fairly regular (weekly or fortnightly) interest-group style activities. This amounts to an average of something like 30 interest-group style activities per U3A, an incredible spread of good practice, involving a bewildering range of variegated concerns, topics and subjects. Barking's four and Sheffield's 117, for example, demonstrate the array of numbers of activity groups.

Because of the small imbalance in the survey toward the larger and more mature U3A groups, it may be unlikely that the average of groups holds good for the 500 and more British U3As as a whole, that is, by simply working out the multiple of 32 interest groups and 522 U3As. The alternative procedure is to proceed by membership rather than U3A groups. Thus the 63,000 surveyed members have at their disposal 5800 interest-groups, or 0.09 groups per member. One may then transform this notional fraction into a national statistic by multiplying it by 130,000, the UK total of membership.

The latter or 'member' calculation results in a total of some 12,000; the former or 'group' calculation leads to a multiple of 16,000. Let us, in a spirit of temperate pride, settle on a happy medium figure of 14,000 interest-groups, as the best approximation to the size of this colourful assortment of self-help educational cells. It is fair to pronounce that the British U3A is currently responsible for the amazing total of 14,000 activity groups. At the same time, it should be recalled, allowing for the fact that many selfless people convene more than one group, that probably over 12,000 group leaders – described everywhere you go in the British movement as the 'life-blood' of the U3A – are devotedly at work.

Using the same set of figures, it is possible to suggest that, on a straightforward computation, the average size of this learning cell is about ten or twelve, although that estimate does not take much account of the fact that many U3A members attend more than one group, with, in the author's experience, the lady in Dunstable attending eleven activities being the current record-holder. Thus the average group size is probably nearer fifteen members. Again, the range of size is wildly extreme, from twos and threes to quite large numbers, depending, of course, on the style and theme of the activity. However, based on calculations done during a similar survey in 1995, it is probable that the British U3As clock up something in the region of 200,000 weekly attendances.

That estimate of, say, ten to fifteen members, enjoying an activity together, frequently in someone's home, conveys something of the intimate trait of the characteristic U3A member's weekly outing. That is the very core and essence of the U3A exercise.

What they share on these occasions amounts to a rich educational pageant. On the one hand, there are what, in the unsuitable language of the football pools, are known as 'bankers'. These are the most popular topics, which most groups offer. Surveys in the mid 1990s suggested that the top ten in order of popularity were: literature, including creative writing; languages; social studies, including discussion groups of varying brands; music; the arts; history; indoor games, such as Bridge and Scrabble; science; crafts, and walking. Together these amounted to over half the activities scheduled.

On the other hand, there is an awesome range of topics. Across the nation it was thought that, in 1995, there were, from antiques to weather forecasting, 150 different subjects being studied, but current estimates place that as high as over 300. In 1995 there was horology at Salisbury; sand-yachting at Burnham; and bamboo-pipe making at Crawley.

iii. Throughput of Membership

As a matter of interest, if the average national U3A has 250 and the average 'survey' U3A has 350 members, with, on par ratings, some 30 interest-groups on offer, then there are some 'survey' U3As that closely align with this template. These include Chelmsford (250 members/25 groups); Hastings & Rother (250/31); Bedford (350/33) and Bakewell (350/27). That anecdotal illustration does suggest that the overall estimates are quite well founded.

The national U3A has naturally prided itself on a count of its growing battalions, from the 40,000 of 1994 to the 130,000 of 2003. The occasion chosen to honour each of the three Founders as a 'Founder Member Emeritus' was, on a wonderfully nostalgic and celebratory day at the Norwich conference in 2000, to note 'the grateful thanks of the first 100,000 U3A members of the movement in the United Kingdom'. It was a reasonable milestone, an acknowledgement that the U3A was a prospering triumph. In the early years there had, naturally, been an anxiety about recruitment, about harvesting new members to give the nascent U3A some institutional *gravitas*.

Furthermore, there was a tacit assumption that people joined the U3A and, give or take a few dismal Jimmies and Jeminas, simply stayed on as members perpetually, rather like the unconditional membership of a church or the unqualified support of a football club. It might also be whispered that numbers were important, because the basic finance of the national organism depended on their affiliation fees. Even in 2000, when that 100,000 target was hit for the first time, there was a sense not just of reaching 100,000 but that U3A had had, since its inception, 100,000 members.

After 20-odd years of endeavour, the issue of throughput may be more sensibly examined. In brief, as well as knowing how many members U3A has now, how many have been members since it began?

Sifting through the testimony provided by the individual U3As, a number of features emerge about turn-over of membership. Most of the tendencies are obvious enough. However positive one is about the Third Age, it is not a passport to immortality. One of Peter Laslett's vital contributions to the 'ageing' debate was to emphasise, not that life endured longer, but that death had been concentrated into later life. Death had not been conquered; it had been manoeuvred into its rightful place at the end of the natural life span. Indeed, John Vincent, an expert in this field, has challenged the pseudo-scientific faith in the possible solution of all problems, including mortality, on the grounds that such a creed creates a cultural and social rift.

He writes (in the learned journal, *Ageing and Society* in 2003): 'Aspirations to immortality nonetheless remain as morally and philosophically problematic as they have been throughout human history. Striving for an ever longer life span represents denial of old age as a valued part of the life course, and allocates old people to a cultural category characterised by reductionism and despair . . . To focus on biological failure sets up a cultural construction which generates and prolongs its low esteem. An irredeemable cultural logic is created: if death is solvable, old age represents a failure. For old age to be its successful conclusion, life requires to be defined culturally not as the continuation of bodily function but in other ways.'

The U3A offers a telling phrase in that definition. It provides a chance of self-fulfilment to older people. In so doing incapacity and death may be deterred but not halted, but death may be more bravely faced without the regret of the wasted life. Writing in *Thriving People*, Eric Midwinter commented on two people who, quietly, plainly, unequivocally, told him they would have committed suicide, had it not been for U3A. That, in itself, is almost worth all the effort.

Thus, over 22 years, there have been many U3A losses. Several individual U3As recorded, with genuine regret, the death of one or more of their founding members. Two of the three founding fathers are deceased, whilst sorrowed mention has been made of the deaths of national figures, such as Charles Braybrook and Len Haynes. It was not felt this text was the right place to supply a long list of U3A deaths over the two decades or so of its existence, for it might have proved invidious and, in any event, degenerated into some sort of war memorial roster.

Nevertheless, it is absolutely proper to pause for a moment to recognise the U3A members who, nationally and locally, gave so generously and selflessly to the making of this history, and to remember them with sadness mingled with pride and affection. Some of these same observations are owed to another group of past members, those who, through severe illness or other handicap, have been forced to yield up membership. What must be added is a comment on the numerous stories of how, all over the country, U3A groups have been vastly supportive of bereaved or sick members. One hears, for instance, of widowed members in receipt of sack-loads of mail from members, anxious to offer condolence and solace.

Others have, for family or other reasons, moved away, although some of these have joined, indeed, started U3As elsewhere – and so, in the strictest sense, would be counted twice in any long-term census. One fascinating development has been people checking out the whereabouts of alternative U3As before moving house. For example, a woman in Cumbria, moving to Hertfordshire to be closer to her daughter, sought advice about which towns in the immediate vicinity had a U3A before choosing a new home. It is like ambitious parents sizing up schools for their children before changing areas. The lady's final comment was as laudatory of the U3A principle as any in a more polished social analysis: 'I walked out of one U3A one week and I walked into another the next week, and it was exactly the same. With that same feeling of friendliness, I immediately felt at home.' For all their manifold differences, U3As do share this highest common denominator: the *ambience* of sociability.

One must not whitewash too uncontrollably. There have been U3A members who have left because they did not like U3A or found it did not meet their needs. Some had higher and some lower expectations of what U3A could provide; either way it was wrong for them. Many of these did not stay long enough to sign on officially as members. As, very occasionally, the individual U3A cameos have hinted, there have also been rows and upheavals and people have stormed off in a huff. It is, after all a bevy of humans, not a gallery of saints. Nor could one expect otherwise. U3A was not invented to answer everybody's case.

Death, illness, mobility, tedium and rancour have been the overt grounds for ceasing membership. There is one other, not often, perhaps, recalled, but peeping through now and then in the various accounts. There are those people who, having attended, even run, U3A groups and activities for several years, have done what students at conventional colleges do. They have, so to say, 'graduated' and moved on to other interests. They have been satisfied by U3A and, in fact, prepared for another interest or responsibility. One should regard these departures as success stories.

One of the flaws of pre-retirement advice has been counselling people, some of them facing 40 years of retirement, to sort out their lives – their money, their accommodation, their health and so forth – and settle down. Much of the advice has been static in tone, with potential retirees instructed on how to cut a rut and stay in it. This new generation of Third Agers have often led dynamic lives. They have fought wars and endured depressions. They have been married and maybe divorced (the divorce rate in the over 60s has shot up to 17% from a long-time plateau of 3%) and probably married again. They have moved house umpteen times. They have had jobs; they have been promoted and then promoted again; and then perhaps they have been made redundant. Then, after this vibrant life-style, they are ordered to dig a fox-hole and bury themselves in it. Of course, some will be glad of the respite, but others may wish to forge ahead and find fresh experiences. However ruefully, we should rejoice at this kind of loss of membership, knowing that U3A has done its job well.

So much for the causes of changing membership. What is the arithmetic? 105 of the corresponding U3As were able to furnish quite accurate figures of throughput. Some were exact, in that running tallies, kept, for example, by sequential membership numbering, had been maintained. Others, on the basis of membership registers, were able to make a reliable estimate. One qualification must be made in that, naturally, the 105 groups have lived varying lengths of time. That was why it was important to point out earlier in this chapter that the date-range of the participating U3As was not too different to the national norm.

In total, the 105 U3As in question have 42,000 members, constituting a sample of a fifth of the national groups and over a third of the membership, altogether an acceptable sample. These 105 U3As have generated a throughput membership of 115,000. Put another way, a net membership of 42,000 represents a gross membership of 115,000.

If that figure holds good for the movement at large, and calculating the outcome by a balance of number of groups and size of membership, it might, very approximately, be estimated that, between 1982 and 2003, no less than 330,000 people have been U3A members.

This is possibly the first time that anybody has been foolhardy enough to risk guessing at this figure and, of course, it must be regarded as a provisional one. Nonetheless, putting aside mathematical doubts and regarding this as an order of magnitude, it clearly illustrates the dimension of U3A's success. It is two and a half times the 2003 membership. It should be a matter of pride, to all U3As locally and to the national leadership, past and present, that, in more or less degree, something in the region of 330,000 have benefited from the U3A experience.

iv. The Social Character of U3A; General

It was not thought necessary to update the overall findings about the social character of U3As included in *Thriving People*, published in 1996, the result of an in-depth piece of social analysis undertaken during 1995. This scrutinised 257 U3As by reference to the social class composition, the age profile and size of population of their local authority locations and little has happened in the few short years since to alter the emergent patterns that were, in any case, painted in broad brush strokes, not delicate tints.

This examination was accomplished to test three oft-quoted descriptors of U3A in the UK, namely, that it was chiefly prominent in avowedly middle class areas, in districts where there were a lot of old people and in compact 'market town' kinds of community. The downside of that anecdotal appraisal was that U3A was not present in working class areas, in 'young' districts and in either large conurbations or sporadically populated rural vicinities.

What the *Thriving People* research did was to attribute to each U3A a three-part coding. There was ABC for above average, average and below average for middle class social component. There was XYZ for 16% or under, 17/19% (18% being the norm) and 20% or over of population 60 plus years of age. There was 123 for district populations under 100,000, between 100,000 and 200,000, and over 200,000.

In summary, the U3As were distributed on this triple pattern as follows:

Social Class:	A: 123 – 47%;	B: 63 – 35%;	C: 72 – 28%
Age profile:	X: 42 – 16%;	Y: 99 – 39%;	Z: 116 – 45%
Population size:	1: 84 – 33%;	2: 121 – 47%;	3: 82 – 20%

What was of significant note was that nearly a third of U3As had, by 1995, gained footholds in what were not conventionally middle class enclaves; that over a half were located in neighbourhoods with average or less than average 'old age' components; and a fifth were situated in sizeably populated localities.

In a further refinement, whereby each U3A was coded 'AX1' and so on, according to its placement in the three indices, it was found that practically all possibilities were represented. As the statistically alert will be aware, there are 26 possibilities. Only two did not show up in these rankings. These were average and below average for social class, each matched with 'younger' age profile and larger population size (that is, BZ3 and CZ3) . Conversely, the top rating – 27 – was AZ2: above average social class; above average age profile; medium population size. Moreover, **all** nine classifications (ABC; XYZ; 123) appear in the top six codings, embracing 120 of the 257 U3As.

The evidence suggested that the anecdotal accounts told something of the truth, as anecdotal accounts are wont to do. U3As have found middle class areas with 'older' populations and in optimally sized districts very propitious for growth. But then the evidence tells the rest of the truth, which anecdotal accounts are wont not to do.

There are no 'no go' areas. Any type of locale is open to the seductive charms of the U3A experience. There is hardly an area where it has not been proved to be a success. This is of the utmost import to U3A developers.

v. The Social Character of U3A; Social Class and Population Size

A few caveats should be entered about these categories.

The usual health warning about social class is the first of these. It is an amorphous topic and is only intended to be a guide to understanding, not some definitive scientific solution. Given the conventional division by vocational standing of professional, managerial and skilled non-manual as against manual workers, retirement obviously makes classification difficult. Furthermore, there are many Third Agers, especially perhaps widows, who missed out on the shift to occupational pensions, who may be tagged 'middle class' in relatively straitened circumstances. Above all, the switch from, as recently as the late 1960s, a middle class/working class split of 30/70 to the present day 50/50 is a telling contextual factor. The best estimate of the division in the Third Age is 46/54, quite close to the national figure, and an indication that the present generation of older people have been involved in what has been termed 'the embourgeoisement of the proletariat'. By that token, it is self-evident that many middle class Third Agers are expatriate working class, either by upbringing or early work experience.

In that the middle class identity has a cultural as well as an economic feature, this bears hardly on the older echelons in society. Education is the formal yardstick in this connection – and about two-thirds of current Third Agers left school at or before fifteen, and the bulk of them, something of three quarters have not studied since. Those without qualifications in the Third Age outnumber those who have no qualifications in the population at large by three to one. Peter Laslett's strictures about the raw educational deal suffered by this generation of older people is sadly confirmed. Of course, middle class Third Agers are three times as likely as working class Third Agers to have taken up some study since leaving school, but there is a further alarming consideration.

Brevity and direness of schooling, often followed by work and domestic experience that called for little deployment of or supplement to even these inadequate skills, led in many cases to dipped confidence, not helped by the later hazards of deficient sight and hearing. This took its toll. Functional illiteracy in the pensionable age-range is higher, at over 30% - some experts put it higher – than the national average, variously quoted at 10% to 20%. It places a different gloss on all those tabloid stories about declining standards in schools today. It is something of a backstairs compliment to the British U3A to comment how well it has progressed against that depressing canvas.

Some commentary on older age as an element in the social equation was offered in an earlier chapter when reference was made to the success of the U3A group in Milton Keynes, the nation's 'youngest' town. It cannot be repeated too frequently that there are now more old age pensioners than there are children on the school registers. Of course, in a well-known base for retirement, there may be a public relations advantage for U3A, simply because of its patent aptness. Christchurch, for example, has some 35% of its population in the pensions bracket, three times as many as in Milton Keynes. However, Milton Keynes's 12% suggests 26,000 Third Agers to target. A dense incidence of older people is a helpful but by no means an essential prerequisite. With 12m people in the Third Age there are full pockets of them everywhere.

Turning to size of districts, at the juncture when this analysis was done, 117 U3As (47% of the sample) were to be found in the 156 local authority districts in England and Wales (38% of the national total of 404, metropolitan and shire based) with a '2' population, viz, between 100,000 and 200,000, a remarkable feat of evangelicalism on the part of the U3A movement. It is now probably complete, with, in several of these districts, more than one U3A, as the previous text has demonstrated.

The provision for '1' populations, that is, of less than a 100,000 was not too bad, with 82 U3As (33% of the then total) serving the 190 (47% of the English/Welsh total) districts in that population band. That, too, has obviously been much improved upon over the last eight years. These areas are often rural and widespread, as opposed to the more compact 30/50 square miles area of the averagely populated district. Even here there are tricks of the cultural light. Towns may be famous without being populous. Bath, for example, with a busy and large U3A, has a population of only 83,000.

vi. The Social Character of U3A; Transport and Gender

In the 1995 survey, the impact of U3A on the conurbations was still comparatively weak, although much has been done since then to repair that flaw. Transport remains a problem both in the rural localities and in the big towns and cities. As the Carnegie Inquiry into the Third Age predictably confirmed in 1992, not only is travel substantially reduced in the Third Age as opposed to the Second Age, the typology of travel – gone are the work and, always allowing for the deployment of grandparents as child carers, the school runs – is radically changed. Yet a half of 'old age' journeys are still made by car, the rest almost equally divided between public transport and pedestrianism. As in the Second Age, money is the key. Three quarters of older people on higher incomes use a car; only a third of those on lower incomes do.

This may affect an issue of particular concern in U3As, for, while only a third of older men do not have access to a car, the fraction springs to three-quarters amongst women. Apart from the factor of income imbalance between the sexes, there is a generational element, in that driving was, traditionally, a masculine pursuit. That is, of course, rapidly changing, although, on average, men in their early 70s travel further than women in their early 50s.

The usual rule of thumb, based on both American and British research, is that older people are reluctant to travel more than five miles or for more than 30 minutes to attend recreational and other facilities. In 1995 137 British U3As answered the question as to whether more or less than half their members travelled 30 minutes for their group meetings. The result was overwhelming. 117 answered 'under 30 minutes'. Interestingly, in terms of this general discussion, the minority of 20 U3As were a mix of rurally and conurbation based groups. In fact, the majority responses conveyed an irresistible measure of proximity. 'Less than six out of 300 members'; only 4 out of 200'; 'very few, most less than ten minutes', were among the comments.

One salutary lesson is that this may mean that people who do live more than 30 minutes away do not or will not bother. It strengthens the case for the rule of thumb of providing a facility, if at all possible, within easy reach.

The transport issue touched on the gender question. The 1995 research suggested that women outnumbered men in the ratio of three to one in the British U3A, although there was also evidence that the bigger the group, the higher the male ratio. An important qualification is that women outnumber men in the Third Age. There are approximately 7.5m women and 4.5m men. There are two strands to this. One is that, on average, women outlive men. This is usually ascribed in part to in-built evolutionary gene-protection mechanisms and in part to environmental features, although, as gender lifestyles grow more similar, some prophesy that the determinants of smoking, drinking, stressful work and so on will narrow that gap.

The other strand is social. Women, at the moment, leave the workforce earlier than men. For instance, only a fifth of men, compared with a half of British women, are 'economically inactive' in the 55/59 age-range.

In the past, 'clubability' has tended to be regarded as a masculine thing, with the school, youth organisations, the work-place, the forces and team sports all taking some of the credit, if credit is due. Joining societies was blokeish. That, of course, is altering and, in older age, there may be a poignant reason for the cultural shift. 47% of older women, compared with only 20% of older men live alone, while 62% of men, compared with just 33% of women, live with their partner, usually another older person. One estimate suggests that of the 7.5m Third Age women, 3.5m may be single, widowed or, a swiftly expanding segment, divorced. Thus both the demographic and social statistics help to explain why women outnumber men in the British U3A. The ratio is nearer to the national canvas than at first sight meets the eye.

A curio of U3A development, experienced from the very beginning by most of those involved with national development, is the chorus of contradictory local interpretations, with pairs of negatives and positives in evidence. Examples of this include: 'there is too much happening here already'/ 'there are lots of activities here; people are keen to try anything' – 'nothing happens round here; you'll never start a U3A/ 'nothing happens round here; what a good place to start a U3A' - 'people are too settled in their ways here'/ 'people are really looking for something to fill their time' – 'a middle class area; people are much too busy for anything like U3A'/ 'a middle class area; people are only too keen to join things' – 'a working class town; no time and money for education'/ 'a working class town; a solid tradition of interest in education' – 'lots of old people here; they won't want to be bothered'/'lots of old people here; it should be easy to start a U3A' – 'there's no university or college nearby, so there's no backing'/ 'there's no university or college nearby, so there's plenty of scope' – 'there's a university/college nearby, so they provide what's needed already'/ 'there's a university/college nearby, so they'll give us good assistance'

In effect, although parochial factors loom large through the local lens, the differences from place to place on our tight little right little island are not so immense when the perspective is a nation-wide one. To repeat, there are no no-go areas. If there were a common factor in the spread of U3As, after all those self-cancellations, it is individuals. Time and again in the tales recalled in this text about the origins of dozens of U3A it was the energy and zeal of one or more personalities in each potential unit who carried the day and made the idea feasible. At least 500 individuals have been, as Joe Gargery ruefully described his wife in *Great Expectations*, 'given to government'. Without those unsung John Hampdens and unheralded Joans of Arc, there would not be any U3As in Britain.

vii. Membership Survey 2001

This is probably the apposite point to introduce the summary of responses to the mapping survey carried out, with the help of the DfES research grant, between November 2000 and April 2001. After a pilot testing in ten U3As, with 186 responses, the finalised questionnaires were widely distributed to 90 more U3As and this elicited a further 2848 replies, making 3034 in all, an eminently satisfactory return of 62%.

This is, without question, the most far-reaching survey of individual members ever undertaken and one can do little more than comment that, apart from the huge value it will have for the next generation of U3A development, it will be of much benefit to practitioners and policy-makers in the allied fields of older age and lifelong learning.

It is possible here only to give a taste of this opulent feast of findings but even these are very savoury indeed.

First, of the sample, the same number – 26% – joined before 1995 and between 1995 and 1997, the remainder became members thereafter. Word of mouth – 73% – is overwhelmingly the way most of them became aware of U3A, with the library, 11% (Frank Pedley will be pleased) and the local press, 9%, being the only other pertinent runners in the awareness race. The reasons for joining are much more disparate. The main motives suggested were to form social contacts, 29%; to develop a specific interest, 18%; to acquire knowledge, 14%; to acquire new skills, 12%; to meet people with similar interests, 10%; to keep the mind active, 10%.

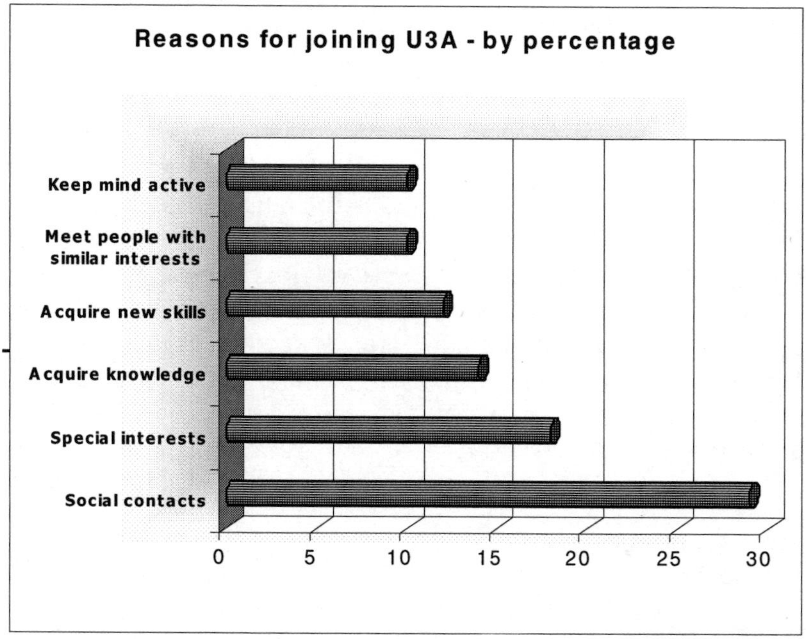

Second, although 88% are members of only one U3A, 8%, 2% and 1% are, respectively, members of two, three and four or more U3As, a fascinating finding that must affect the overall membership, *apropos* actual human beings, somewhat. The degree of commitment is quite high, in so far as 16% have held or do hold committee office and 11% are or have been group leaders. Similarly with group membership: while 26% are in just one group, several are in more than one, as has been noticed in previous surveys. In these figures, 25% are in two interest-groups; 19% in three; 10% in four and 11% in five or more. 5% are on a waiting list for a group and 26% mentioned subjects that were not available in their local U3A. In terms of attendances, 31% attend meetings once or twice a month; 34% three or four times; 32% five or more, and 4% ten or more.

Third, although 38% found no restricting factors barring them from participation, 45% averred that lack of time was a problem, while inconvenient meeting times, 14%, and transport, 8%, were the main other stated hurdles. When U3A could not be attended, 29% missed it very much indeed and 40% very much, against not very much at 4% and not at all at 1%. A compelling finding, recalling the 29% who opted to join for social contact, is that 55% give social contact and companionship as the aspect most enjoyed, much to the credit of the social ethos of the organisation. 19% spoke of the mental stimulation and 17% of meeting like-minded people, which is not a far cry from social contact. The evident friendliness of the U3A experience, witnessed throughout this study in anecdotal fashion, is borne out by the strength of these responses. Organisers, both local and national, should be pleased at the 73% credit rating, in the shape, that is, of three quarters of the sample that had no suggestions to make about how this fine movement might be improved. 91% claimed to receive *U3A News*; 74% state that they read all three copies annually; only 1% does not read any edition; a very gratifying outcome for the long-established newspaper.

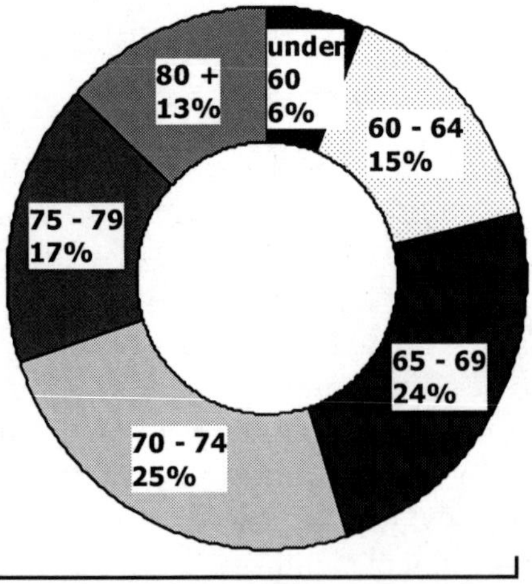

Fourth, turning to a more personal profile, and one lacking in most of the previous national research, the age range is from 6% under 60, via 15% 60-64, 24% 65-69, 25% 70-74 and 17% 75-79, to 13% over 80. This is a rather more even spread than most anecdotal comment has allowed and is rather reassuring. It gives an average age of 70.6 years. As expected, the gender ratio is 26% men to 74% women, with the huge majority either living with a spouse or partner, 56%, or alone, 39%. The previous job is a useful steer on social class and it again bears out some of the social observations made about the U3A. The range is 40% professional; 15% each managerial and administrative, against 4% each technical and manual, with 5% having had only occasional or no employment – and the high sum of 84% have some form of occupational or private pension. However, it is interesting to observe that the relatively high figure of 65% had had no recent learning activities prior to joining U3A; that 51% had completed full-time schooling by the age of sixteen; and that whereas a high percentage for this generation– just over 40% - have higher educational qualifications, 23% have no formal educational qualifications at all.

It is impossible to tease out an average U3A-er from this swirl of statistics. Possibly the nearest to a prototypical member, peering hazily out from the mist of numerals, might be the 70 year old woman who, on leaving school without any qualifications, had had the sense and drive to do well vocationally and retire fairly comfortably, but who had had no further dealings with formal education before discovering the solace and stimulation of U3A. Above all, this significant mapping survey spells out the U3A watchword: 'good learning in good companionship'.

Now we may turn to four or five topics that may be worth considering during this round-up of U3A at the start of the 21st century.

viii. When Large may be Beautiful

When *Thriving People* was published in 1996, the development prescription was for 500 U3As where there were then 266, and 250,000 members where there were then some 40,000. The first test has been passed with flying colours, *honore cum laude*. That is almost too good to be true and one is tempted to guess that the target might have been too easy. Looking back, however, the development plan was a rational attempt to ensure that there were sufficient U3As strategically located so that any Third Ager desireth of joining a U3A could approach one with relative comfort. 539 inside eight years is a remarkable achievement.

It is true that the ideal of strategic location has not always been met. Parts of Scotland and some conurbations, including areas in the London and Manchester metropolitan regions, could still benefit from a few more carefully sited U3As, whereas the majority of England and Wales (31 suggested in Wales in 1996; 29 in 2003) have excellent cover, apart from odd anomalies like Northamptonshire, where there were, in 2003, only two U3As.

So far, so good, but the tickled palate whets the developmental appetite. The membership has, in the same period, grown more than threefold, which is an undeniable success rate. Most voluntary organisations would weep in their beer at such headway, given the paucity of take-up for many of them. Where, in 1996, one in 250 Third Agers were members, by 2003, it was one in 100, a major advance. Was asking for 250,000 members in 1996 as severe a challenge as asking for 500 groups was an easy one?

Retrospectively, the same judgement applied. The gauntlet of 250,000 was thrown down on the basis of the 'ratio of potential' that was calculated. This was founded on the best practice of U3A recruitment in districts countrywide, if, chiefly, in the southern counties where U3A had taken such a firm grip in its early years. This piece of arithmetic was humble enough. It merely opined that, where U3As had recruited most vigorously and over reasonably long periods, it appeared that about 1 in 40 of Third Age people would, if the physical and cultural welcome were cheerfully offered them, follow the U3A flag.

Did that prophecy come to fruition, the national U3A membership would be 285,000; hence the suggested 250,000 as the next target.

Seven years on and two facts are pertinent. One is that the U3A in the UK is over halfway to that objective, with one in less than every 100 Third Agers a U3A member, although some earlier strictures about throughput may be properly recalled.

The other is that, in many of the areas of intense involvement, the base for that 'ratio of potential' has been radically shifted. It might even be necessary to revise that proportion to one in 20 and envision an endgame of 500,000 members. Indeed, in some districts, U3As have 1 in ten of the potential clientele on their registers, which, if emulated nationwide, would result in an astronomical figure of over a million members.

Mike Long, with some adroit arithmetic, has produced fascinating calculations about recent membership growth, which, with a hearty nod of gratitude in his direction, we summarise here.

What he calls the '500+ Club' currently has a membership of 57, as the year 2003 witnessed another ten U3As reach a membership of 500 or more, with a couple of U3As just ducking under that figure during the year. Sheffield, advancing on 2000, is the leader in this regard, followed by Bath, Bromley and London, with, in all, nine U3As beating the thousand mark. The 57 U3As contribute 44% of the total UK membership.

Of course, with such success, growth begins to dwindle. Sheffield, with 450 members more than anyone else, welcomed 'only' 59 new members in 2003, just 3% as a growth rate. In Mike Long's 'growth table' for 2003, 20 U3As showed 10% or more increase. Crewe and Nantwich came closer, in this regard, to emulating nearby Manchester United than lowlier (but always trying) Crewe Alexandra. Topping the 'growth' premiership, Crewe and Nantwich had a spectacular 31% rise, up to 736 members, a really impressive performance. Camberley and Thornbury both had just over 20% growth, and, in general, 2003 was a good season for harvesting new members.

We are nowhere near the terminus of this exhilarating journey.

ix. Communication

U3As were asked in 2003 to send samples of their bulletins, newsletters and other literature, as a help in judging how well U3As communicated with established and approached potential new members. The study floor was soon creaking under what seemed like a geological layer of paper. It was all so comprehensive and so colourfully presented that it leaves little to add by way of commentary. As the old song warbled, 'everybody's doing it.' Quite simply, every U3A is conscious of the need for reasonable communication, and many U3As obviously have access, in this technocratic age, to very efficacious apparatus, to say nothing of the number of U3As who have websites and commune with members via e-mail. In almost all cases the standard of editing and the range of contribution was excellent.

Occasionally, U3As undertake local surveys among their members to elicit some data on how well or how badly those members are reacting to their experiences. Ian Yates, Chairman of the Carlisle U3A, kindly forwarded the results of such a scrutiny conducted towards the end of 2002. It had 42 questions ranging over seven areas of interest. There was a 32.5% response, that is from 162 of the then 598 members. Apart from some disappointment at the large proportion of 'neutral' answers, there was a generally positive reaction, coupled with many practical suggestions. For example, the content, format and style of the newsletter gained 'overwhelming approval', while many took the opportunity to congratulate the committee and group leaders on their efforts: 'a common theme was the desirability of maintaining, if not increasing, the social dimension to our learning opportunities.' Such a far-reaching questionnaire must have been highly useful to the leadership of Carlisle, as they sought to plan ahead, and there were indications from the membership that a repeat survey every few years would be welcome and beneficial.

By way of finale to this largely statistical section, we provide a cameo of one U3A, the Dunstable U3A, where Peter Capp is the wizard of the arithmetic. It offers a mathematical x-ray of the innards of a British U3A. As of October 2003, there were 626 members. Of these, 44 had joint membership with Toddington U3A, which Dunstable members had been instrumental in establishing. During the year 85% of the members had attended at least one monthly general meeting, at which there was an average attendance of 245 (42%), while 437, three quarters of the register, were members of at least one interest-group, leaving 152, a quarter, as uninvolved with any regular group activity. 41 of those involved with interest-groups had not attended a general meeting, but, oddly (although it is a phenomenon experienced in several U3As) there were also 44, inclusive of five couples, who were not in an interest-group and had not attended a general meeting. It is suggested in some of these U3As that some people simply wish to contribute financially and enjoy getting a newsletter or other bulletin.

Dunstable, at that stage, offered 64 groups, covering 45 topics, variously categorised as primarily 17 'physical', 25 'interest' and 22 'learning', although it was conceded that the overlaps were often emphatic. The 64 groups are stewarded by 45 leaders and the attendances demonstrate the point about the devotion and diligence of U3A members. 116 attend one group; 110 two groups; 71 three groups; 49 four groups; 20 five groups; 20 eight groups, as well as the super-student, already marvelled over, who attends eleven groups. 27 of the interest-groups are, for the usual variety of logistical reasons, full, and Peter Capp is able to utilise his findings to direct his U3A along the lines of what sort of new groups need to be launched.

Peter Capp crowned his investigative deeds with a spot check on the coach trip to Windsor and one of the theatre outings. Of the 53 visitors to Windsor, there were only six non-active (that is, not members of an interest-group) members and three of them were partners of three who were, leaving 47 who were active in groups. Of the 200 on the theatre trip, only six were not in groups and only 28 had not attended a general meeting, of whom four were with partners who had, leaving 116 stalwarts who were both interest-group members and attended general meetings. Peter Capp undertook this piece of research to deny the part-myth that the more purely social ventures were being dominated by the educational non-combatants.

It forms a fascinating little study, admirable for its adept identification of what members are doing and not doing and valuable to the Dunstable leadership as they continue to expand. And all this for a £7.50 annual subscription . . .

x. Inertia and Trivial Pursuits

In turn, this forms an apposite introduction to a further point about the U3A construct. From the beginning there has been some occasionally harsh criticism about the lethargy of some members and the triviality of some subjects.

The first of these – the failure of members to jump to it and shoulder responsibility – is not uncommon in associations. What Karl Marx called, in other contexts, the 'Iron Law of Oligarchy' seems to operate everywhere, whether it is the House of Commons or the local tennis club, with a minority rising to hold the reins of authority. However, such inertia comes hard to a body predicated on self-help. Several U3As have tried several ways of improving the active component, including, at the very least, insisting that all members belong to at least one interest-group or by splitting tasks, so that, for example, each interest-group has an administrative clerk and maybe a caterer as well as a convenor. There are all kinds of methods for boosting the confidence of the more diffident member, but one rule is paramount.

It was informally pronounced by Peter Laslett, no slacker, to put it mildly, when it came to intellectual endeavour. One might have expected him to be severe on scholarly backsliding, but, perhaps remembering his childhood in a nonconformist manse, he said firmly that there was more chance of a person becoming more involved with U3A if they were already a member than if they were not. He readily drew the analogy with church membership, where 'four-wheeler' Christians (baptismal pram, wedding car and hearse) should not be scorned, the hope being that they would become more engaged: 'in my father's house, there are many mansions.'

That simple piece of good sense applies to the other poser about the triviality of some interests and activities. Rather one of the more recreational groups than no group at all. Next year the choice made might be more ambitious. But that is only the first element in this discussion. Next there is a false and sometimes snobbish ambivalence about these arbitrations. Whatever the exercise, the group is a social construct with some form of design and some objective. It is not aimless and it is not solitary. That purposeful, collective endeavour is rewarding, for mental effort and social involvement are clinically as well as psychologically wholesome. One must also be careful how one measures these matters. The mental exercise involved in a game of Scrabble or Bridge may be more potent than listening, perhaps languidly and occasionally distractedly, to a talk on Geology, although the latter sounds more intellectually upmarket.

With social events there is conversation, some of it quite meaningful. One is impressed by the U3As where the theatre visit may be prefaced or 'epilogued' by well-led discussion of the play in question, or the 'pub lunch' series, where each pub is the focus for study. The walking and travel groups are perhaps the most large-scale examples of this tendency. Moreover, those who seethe at the lack of earnestness of some of their fellows, and some of the selections for which they opt, have obviously forgotten the ways of the conventional universities. Playing football, acting in plays and joining numerous clubs was supposed to be part of the all round experience, with many students possibly contriving to devote more of their energies in such directions than towards study.

The pattern of shared learning is plainly a social exercise. In its recognition that everyone's experience is grist for the educational mill, the purported border line between 'social' and 'intellectual' is erased. During one workshop for group co-ordinators arranged by Audrey Cloet in the early 1990s, a class was described in which the tutor arrived, gave a talk on a highly scholarly subject and left, without even so much as a question and answer session. The chairs were formally ranged behind tables, classroom style. Members of the committee had tried sneaking in beforehand and moving the furniture into a more comfortable circle, a heavy hint, if ever there were one. It was to no avail. The tutor arrived and shifted it all back into regimental configuration. There would have been more 'shared learning' had the group members had a pub lunch together and just had a good conversation.

xi. A Philosophic Interlude

The term 'tutor' was advisedly used in that last paragraph. It gives the wrong impression of the genuine U3A process. True education is about thinking through and problem-solving in the broadest sense, as in what one might gain from the organised ramble or the French conversation circle, as well as from the highly valuable study of Geology. It is in this interaction of self-directed experience and reflection that progress is made. It is about understanding rather than instruction, more about using than acquiring knowledge – and many experts – as chapter six made clear - regard the small scale learning circle as the prime method for so doing. It is conducive to that process of thought, reflection, exchange, action and practice that is the best educational route, with, ideally, all contributing as both teachers and learners. Process is as important as content. It is a method of questioning, leading to more efficient performance, all on a collective basis. Mutual respect and joint consideration are the courteous hallmarks of the self-help learning *credo*.

It would be unduly fanciful to claim that there are 12,000 interest-groups in the U3As of the UK that consistently abide by these counsels of perfection. It would be unduly sceptical to scoff that there are thousands that do not. All over the land, there are learning circles and activities that are operating on these lines. The truth of that statement is mathematical. The better proportion of 140,000 older people are turning out once or more a week or a fortnight to attend these groups, not for qualifications, not for glory, not for kudos, but primarily to enjoy themselves, and, importantly, to enjoy themselves positively and to realise aspects of their being heretofore unrealised.

They are, in a hyphenated word, self-motivated. One never hears the word 'truancy' in U3A circles, in a society that has to have acts of parliament to corral its youngsters into schools. At a mundane level, what U3A members are doing is having a bloody good time.

The radical thinkers about education argue that, fundamentally, learning without enjoyment is harshly deficient and that enjoyment without learning is idly fruitless. This is what made British pre-school and primary schooling, in its post-Plowden liberalised and humane years, the envy of the world. In shorthand phrasing, it was called 'the play way', a combine of tough application and unbounded satisfaction. It is the key to U3A's learning programme. It epitomises an acknowledgement that education and life are intermingled at the here and now. There has been no more cogent expression of this than in the famous dictum of the American educational philosopher, John Dewey. Education was, he espoused, 'participation in, not preparation for'.

The organisational consequence for U3As of this revolves around the role of the group leaders. They must be facilitators not didacts. Many U3A group leaders are former teachers and lecturers, many of whom are keen advocates of mutual learning methods. Others, with, educationally speaking, a non-educational background, have equally taken to shared learning like dialogic ducks to water. Some, of course, from both professional and lay backgrounds may have been less conspicuous in this regard, maybe adhering to the monologic mechanics of traditional teaching. In encouraging these and, now and in the future, many more thousands to master these skills, one basic tenet must be accepted.

These 'animateurs' (or, as one irritated member of a U3A workshop, wanting no truck with franglais, insisted, 'animators') must be facilitators first and experts second. That should be the ultimate target. It is pleasing if both skills are in evidence, but it is necessary to place a marker against the primary proficiency required. The ability to steward mutual learning should be prior to the grasp of subject matter. The defining traits are enthusiasm, sociability and confidence, all malleable in good workshop practice.

Twenty-two years of pioneering has given the British U3A an unparalleled reservoir of experience in the management of small study circles. It should be possible to capitalise on that valuable asset over the next twenty or so years, for the sake of the Third Age – and, one hopes, the First and Second Ages as well.

xii. A Sociological Intermission

The political canvas against which the U3A in the UK evolved is rarely alluded to, but, in evaluating its sturdy place in the body politic today, it merits a comment.

The 1980s and the 1990s were unpropitious climes for co-operative endeavours, indeed, one would have to time-travel back perhaps to the 1840s to find a decade so barren in terms of mutuality. The pre-school playgroup movement, already cited as a precursor of the U3A experiment, blossomed, for instance, in the more fertile preceding years. There were many reasons for this change. In brief, the oil crisis of the early 1970s triggered off the inflationary spiral and economic recession that toppled the 'Butskellite' consensus of the post-1951 era. This was coupled with the rise of consumer materialism as the new Mammon. A major aspect of the emerging critique was a fierce and often accurate attack on the hidebound, wasteful, blunt-edged anonymity of 'nannying' state bureaucratic machinery.

Possibly there was simply a swing of the emotional pendulum, away from a statist to a personal mind-set. Aneurin Bevan said that societies did swing inexplicably from being cat-like, fiercely nursing introvert independence, to dog-like, happily joining in extravert pack-like togetherness. Certainly the 1980s found us in the feline basket and not the canine kennel.

In reaction, the national mood increasingly adopted individualistic flavours, with an accent on privatism and, in the non-pejorative sense, self-ishness. There was a lurch toward the free market as the main governor of social as well as economic issues. This, of course, was associated with the name of Margaret Thatcher, although social historians are now readier to suggest that the Conservative leader rode rather than created the individualistic, privatising tiger. A curio, from the stance of local voluntary effort, was that, as often happens where governments are eager to release the citizenry from the thrall of collectivist shackles, there was a shift to very powerful centralised controls, ostensibly to clear the social arena for freedom and choice. Local authority, for long years the counterpoint to central dictation, suffered badly, as major services – health, education, police, above all, finance – became more and more subject to Whitehall control.

Whatever the rights and wrongs of these positions, it was scarcely an auspicious moment for localised co-operative action. In Bevanite terms, U3As were a few puppies scampering in Cat World. It is not the least surprising element in the history of U3As that they worked against what was then, and, in some measure, still is, the social grain, and succeeded.

There are three explanations of why the U3A triumphed against the sociological odds, each of them with a pertinent relevance to the work and belief of the three Founding Fathers. The first, and one that Peter Laslett, demographer and gerontologist, would have pressed, was that the Third Age hordes were ripe for quiet uprising. They were ready for the fray of shifting the imagery of older age from the medical to the civic design. The second, and one that Eric Midwinter, social historian, would urge, was that it was among this generation of the Third Age that the residual strengths of civic virtue and 'voluntaryism' remained. These sturdy values, bred in school and youth associations, in the rigours of war-time and thereafter, in the running of a thousand and one societies, from light operatic and rose gardening to trade union branches and chambers of commerce, perhaps these burned through again and aided the U3A crusade. The third, and one that Michael Young would have emphasised, is that people had perhaps spotted that mutual aid is a wiser socio-political course to pursue than either state socialism or state-monitored private enterprise. From 1951 on, and increasingly, he wished a plague on both their houses. For him, there was little to choose between a huge nationalised industry and a huge privatised, possibly multinational, business: ordinary folk were outgunned by both and he hoped the day of the little man and woman was at hand.

Explanations there may be, but the prosperous outcome for U3A is as undeniable as it is astounding. Many another co-operative experiment, especially in the workplace but also in the field of health and social welfare and in housing, was tried in the same period and most of them were found wanting, usually ground down by the adverse climate. The British U3A won through, not only here and there, but also on a widespread national scale. 500 U3As and 140,000 members now constitute the chief practical memorials in Britain to Peter Laslett's absolute belief in the rich promise of the Third Age as 'the crown of life' and Michael Young's no less vehement faith in the resilience of the common man and woman in the conduct of their own social affairs.

Twelve: TOMORROW

Two questions remain as to the future. One is about how the U3A in the UK should develop. The other is whether the U3A model may, in a number of ways, be replicated in British society.

---

i. Whither U3A

Chairman Keith Richards, in a perceptive and sensitive piece of writing, introduces some aspect of both those issues.

> 'A 21st birthday is a time to pause, reflect, take a snapshot and then indulge in some modest forward projections. Over 130,000 members – a cause for wonder and, of course, as many as our small national resources can at the moment handle – but a very tiny percentage of those 'no longer in gainful, fulltime employment'. The delicate task of widening membership to reflect more closely our multicultural society is beginning; we are gradually becoming more bold in seeking government support for our radical educational experiment.
>
> During the next few years the U3A may, on entering its own 'second age', have more to contribute to the ongoing national

debate, emphasising the real nature of lifelong learning. In doing so, it needs to proclaim its own reliance on the experiential learning of its own members and the daring notion of basing its activities upon the conviction that everyone has something to contribute to the educational experience. In this university the curriculum is infinite and the challenges are daunting. Learning for its own sake offers no sticks or carrots and the group will close unless the participants realise their own expectations.

I hope for greater understanding of the nature of the enterprise – not least among the members themselves – and closer links with the international community of Third Agers. Technological advances, with which the next generation of members will be comfortable, offer the opportunity of communicating with and learning with people outside of our group, region and country. At the heart of U3A, though, there will always be a community of learners, probably sitting in a circle, 'leading out' the essence of an artefact through the medium of each other's enjoyment.

Autonomous, non-institutionalised U3As may remain difficult to forge into a thoroughgoing national movement but my main hope for the future is that the excitement generated will do its work anyway and that the return of student-centred learning at its best for all is not too far distant.'

These are indeed wise words. In this concluding chapter, both the internal U3A ramifications and the possible external repercussions of that challenging statement will be examined.

ii. Inside the U3A – the More the Merrier

The NEC theme for the 2004 conference at Leicester is 'Widening the Net'. It begins with a realisation that, with its strong base of 539 groups representing a vast number of the UK's localities and providing coverage of virtually all the land, the time is ripe to promote extending the membership and developing the product and services made available to that burgeoning membership. Eight aspects will be under review. These are diversification of membership, not least among disabled people and with the multi-ethnic populace of the UK in mind; links with other bodies and agencies of a like interest and intention; participation, in the sense of encouraging more members to be more active; relations with the international movement; the use of new technology, especially electronic communication; the organisational implications of growth; shared learning projects; and improved support for U3A groups and the individuals within them.

An American historian has said that 'history is made forwards and written backwards'. It would be wrong to attempt to pre-empt the outcome of such an august discussion in this essay on U3A retrospect. Nonetheless, it might be possible to suggest a few pointers from the past, finding directions from what has gone before.

The salient analysis was that which proposed there was a 'ratio of potential', originally calculated at one in 40 Third Agers who might, given the right conditions, be prepared to join a U3A group. The conditions, by way of reminder, are twofold. There is physical proximity, with, as a rough and ready yardstick, the hope that there would, normally, be a U3A within five miles or 30 minutes travelling time of a potential customer's residence. There is a social proximity, in that the hopeful member might find the organisation immediately appealing and welcoming. If that were open to psychological measure, it would be the cultural equivalent of within five miles or 30 minutes travelling time.

If there are half as many again in the British Third Age who would find the U3A experience beneficial, then the first priority must be to track them down, whether they are in the traditional courses for U3A hunting or in less likely confines. The premier rule must be that the U3A is good for those for whom the U3A is good.

To begin at the worst end, some 30 of the 187 U3As that so kindly recorded brief notes of their history for this study referred to waiting lists. Often this was in the context of helping to start another U3A in the neighbourhood, almost always keeping good relations with it thereafter. These were honourable solutions to the poser of feeling that groups had grown overlarge.

This text has been complimentary throughout about the unpaid vigour and vim of hundreds of people who have made a success of the U3A story. It has waxed almost hagiographically about some of the movement's important leaders and it makes no apology for so doing: it has been a marvellous tale of voluntary endeavour. The waiting list is a slight stain on this proud record. It directly transgresses the original and implicit concept of the U3A as an agency created to gather together older people regardless of qualification or expertise. It imposes a numerical standard and barrier. It ignores Peter Laslett's telling gloss on survival as opposed to longevity: the Third Age is a factor not so much because some people are living longer lives but more because most people are living normal lives. Waiting lists may be acceptable for First and Second Agers. However, all Third Agers are already on a waiting list besides the awesomeness of which whether or not one may join Warmington-on-Sea U3A pales into feeble insignificance.

Waiting lists appear to have arisen for a number of reasons. Somehow the sense arose that a certain number represented a compact unity, beyond which social coherence would be lost. This is sometimes portrayed organisationally, that is, as the point at which one has to jettison highly individualised administration – 'this is as many as I can manage from my sitting room', as one leader put it – and organise a more complex formal system. It is sometimes epitomised in social terms; the loss of what is inevitably called 'the personal touch' is much feared and it would be foolish to dismiss this as a mere whim.

What some of the successful large U3As have done is to have managed the administration by involving more people, often on a grouped basis, like a team, rather than an individual, editing and distributing the newsletter. They argue that the bigger the membership, the more chance there is of conquering that old bogey of all associations, the reluctance of people to advance and be recognised as committee material. On the social side, they have met the issue by using the interest-group as the focal point, but also by generating many more social events and trips (another bonus for larger memberships) and also by developing some 'faculty' type ventures, that is, with 'groups of groups' enjoying some shared enterprise.

One must always be aware of the sociometric problem of the inward-looking nature of any group formation, a proclivity illustrated by the old village saying 'here's a stranger; throw a brick at him'. Groups, once settled, tend to form, psychologically, a tortoise shell, a defence against the outside world. Some community developers claim that it is easy to recruit the first twenty for some pursuit but that, once the twenty are ensconced, recruiting the twenty-first is arduous.

As with patients presenting themselves to the medicos for diagnosis, the symptoms often hide the ailment. A very noticeable example has been the size of the general meeting room. Several U3As have deployed the fact that, what with fire, health and other safety hazards and the knotty pull of insurance, the hall will only hold 250 for the monthly meeting, so the cap goes on at 250. Experienced speakers at U3A assemblies will be familiar with the following dialogue, perhaps when seated with the chairman, awaiting the start of the meeting:

Speaker: *What is the size of your U3A?*

Chairman: *250. We have a waiting list. This church hall only holds 250, so we had to draw the line at that number.*

Speaker: *How many are here today?*

Chairman: *It's one of our best turnouts ever – there must be 150 here.*

The words 'dog', 'tail' and 'wagging' immediately spring to mind.

Apart from possible solutions already practised – a second meeting, maybe in another hall in a different part of the town; tickets (free, of course) to guard against overcrowding – the notion that the viability of the monthly meeting should rule the roost is wrong-headed. The suspicion must be that it masks an unwillingness to expand.

Once more, much credit redounds on those many U3As who, rather than have a waiting list, have sought to launch complementary U3As, although, reading between the lines of one or two such cases, the thought occurs that some members were 'volunteered' for alternative duties in the strictest military sense. Moreover, the bifurcation of many U3As may account for any slight imbalances in U3A coverage. It was suggested in 1995 that 500 U3A groups would be about sufficient to cover the nation, but, of course, they had to be rationally located so to do, and there are many examples of places with two and more medium sized U3As that distort that pattern a trifle. However, all of this activity is much to be applauded over against the occasional example of the small U3A group that does not have a waiting list for, one conjectures, they are reluctant to advertise their whereabouts and activities and thus no one knows of their existence. These are the likeliest to decay and die. The mid-term peril of a stagnant membership is petrifaction. All groups need a flow of fresh (let us avoid the ageist adjective 'young') blood.

For several reasons of logistics and geography and style, there is room for small as well as large and medium-sized U3As. There is no place for central dictation, even if a pennyworth of friendly persuasion might not go amiss. The breadth of types and sizes, within the general umbrella of self-help learning, is one of the glories of U3As. What needs, however, to be urged is the primacy of reaching all those for whom U3A would offer a lifeline to a fuller and more bountiful life. Surely all U3As – all U3A members – have some onus upon their shoulders not to deny others the participative enjoyment that is already theirs.

In the spring of 2003 a workshop was organised at Peterborough, masterminded by that zealous U3A warrior, John Knight, on this very subject. The aim was to discuss the working of the larger group and draw together the important experience of founders and developers of large groups, in the hope that this collective know-how could be made available and be instructive to others struggling with the questions resultant on expansion. There was some serious debate about the quandaries facing the expanding U3A, but there was also a countervailing flavour. There was a definite feeling that one should not be defensive about largeness, always seeking to solve the puzzles with which it confronted U3As, but eagerly ready to trumpet the advantages. The financial element, the range of people to draw on for tasks, the splash one is able to make locally and other bonuses were described, together with the self-evident characteristic that the more the members, the broader the range of activities one could offer – and the broader the range of activities one could offer, the more attractive the bait for new members.

There was some discussion of a simple training pack being made available on this front and it might be further suggested that the regional networks be asked to consider, where necessary, membership development plans. These might include new U3As; sets of U3As working in harness; aid to U3As who might wish to expand, and so on. First, perhaps, there is the cultural hurdle that must be overcome. There is little doubt that, within the U3A movement, an understandable impression has become entrenched about what constitutes normalcy of size. At the 2003 workshop, by far the most perceptive remark issued from the sage-like mind of Ivor Manley: 'it was only when, as a member of Farnborough U3A (membership 1270), I became involved more with the national situation and visited other U3As that I realised I **was** in a 'large' U3A.'

iii. Outside the U3A - More of the Same

Were the U3A 'rate of potential' one in ten Third Agers and thus the national membership an amazing one million, it would still leave 91% of those in the Third Age outside the U3A movement.

It has been, in a phrase borrowed from *The Yeomen of the Guard*, a 'strange adventure'. A paradox presented itself in the very success of the U3A notion that muted the joy of its founding brethren, particularly Peter Laslett. He strongly believed that the Third Age echelons should invent dozens of new institutions and associations that would carry their positive trademark. These might be in the arts, for instance, with the Third Age finding its own voices or depicters, its own Mozart or Dickens, or in such fields as architecture, design, fashion, politics, television, in fact, everywhere. His prayer was that the foundation of the University of the Third Age would trigger off an explosion of such visionary experiments.

Even in the single arena of education, the Founding Fathers were pluralists. The U3A was, they hoped, the first of a dozen or more educational initiatives that might be implemented. They courteously accepted that some older people found the educative solace they required in the traditional fodder and politely wished them the best of good fortune. Peter Laslett, for instance, was always hopeful that a mass television-based education service for older people might emerge.

There was also the desire to see some intergenerational projects. It was never claimed that older people could only learn in their own peergroup. What was pressed – and what has proved to be the case – is that many of them learn well in their own peergroup, always with the qualifier that there might be many others for whom cross-generational groupings might be preferable. And, additionally, this might be true in either instance for some of the time or some of the elements of study. By analogue, there used to be sombre debates about whether older people were more beneficially housed in specialist 'old age' accommodation or in broadband settlements. It was a long time before the old penny dropped and housing experts began to realise that some old people would hate to be crammed together just with other old people, whilst there were others for whom, if they never again heard a motor bike rev up or a baby scream, it couldn't be too soon.

Little of this has happened. In fact, one of the few illustrations of progress in the Third Age institutional field was through Michael Young, whose motto was, 'when in doubt, start an organisation'. The very last agency he had a major hand in starting was Grandparents Plus, led by the redoubtable Jean Stogdon. It is geared to a better understanding of grandparents' functions, and a campaigning for their improved rights and support, in a world where the demographics and the economics and the moralities have altered the age-long traits of that role. In drawing up his plans for this organisation, he was insistent that one of its first partners should be U3A, for, obviously enough, the Third Age is the haven of the modern grandparent.

Apart from Grandparents Plus and one or two other instances, the curio – the 'strange adventure' - is that the very triumph of U3A appears to have halted the march of the institutionalised Third Age in its tracks, almost before the order to 'quick march' had rung out. There soon arose the thought that U3A was at least the educational answer and no one need think about other solutions. Worse still, critics questioned U3A and tried to make its leaders feel guilty or embarrassed that they had done little for this group of people or that type of place.

Once more it must be repeated: the U3A works for those for whom the U3A works. At top weight, that might be a million – but that still leaves 11m with precious little in the way of educational or, for that matter, other social and cultural outlets that have, like U3A and as Peter Laslett had hoped, emerged spontaneously from and for the brand-new Third Age phenomenon. The U3A suffers from the glow of its success. It is too easily seen as a catch-all for all the educational and, by extension, even the social and political questions of older age.

These words are not scribbled by way of comfort. There are still hard tasks for the U3A in Britain to accomplish and hard yardage to win. However, the primary aim must be to recognise that the U3A's first objective is to ensure that all Third Agers who wish to are accommodated within its ranks. Then it should seriously consider whether or not it has some responsibility to examine the wider perspective. That question arises again because of the success of U3A. Like it or not, it is just about the only national organisation of its kind, declaring the value of a civic role for Third Agers, as the inventors and managers of their own service. It is, to borrow and then mangle a famed saying of Abraham Lincoln, education of the older people, by the older people and for the older people.

There are a couple of possibilities. On the one hand, there is the campaigning possibility. This is not to suggest an overtly political role for U3A and, for example, there are organisations that already campaign for older people on issues such as pensions and health matters. It is about underpinning the civic rights of older people and ensuring the voice of U3A is heard when aspects of the Third Age lifestyle, especially those concerning education, leisure, the arts and other cultural 'quality of life' issues. As this text has shown, the NEC has already made some headway in this direction. It should be applauded and backed and, regionally and locally, it should be emulated. At all levels, it should be proactive. It should be one of those organisations that decision-makers and opinion-formers turn to automatically for comment and advice when these relevant matters are considered.

On the other hand, there is the research possibility. Peter Laslett was very keen on the research element, saying it was a well nigh indispensable component of university existence. It would be misleading to suggest that he was not disappointed that the research element was not bigger in U3A life. He was even more disappointed to find that some U3A members thought that research was not for them; that it was some sort of arcane mystique that was best left to the professionals. Like Michael Young, he was wary of professional claims. Both men believed that, at worst, the laity should always be the masters and not the servants, or, at best, with the U3A as their prime example, the amateur/professional division should be erased. As the man who had produced demographic findings over a longer period and of a more complete exactitude than in any other country, all on the base of massive voluntary lay assistance, Peter Laslett did know what he was talking about on this subject.

Of course, there has always been a research shot in U3A's locker, but perhaps the *motif* could be more oriented to the Third Age itself. What are the needs? Where are the gaps? What sort of institutions and agencies does the Third Age require? U3A members are ideally placed to muse over and scrutinise these notions. Maybe it is one of the next tasks of the U3A, not merely to preside over its own coming to ripe maturity, but to conceptualise the formulae of its complementary organisations.

iv. U3A and Society

The three Founding Fathers were Utopian Socialists. Peter Laslett leaned a little toward more orthodox left-wing opinions, but Michael Young was the *guru* of the modern incarnation of Utopian Socialism in Britain, and Eric Midwinter was his devoted disciple.

A word in season about definitions: the epithet 'Utopian' was contemptuously conferred on some of their rivals by Karl Marx and Fredrich Engels in the 19th century, to differentiate between what they considered the dreamy *reveries* of these opponents and what they rather over-fondly referred to as 'Scientific Socialism'. The Marxist analysis was Messianic in its triumphalism: history would determine the downfall of the class system, the state would, in Engel's famous words, 'wither away', and 'the administration of things would replace the management of people'.

The Utopian Socialists were, by and large, not quite so dreamy as the Marxists insisted, sensing that the realities of human experience were not so immutably carved out by historical law. This was particularly true of the British tradition, sometimes referred to as 'English Ethical Socialism', with, in R H Tawney, its major 20th century protagonist and the direct political ancestor of Michael Young. They acknowledged that the struggle was different in kind to that described by the Marxists. It was more mundane. Progress might be limited or even halted. Victories in one era might be lost in another. It might be a question of one step forwards and three steps back. Where the exultant anthem of the Marxists was *The Internationale*, the Utopian Socialists might have opted for Fred Astaire performing *Pick Yourself Up, Brush Yourself Down and Start All Over Again.*

It was a creed that did not follow strict party lines. Indeed, Michael Young, drafter of the Labour Party 1945 election manifesto, *Let Us Face the Future*, and head of the Labour Party Research Office during the Clement Attlee ministry, came to deplore the huge statist bureaucracies – the National Coal Board; the National Health Service – constructed during that time. It is the mark of the journey travelled that Michael Young's coinage of the 'meritocracy', which he used perjoratively or, at best, satirically and ambivalently, has become one of the trademarks of New Labour. Similarly, as in his pioneering work with the Consumers Association and the National Consumer Council, he developed his telling critique of the equally dreadful traits of big business corporations.

Conversely, the old-style Conservative Party had, before it became, in the term of one of its own members, 'garagiste', a distinctive and intuitive thread of affection for the little man and the little woman, struggling against the controls imposed by large anonymous enterprises, together with an engaging sense of obligation to those who needed aid. This Disraeli-like warmth was, for a century, a mellowing and honourable factor of 'one nation' Toryism. Michael Young was not entirely joking when he gave this advice to those carrying his message to local government: 'if it's a Labour authority, call it mutual aid; if it's a Conservative authority, call it self-help'.

The essence of the creed is anti-state, popularly democratic, decentralising, de-institutionalising and co-operative. The Sunday-go-to-meeting name for this type of governance is **anocracy**. It is about people associating locally to meet their social and other challenges at a human scale – and then meeting on equal terms with other circles of similar associations, even unto international co-operation. The eventual outcome was described by Kropotkin, one of the 19th century adherents to this noble cause, as 'a league of leagues.'

It is no coincidence that the British U3A exactly corresponds to that template. From the self-help learning circle that, at its not uncommon best, is the cell of the organism, through the autonomous U3A group, increasingly via the largely spontaneous growth of its regional networks, to the Third Age Trust, with its constitution valiantly grappling to balance the democratic rights of its member groups and regions, with, finally, a foot in the international door, urging the excellence of the British U3A case – the University of the Third Age in the United Kingdom is 'a league of leagues'.

We may revisit the three concepts that drove the U3A vehicle at the time of its planning, as was discussed in chapter two. They are old age as citizenship, not as social casualty; recurrent education, and mutual aid. To what degree does the British U3A offer a *modus operandi* for these ideas in society at large?

The notion of Third Age citizenship may be briefly considered. Each U3A meeting is a statement about the ability of older people to manage their own affairs. It reverses the administrative relationship in which, conventionally, others, normally Second Age professionals, did unto older people. Simple as that is to opine, it is a major theme, for the ageism of society, with its shunting of older people into the sidings of national life, is still not properly addressed. Recollect, apart from the ethical issue of civil rights involved, the United Kingdom has been, as Peter Laslett demonstrated, an officially 'ageing' society since 1951, but it is only recently, not least through the ramifications of the U3A experiment, that much notice has been taken of what is probably the most compelling social revolution since the onset of industrialism. To give some order of where ageism stands in the political reckoning, it might be estimated that it is where sexism was in the 1860s and racism in the 1920s. From this angle, the U3A is still something of a gleaming light in a naughty world.

There may be other areas of concern where the model of Third Age citizenship could be adopted. Eric Midwinter, for example, has already commended the hypothesis to the charities dealing with the care and repair of older age housing. Self-mobilised teams of skills-sharing older people might be one answer to what is becoming a very difficult problem. Shopping and other domestic needs are another possibility; the examples chosen are consciously at variance with the educational *motif* in order to stress the broad gamut of the opportunities.

As for the question of lifelong learning, each U3A gathering, large or small, sends out another statement, this one emphasising the power of shared learning and, in the minds of its convinced promoters, its superiority to the formal version. The idea that older people are capable of learning, and that all people should have the chance to learn at all stages of their lives, is a gracious enough sentiment and one that is far from being realised. However, the British U3A goes much further than that, arguing, by its everyday practice, that co-operative learning is more effective and more satisfying.

It is a credit not a debit model. The assumption is that everyone brings a present to the party, rather than that they arrive empty-handed. It turns on its head the ancient but still extant psychology of the teacher jug pouring some artificial brew into the pupil mug. Both have quantities of real ale to exchange. It dashes aside the persistent cynicism that education is that which is conveyed from the notebook of the lecturer to the notebook of the student without passing through the mind of either or that it is a system whereby artificial pearls are thrown before real swine.

Thus one might innocently hope that, far from being a second-rate, market stall brand of education for old people, the U3A philosophy might come to gain footholds in mainstream education, not only in its adult and continuing but in its school and college components. The technological revolution has galvanised some of the thinking on this issue. There has been exciting talk of 'Community Centres for Lifelong Learning', providing everyone with an open-ended focus, not an insulated location, for their studies, a service rather than a system, facilitating the studies of all, in 'Neighbourhood Learning Centres', in 'Universities of Industry', in the local library or at home: 'the picture of the 75 year old learning and qualifying for a new trade alongside the 15 year old, their computers side by side in, say, the local café is unusual – but it would be very welcome.'

Above all, U3A teaches the relishable lesson that there is no genuine education without enjoyment and that people, children as well as adults, should be attracted thereto. There remains in the education system a puritanical feeling that if the medicine does not taste nasty then it can't be doing much good. Eric Midwinter recalls, in one of his first years of teaching on the Manchester Wythenshawe estate, the head entering the classroom unannounced. He afterwards apologised for the unnecessary interruption: 'I heard laughter', he explained, 'and I thought it meant trouble.' One thinks of the hoary chestnut of the evangelical pastor who preached to his flock that it was not sinful to have sexual intercourse on the Sabbath day, so long as they didn't enjoy it.

Not the least of the joys of U3A is that it is not compulsory. For over 150 years the British schools system has relied heavily on legislative compulsion, something of a soft option for the operation, for there has been no fundamental pressure to ensure that what was on offer was so enticing that no one would dream of absenting themselves. When one strolls across a dreary shopping mall or round a desolate street corner and observes the young truants, aimlessly idling, one may only wonder at the unattractiveness of the school experience if this desultory one is preferable.

The British U3A, where truancy, by definition, does not exist, has much to teach the rest of the education service. May, in 50 years time, the organisation of British education look much more like the British U3A than it does today.

Finally, there is the portentous question of society at large. Dare one risk even the faintest dream that, in time to come, the mutualism of the U3A in the UK will be adopted in other fields and for other purposes, so that the vision of a humane and co-operative honeycomb of civilised communities might, in part, be realised? To recycle Peter Laslett's dictum on the inert member, there is more chance of this happening in that one more successful pioneering project on co-operative principles has been secured than if it had not.

Today, Bruddersford U3A (borrowing from J B Priestley's *The Good Companions*); tomorrow, the world!

v. The Objects of U3A

The U3A experience may be enjoyed and participated in at a number of levels and degrees. It is, of course, as unnecessary as it is unlikely that all U3A members would share the Founders' peculiar combine of beliefs and aspirations. Nonetheless, it is perhaps of value for all members to realise how profoundly important the U3A project was deemed to be by its originators.

Peter Laslett drew up the original Objects and Principles. They were summarised in the third chapter and they were further discussed in the ninth chapter. What has perhaps not been sufficiently recognised is that Peter Laslett's two co-founders, Michael Young and Eric Midwinter, tacitly agreed not to discuss the printed statement of Objects and Principles with him. They simply received them. This was not because they agreed with every word – there were aspects they did not altogether accept – but because they believed that the impact of the message would be more profound were they phrased in the distinctive style of one person.

Experience had taught them that drafting a statement of that kind by committee, with compromises and amendments and substitutions and corollaries, could result in a dog's dinner. Thus the ascetic, cold-water clean tones of Peter Laslett were judged to be the most effective way of challenging the Third Age public. It is the inspirational message that is important, rather than the specific clauses. Michael Young and Eric Midwinter would have no more thought of negotiating about and commenting on Peter Laslett's individualistic and commanding phrases than the Sons of Israel would have submitted amendments to Moses when he presented to them the tablets of the Decalogue. ('There's good news and bad news: we've got them down to ten but adultery's still in', as the ancient New Yorker gag had it.)

It is as highly important to revisit the Objects and Principles as it is the Ten Commandments. Kate Wedd was right to call for such a debate and Stan Miller and Ivor Manley, with the contributions of many others, have responded vigorously and thoughtfully. What is most telling is the overall message; there is no need to perform the equivalent of medieval churchmen counting the number of angels dancing on the point of a needle. More than 20 years have passed and, in common with other members, the author has, with some trepidation, but with all that weight of U3A history in mind, given much thought, not to anything so blasphemous as a replacement for the Laslett manifesto, but to some updated guidelines. He strongly believes that there are three simple approaches steering the U3A vehicle, each of which may be stated briefly and without any of them becoming too prohibitive or inhibiting. They are by way of being signposts, not blueprints – and Eric Midwinter commends them to all members present and yet to be.

The Three Guiding Principles of the U3A in the UK

1. THE THIRD AGE PRINCIPLE

The U3A in the UK is open, without other condition, to all those in the Third Age. Third Agers may be defined, not by birthdays, but as those who have either ceased full-time employment and/or completed their mainline parenting duties, in that their children have reached years of (notional) independence.

Members are expected to take some responsibility, in particular, to ensure that any potential members might have the opportunity to join the U3A ranks; and, more generally, to promote the values of lifelong learning and of the positive attributes of the Third Age lifestyle, especially in regard of activities, educational or otherwise, that Third Agers might find beneficial.

2. THE SELF-HELP LEARNING PRINCIPLE

The U3A in the UK is devoted to self-help shared learning. Its members gather and mobilise themselves into learning circles, utilising as broad a selection of themes as they think fit, with intellectual, artistic, recreational, physical, technological, research and social elements intermingled according to taste. No tests or qualifications will be offered or sought, with all agreed to learn together in concert. Although there may be interest-group convenors and facilitators, it is recognised that all members are on an equal footing, with the traditional distinction of teacher and student shelved.

The sole criterion of what is done and how it is achieved is the members' wishes, with the accent on learning for its own sake – and with an emphasis on sheer enjoyment as a prime motive.

3. THE MUTUAL AID PRINCIPLE

The U3A in the UK is organised on the co-operative precept, with each local U3A group autonomous of itself, within the greater circle of and enjoying a confederate relationship with the national body, the Third Age Trust. According to choice, a local U3A group and its members might participate in regional groupings or subject networks and other such activities. As befits a basically decentralised, mutual aid organisation, the normal tenets of popular democracy shall be sovereign at all times and at all levels.

This self-help principle requires that, ordinarily, no payments will be made to members for services rendered, while, at national, regional or local level, acceptance of outside financial or allied assistance should not be contemplated where it imperils the integrity of the mutual aid principle.

Floreat U3A

Now there are well over 500 beacons. The metaphor is deliberately savoured. At varied times in British history – in 1588 at the time of the Spanish Armada or on other more festive occasions – bonfires have been lit in sequential chain across the land by way of warning or of celebration. The 500 beacons of the U3A groups likewise shine brightly across the nation. They blaze away with a message about the positive traits of older age citizenship, about the benefits of lifelong learning on a self-mobilising basis and about the virtues of co-operative living. They blaze away the more brightly because of the darkness that still shrouds public attitudes to the causes they represent. They glitter in a society that still largely views older age as a period of decline, education as the chiefly vocational prerogative of young people, and social existence as frequently deracinated and cut-throat.

The Founders knew and hoped that what they were embarking on was some sort of crusade. Their first wish was that U3A members would find value and enjoyment in what they did and that has indubitably been the case. 140,000 current members testify to the attractiveness of the U3A proposition. Their second wish was that, in time, the U3A activity would come to be seen as a model for how older age should be perceived, of how education should be realised and, as a very distant dream, of how society might be organised. It was their hope that, in 50 or a hundred years, such things might gradually come to pass.

Each time you, the ordinary but much valued U3A member, sallies forth on a Tuesday morning to attend an interest-group gathering aimed at the study of local history or French conversation, it is worth recollecting that your little learning circle is part of the neighbourhood or township U3A group, which, in turn, is almost certainly part of a regional network, and is assuredly a cog in the national wheel of the Third Age Trust, touching, too, on an international fellowship of U3As. Each time you join your peers in so doing, you are part of that crusade and the beacon fires gleam that much more fiercely.

So let an 'ordinary' member have the last word. It might be one of a thousand such tributes that arrive at the national office or as missives for *U3A News*. Eric Midwinter, nearing the completion of his text, happened on this one during a fact-finding mission to the Bromley headquarters and pounced on it. It comes from Carrol Conroy and, in a covering note, she wrote of how 'so many people tell me how well I am looking now. It's taken nine years to come to terms with my life and I now feel I am living again. It might give other people hope for the future, after a bereavement.'

What the U3A Has Done For Me

Ten years ago my husband died.

I went through all the emotions (numbness, denial, anger, guilt, self-pity)

I took a part-time job and did some voluntary work; I joined various groups (painting, embroidery, bowls)

I went to college to train as a counsellor person.

All this did nothing to help me; I just foundered on the sea of life for nine years, gradually going deeper down a dark tunnel.

Last year I reached the depths. I had no confidence, no self-worth; I did not like myself.

I was no good at anything and could see no further life for myself.

I really had tried very hard for nine years to come to terms with life on my own.

Then I joined the U3A. I went to meetings (I did nearly leave at the beginning) I enjoyed the walking group and enjoyed the walks and the company of the other members.

I now run the walking group, planning and organising the walks for my group.

I am also now on the Committee and organise the speakers for the monthly meetings . . .

. . . The members are all very friendly and have made me feel I belong.

I now have confidence and self-worth and there is a future for me with many new friends, who have shown they have faith in my ability to perform these tasks for the U3A.

A big thank you to everyone at the Alnwick U3A, Northumberland.

I am so pleased I did not leave at the beginning.

The one regret is that two of the Founders, Michael Young and Peter Laslett, to whom this study is respectfully and lovingly dedicated, did not extend their long and fruitful lives a little longer, so that they might have witnessed the number of U3As in Britain reach the 500 mark and had the chance to read letters of that character. Like Carrol Conroy they did not 'leave at the beginning' but rather gave so much of energy and intelligence that the nation's Third Agers might have this supreme opportunity to be the pioneers of this wondrous social and educational experience.

Acknowledgements, General Reference & Sources

1. Local U3As

The following 187 local U3As forwarded information for use in this study, for which the author would like to express his gratitude to the many officers, several of them named in the text, who took the time and trouble to assist him in this way.

Abergele
Alnwick
Arbroath
Arun Valley
Aylesbury
Bakewell
Bangor
Banstead
Barking & Dagenham
Barnsley
Barnstaple
Basildon & Billericay
Bath
Bebington
Bedford
Bexley
Bolton
Borehamwood & Elstree
Bournemouth
Bracknell Forest
Bromborough
Bromley
Bude
Burgess Hill
Buxton
Caldicot
Carlisle
Carmarthen
Carrick
Causeway
Cefn Sidan (Burry Port)
Chandlers Ford
Cheadle
Chelmsford
Chester
Chesterfield
Chichester
Chorley
Christchurch
Cirencester
Clitheroe
Colchester
Congleton
Costa del Sol
Coventry
Crawley
Crewe & Nantwich
Crossmaglen
Dacorum
Darlington
Derby
Doncaster
Dukeries
Dundee
Dunstable
Dwyfor & Meirionnydd
Ealing
Easingfold
Eastbourne
East Lothian
East Suffolk
Elmbridge
Exeter
Farnborough
Farnham
Ferndown
Fleet
Flintshire
Foyle
Frodsham
Gloucester
Great Glen
Guildford
Gunnislake
Haddenham
Hadleigh
Hall Green
Harborne & Edgbaston
Harpenden
Harrogate
Harrow
Hastings & Rother
Havering
Haywards Heath

Headington
Henley
Hertford
Hessle
Hinckley
Huyton
Kennet
Lea Valley
Leek
Leicester
Leighton Linslade
Lewes
Lichfield
Lincoln
Llanelli
London
Looe & District
Looe Valley
Ludlow
Lytham St Annes
Macclesfield
Maidenhead
Maldon
Melbourn
Merton
Mid-Bucks
Milton Keynes
Monks Brook
Monmouth
Newcastle-upon-Tyne
Newport (Mon)
North Norfolk
North Northumberland
North Wilts
Norwich
Oadby &Wigston
Old Basing
Orpington
Peterborough
Petersfield
Plymouth
Poole
Porthcawl
Princes Risborough
Reading
Redbridge
Reigate & Redhill
Richmondshire
Ricksmanworth
Ringmer
Rugby
Ryedale
St Albans
Sale
Sarum
Sevenoaks
Shaftesbury & Gillingham
Sheffield
Shoreham & Southwick
Shrewsbury
Sidcup
Sleaford
Soar Valley
Solent
Solihull
South Durham
South Leicestershire
South Molton
South Lakes
Southend
Spelthorne
Stamford
Stevenage
Stockport
Sutton
Sutton Coldfield
Swanland
Swansea
Swindon
Taunton
Taw & Barnstaple
Tendring
Tewkesbury
Thanet
Thornbury
Waltham Forest
Warminster
Washington
Watford
Wear-Tees
West Dartmoor
West Oxford
West Wilts
Whitby Whaler
Whitchurch
Wirral
Witney
Woking
Wokingham
Wonersh
Wrekin
Yardley
Yeovil

2. Individual U3A Activists

The following senior U3A officers, past and present, and others close to the U3A movement, furnished the author with specific information on regional and national issues, for which he also wishes to express his appreciation. It is by no means an exclusive list, for many people have been helpful with items of information, and the author would like to take this opportunity of offering his thanks to everyone who has been of assistance in this fashion. Wherever possible the names of informants have been included in the relevant text as well as in the index.

Barbara Adkins, Sharon Ahtuam, Francis Beckett, Audrey Cloet, Roger Cloet, Elizabeth Gibson, Hilary Greenwood, Brian Groombridge, Ann Hayes, Gerry Hitchen, Lin Jonas, John Knight, Derek Legge, John Lloyd, Mike Long, Dianne Norton, Frank Pedley, Harold Potts, Ivor Manley, Stan Miller, Margaret Minns, John Newcombe, Don Rankin, Keith Richards, Norman Richards, Jim Soulsby, Len Street, Jean Thompson, Glenys Tuersley, Alan Willey, Mike Williams, Kate Wedd.

The author and the publisher would especially like to thank Lin Jonas, Barbara Adkins and Gill Birchall very sincerely for their full and careful reading of the complete text. Lin Jonas has also generously supplied a wealth of detail, as a result of which errors, both of commission and ommission, have been avoided.

3. List of Selected Books and Documents Consulted

A Briggs *Michael Young; Social Entepreneur* Palgrave 2000

M B Brodie *University of the Third Age; A Review* NEC 1994

K P Cross 'Adult Learners; Characteristics, Needs and Interests' R E Peterson et al. *Lifelong Learning in America* Jossy Bass USA 1979

B Groombridge *Education and Retirement* National Institute of Adult Education 1960

W Hawes Survey of Central Office and Regional Plans NEC 1994

P Laslett *The Education of the Elderly in Britain,* Elmgrant Trust/ National Extension College 1979

University of the Third Age: Objects, Principles and Institutional Forms and *All Our Futures* 1982

'The Emergence of the Third Age', *Ageing and Society,* Vol 7 Part 2 1978

A Fresh Map of Life Weidenfeld & Nicholson 1989

E Midwinter *Age is Opportunity; Education and Older People* Centre for Policy on Ageing 1982

The British Gas Report on Attitudes to Ageing British Gas 1991

(ed) *Mutual Aid Universities* Croom Helm 1984

Thriving People Third Age Trust 1996

Thriving People Revisited Third Age Trust 2002

NEC *Facing the Future; the Business Plan* NEC 1995

Investing in the Future NEC 1996

N Richards (ed) *U3A Policy Review* NEC 1993

R Swindell & J Thompson 'An International Perspective on the University of the Third Age' *Educational Gerontology* no 21 1995

R H Tawney *Equality* 4th edition Unwin Books 1952

K Taylor *The Political Ideas of the Utopian Socialists* Cass 1982

C Trinder, G Hulme & U McCarthy *Employment; the Role of Work in the Third Age* Carnegie Inquiry into the Third Age 1992

J Vincent 'What is at Stake in the War on Anti-ageing medicine' *Ageing and Society* Vol 23 Pt v 2003

M Young *The Rise of the Meritocracy* Thames & Hudson 1958

Mutual Aid in a Selfish Society Mutual Aid Press 1978

The author and publishers have endeavoured to trace the provenance and, where possible, test the accuracy of all the material used in this book and apologise for any shortcomings in this regard. They would welcome suggested amendments or additions in respect of such references for use in any future edition.

Index of U3A People & Places

Third Age Press

THIRD AGE PRESS

. . . a unique publishing company inspired by older people

Third Age Press books are available by direct mail order from 6 Parkside Gardens London SW19 5EY

Email: dnort@globalnet.co.uk Website:www.thirdagepress.co.uk

All prices include UK p & p. Cheques payable to *Third Age Press.*

Other *Third Age Press* books by Eric Midwinter
[at special U3A prices]

Novel Approaches: a guide to the popular classic novel
. . . 35 novels that have stood the test of time, embedded in historical and literary commentary 180 pages **£8.00**

Best Remembered . . . a hundred stars of yesteryear

. . . presents a galaxy of 100 stars from the days before television ruled our lives. 168 pages **£9.50**

A Voyage of Rediscovery: a guide to writing your life story 36 pages **£4.50**

Encore: a guide to planning a celebration of your life
20 pages **£2.00**

The Rhubarb People . . . Eric Midwinter's own witty and poignant story of growing up in Manchester in the 1930s.
32 pages **£4.50** or audio cassette **£5.00**

As one stage door closes . . .
The story of John Wade: jobbing conjuror 174 pages **£12.50**

. . . and other Third Age Press books ----->

On the tip of your tongue: your memory in later life ~ our best seller! Dr H B Gibson **£7.00**

A little of what you fancy does you good: your health in later life Dr H B Gibson **£8.50**

[or both the above for £10.00]

Our Grandmothers, Our Mothers, Ourselves: A century of women's lives Edited by Charmian Cannon **£8.00**

Changes and challenges in later life: learning from experience Yvonne Craig (ed). Foreword by Claire Rayner **£5.00**

Consider the alternatives: healthy strategies for later life ~ Caroline Nash & Tony Carter **£5.00**

Lifescapes: the landscapes of a lifetime by Enid Irving . . . introduces a whole new art form . . . a '*Lifescape*' is a collage of memories. **£4.00**

No Thanks to Lloyd George:The forgotten story ~ how the old age pension was won Dave Goodman **£3.60**

Europe at Walking Pace by Ben & Betty Whitwell **£9.25**

An Experiment in Living - Sharing a House in Later Life by June Green, Jenny Betts & Greta Wilson **£5.00**

---

perspectives. . . *offers a comprehensive publishing service for people wanting to produce a memoir for sale or distribution to friends or family.* **For clubs or U3As**, *Third Age Press can advise or produce books, booklets, pamphlets or newsletters. Every project is individually priced and given our expert, personal attention. Please write for details.*